"Within the tradition of *tajdid*, or 'renewal', in Islamic heritage, there might be disputes as to who is considered the *mujaddid* ('renewer') in each century—not so with *Hujjat al-Islam*, Imam Abu Hamid al-Ghazālī, who is so widely recognised as that figure in the 5th century. Unsurprisingly so, considering his width and breadth of knowledge in so many different sciences, particularly in law, jurisprudence, theology, Qur'anic commentary, and spirituality. One area that remains sorely understudied, nevertheless, is that which pertains to al-Ghazālī's thoughts on the political realm, which, though profane and secular, can, in al-Ghazālī's schemata, become a source of sacredness, if the correct approach and intention are taken. It is a pleasure to see this volume, *Al-Ghazālī's Political Thought and Other Essays on Hujjatu'l-Islām* that engages with that area of his work."

Hisham A. Hellyer,
Centre for Islamic Studies, University of Cambridge (UK)
& the Carnegie Endowment for International Peace

"It is a testament to al-Ghazālī's scholarship that his writings are still hotly debated by Islamic studies specialists, both by his proponents and the detractors. In this edited volume, Prof. Muddathir 'Abd al-Raḥīm casts a spotlight on a less studied aspect of al-Ghazālī's ideas—political and economic thought. The introductory essay by Prof. Muddathir, in particular, should be a starting point and a great introduction to any future work on al-Ghazālī's political thought. This book is a highly recommended reading for anyone interested in the medieval Islamic political and economic history and thought."

Ermin Sinanović,
Executive Director, Center for Islam in the Contemporary World
at Shenandoah University (USA)

Al-Ghazālī's Political Thought and Other Essays on *Ḥujjatu'l-Islām*

AL-GHAZĀLĪ'S Political Thought and Other Essays on Ḥujjatu'l-Islām

Edited and with an Introduction by
Muddathir 'Abd al-Raḥīm

CONTRIBUTORS
Muddathir 'Abd al-Raḥīm
Sabri Orman
Cemil Akdogan
Mustafa Mahmoud Abu-Sway
Mohd Zaidi bin Ismail
Asmaa' Mohd. Arshad
Ssekamanya Siraje Abdullah

IBT
Islamic Book Trust
Kuala Lumpur

Published by
Islamic Book Trust
607 Mutiara Majestic
Jalan Othman
46000 Petaling Jaya
Selangor, Malaysia
www.ibtbooks.com

Islamic Book Trust is affiliated with The Other Press Sdn. Bhd.

Perpustakaan Negara Malaysia   Cataloguing-in-Publication Data

Muddathir Abd al-Rahim, Prof., Dr., 1932-
Al-Ghazali's Political Thought and Other Essays on Hujjatu'l-Islam / Edited and with an Introduction by Muddathir 'Abd al-Rahim ; Contributors Muddathir 'Abd al-Rahīm, Sabri Orman, Cemil Akdogan, Mustafa Mahmoud Abu-Sway, Mohd Zaidi bin Ismail, Asmaa' Mohd. Arshad, Ssekamanya Siraje Abdullah.
ISBN 978-967-0526-98-0
1. Ghazzali, 1058-1111. 2. Political science.
3. Philosophy. 4. Theology.
I. Sabri Orman. II. Akdogan, Cemil.
III. Abu-Sway, Mustafa Mahmoud. IV. Mohd. Zaidi Ismail.
V. Asmaa' Mohd. Arshad. VI. Abdullah, Ssekamanya Siraje. VII. Title.
320

Printed by
SS Graphic Printers (M) Sdn. Bhd.
Lot 7 & 8, Jalan TIB 3, Taman Industri Bolton,
68100 Batu Caves, Selangor Darul Ehsan.

Dedicated to the memory of

Dr. Sabri Orman

(1948-2020)

Al-Fatiha

Contents

Introduction xi

ESSAYS

1. Al-Ghazālī's Political Thought:
Its Nature and Contemporary Relevance 1
Muddathir 'Abd al-Raḥīm

2. Abu Ḥāmid Al-Ghazālī on the Formation and Development of Economic, Social and Political Life 39
Sabri Orman

3. The Ghazalian Origins of Modern Philosophy 59
Cemil Akdogan

4. Al-Ghazālī's "Spiritual Crisis" Reconsidered 109
Mustafa Mahmoud Abu-Sway

5. Logic in Al-Ghazālī's Theory of Certitude 127
Mohd Zaidi bin Ismail

6. Major Terms in Al-Ghazālī's Child-Educational Theory:
An Example of Islamization of Contemporary Knowledge 159
Asmaa' Mohd. Arshad

Introduction

Ḥujjatu'l-Islām Abū Ḥamid Al-Ghazālī (450 AH / 1058 C.E-505 A.H/1111 C.E) was a towering monument of intellectual brilliance and spiritual enlightenment. His seminal creativity across a breathtakingly wide range of subjects, together with the shining example of his life experience, have continued to inform and inspire generations of thinking people for nine centuries—and will almost certainly continue informing and inspiring people for as long as there are thinking men and women on earth.

It can safely be said however that, for most people, Al-Ghazālī's rich heritage is identical with his profound and many teachings on spiritual, ethical, educational, juridical, and philosophical issues. A typical example of this general tendency is the fact that five of the seven papers that constitute the present volume have been randomly dedicated to analyzing and commenting upon different aspects of Abu Ḥamid's numerous and profound contributions in the said fields.

By contrast, only two of the seven papers that constitute the volume—the first and the second—focus on the immensely interesting and undoubtedly significant and important, but relatively less frequently discussed, subjects of Al-Ghazālī's political thought on the one hand, and his views on the formation and development of economic, social and political life and institutions on the other.

It may not be out of place to add in this connection that when the subject was first considered by the ISTAC Management Board some two years ago, under the then Dean of the Institute, Prof. Dr. Ibrahim M. Zein, the decision initially taken was to publish the paper titled *"Al-Ghazālī's Political Thought: Its Nature and Contemporary Relevance"* as a monograph on its own. In the course of further discussions however it was later decided to publish the said paper together with all others on Al-Ghazālī's thought that had similarly been published in *Al-Shajarah*, ISTAC's journal, and that I should be entrusted with the editing, or reediting, of the said collected papers as may be deemed necessary.

Considerable efforts have accordingly been vested in the preparation of the volume at hand. It is hoped that it will be found of some value and interest for all those who wish to acquire or develop a more comprehensive and balanced appreciation of *Ḥujjatu'l-Islām's* heritage and its contemporary significance.

Before bringing these brief introductory remarks to an end one more important point needs to be made. It is that both the editor and the prospective readers of this collection of essays are deeply indebted to Prof. Dr. Hassan Ahmed Ibrahim, the present Dean of ISTAC. Without his financial and moral support—along with his generous personal interest and enthusiasm—this book would not have materialized.

A special word of thanks is also due to Mohammed Muneer'deen Olodo Al-Shāfi'ī, a doctoral student at ISTAC, for the dedication, skill and patience that he has consistently shown in typing and retyping several drafts of the manuscript over the past three months or so until it was finally ready for submission to the publishers.

Wa'l ḥamduli 'Llāhi awwalan wa akhiran wa 'alā kulli ḥāl!

Muddathir ʻAbd al-Raḥīm
ISTAC-IIUM
31 August 2011

Al-Ghazālī's Political Thought: Its Nature and Contemporary Relevance

Muddathir 'Abd al-Raḥīm

I. The Historical Setting: Challenges and Stimulants

Universally recognized as theologian, philosopher, master-sufi and jurist, the celebrated *Ḥujjatu'l-Islām* (Proof of Islam), Muḥammad Ibn Muḥammad Ibn Muḥammad Ibn Aḥmad al-Tūsī, Abū Ḥamid al-Ghazālī,[1] was also an outstanding and highly original political thinker.

A prolific writer, al-Ghazālī's political ideas-especially as expressed in *al-Iqtiṣād fī al-I'tiqād, Mizān al-'Amal, Naṣīḥat al-Mulūk, Faḍā'iḥ al-Bāṭiniyyah* (or *al-Mustaẓhiri*) and *Iḥyā' 'Ulūm al-Dīn*—are closely intertwined with his views on theology,

[1] Al-Subkī, *Tajuddīn, Ṭabaqāt al-Shāfi'yyah al-Kubrā*, 10 vols. (Cairo, Dar al-Kitāb al-'Arabī, 1969) vol. 6, p. 191. Al-Ghazālī's first mentioned *nisbah*, al-Ṭūsi, derives from his birthplace, a suburb of Tūs, near present day Meshhed in Khurāsān, but he is, of course, much better known as al-Ghazālī (sometimes spelt al-Ghazzālī (with two 'z's or *shadda*) preceded with the kunya, Abū Ḥāmid.

philosophy, ethics, law and jurisprudence. A major expositor and interpreter of Islam in its many and all-encompassing facets, al-Ghazālī's ideas in fact constitute an integral whole none of which can be fully comprehended in isolation from the others.

Like many other major political thinkers in both the Western and the Islamic traditions-Plato, Hobbes, Marx, al-Mawardī, Ibn Taymiyyah and Ibn Khaldūn included—al-Ghazālī's interest in the theory and practice of politics was at least partly aroused and sustained by the fact that the political conditions in which he happened to live (born in 450 A.H. / 1058 C.E., died in 505 A.H. / 1111 C.E.) were far from perfect and the principal Islamic political institution, the caliphate, had for decades been in serious decline.[2] Under the Buwayhids (945-1055) in particular, it had become little more than a plaything in the hands of the dominant war-lords who, as Shī'ites moreover, could not and, of course, did not, recognize the legitimacy of the Sunni 'Abbasid caliphate even in theory.[3]

No less disconcerting for al-Ghazālī was the fact that corruption, long known to have been widespread among the administrative and business classes, had also engulfed many among the *'ulamā'*. This was particularly depressing because as bearers of the *Sharī'ah* and Islamic ethics, the *'ulamā'* were, individually and collectively, expected to be not only examples of propriety and personal integrity but also leaders and standard bearers in the struggle for social reform, which for all Muslims was and remains a basic religious duty if not an article of faith.[4]

---

[2] See, for example, Al-Qalqashandī, *Ma'āthir al-Ināfa fi Ma 'ālim al-Khilāfah*, ed., 'Abd al-Sattār Aḥmad Farraj (Kuwait: Wizārah al-Irshād, 1964); reprinted (Beirut: 'Alam al-Kutub, 1980), vol. I, p. 217 *FF.*

[3] Ibid, pp. 284-338.

[4] For a thorough and thoughtful treatment of this subject in English, see Michael Cook, *Commanding Right and Forbidding Wrong in Islamic*

In 1055 (i.e. three years before al-Ghazālī was born) the Seljuks, already in control of Khurāsān and Western Persia, finally destroyed the 110 year old Buwayhid hegemony over the enfeebled caliphate in Baghdad. Like the Buwayhids, the Seljuks were war-lords who, as such, continued to dominate the caliphate. Unlike their predecessors however, the Seljuks were Sunni Muslims and ardent defenders of the faith as articulated by al-Ash'arī and his followers including al-Ghazālī's renowned teacher, Imām al-Ḥaramayn al-Juwaynī and subsequently, al-Ghazālī himself.

Under the leadership of such able men as Tughrul-Beg, Alp Arslān and especially the brilliant *wazīr*, statesman and administrator, Niẓām al-Mulk, the Seljuks did not only bring an end to the chaotic and unstable situation which had prevailed for several years previously—establishing important reforms of enduring value—but they also played crucial roles in the development of science and scholarship, especially through the establishment of a number of *madrasahs* (colleges of higher learning), generically known as *Niẓāmiyyahs*, named after their great sponsor and benefactor, Niẓām al-Mulk. The most renowned among these was the Niẓamiyyah of Baghdad where both al-Juwaynī and al-Ghazālī were professors.

Under these circumstances, caliphs naturally began to feel more confident as well as more comfortable than they had been for several decades. Many others, including al-Ghazālī, who deemed the caliphate both guardian and chief executive of the *Sharī'ah*—the fountain of legitimacy for the *ummah* constituting the singular lynchpin that held the entire body politic together—the welcome change that ensued from the rise of the Seljuks gave renewed hope. Although it was perhaps impossible, they wished to recapture or reinvent the vigor and the glory, for example, of

---

Thought (Cambridge, U.K.: Cambridge University Press, 2000).

the days of Harūn al-Rashīd, so that much would be done to strengthen and reinvigorate the caliphate in order to revive both the ummah and the state. Needless to say however, the identification and structuring of those components necessary for the required reform and formulation of these into a coherent and workable programme of action were tasks by no means easy to accomplish.

But there was another and more immediately pressing challenge: i.e. that of the Ismā'ilites or Sevener Shī'ites, also known as Bāṭinites and Assassins (a corruption of (*ḥashshāshīn* or *hashīshmen*). Because of the methods, for which they became famous, this group has been described as "the most radical and dangerous type of revolutionary Shi'ite sects."[5] The Ismā'ilite, or Bāṭinite challenge to the 'Abbāsid caliphate was in fact twofold: i.e. military-strategic, and political-ideological.

As a militant movement skillfully organized and ruthlessly led by Ḥasan ibn al-Ṣabbāḥ, the Ismā'ilites took the fortress of Alamut in southern Persia in 1090. From that stronghold they continued to harass the caliphate and the Seljuks. Two years later (October 14th, 1092) they assassinated Niẓām al-Mulk. The Bāṭinites thus dealt a hard blow, not only to the Seljuks and the caliphate, but also to the whole community of Sunni Muslims, especially the many scholars and students throughout the realm whose patron and benefactor the great statesman had long been.

Politically and in terms of religious belief and doctrine, the Ismā'ilites, the Qarāmiṭah (Carmathians), together with the followers of Bābak of Adharbaijan and the Khurramādins of

---

[5] Bertold Spuler, *The Age of the Caliphs* (Princeton: Markus Wiener Publishers, 1995), p. 67. For a comprehensive and sympathetic account of the Ismā'ilites from their inception to the present day, see Farhad Daftary, *The Ismā'īlīs—Their History and Doctrines* (Cambridge: Cambridge University Press, 1990).

Isfahan, had been vigorously denounced by Niẓām al-Mulk as heretics and subversives. Clearly reflecting the views of the majority Sunni community, Niẓām al-Mulk stated in his *Siyāsat-Nāmah* (Book of Government) that "the constant object of them all [was] to overthrow Islam."[6] The charge of heresy and its attendant corollary, subversion, were rooted in the fact that the Ismā'ilites believed that the Holy Qur'an has a hidden or esoteric (Arabic: *bāṭin* or *bāṭini*) meaning distinct from its *ẓāhir* (i.e. plain or exoteric) meaning, hence the designation "Bāṭinites" by which they came to be known. They also held that only their imam, whom they believed was an infallible charismatic leader, could know the truth and correctly understand the real or esoteric meaning of the Holy Book. Other mortals, Ḥasan ibn al-Ṣabbāḥ insisted, could acquire such understanding only by means of *ta'līm* (i.e. authoritative instruction) given by the imam,[7] hence the designation "*Ta'līmiyyah*" by which Ismā'ilites also came to be known. This implied, inter alia, that the methods of *ijtihād* (personal intellectual effort), *naẓar* (reasoning) and *ra'y* (thinking) which were favored by the Sunni *'ulamā'* could not lead to the truth. This constituted "a direct attack on the scholar-jurists"[8] as well as the basic principles of Islamic jurisprudence.

The decline of the caliphate and the spread of corruption even among the *'ulamā'*, together with the bitter and long drawn-out

[6] Niẓām al-Mulk, *The Book of Government or Rules for Kings* (*Siyar al-Mulūk* or *Siyāsat-Nāmah*), translated by Hubert Drake (London: Routledge and Kegan Paul, 1960) p. 238.

[7] Al-Ghazālī, *Faḍā'iḥ al-Bāṭiniyyah*, ed., 'Abd al-Rahmān Badawī (Cairo: Wizārat al-Thaqāfah wa'l-Irshād, 1964), p. 11 *FF*. Also, W. Montgomery Watt, *Muslim Intellectual—A Study of al-Ghazālī* (Edinburgh: Edinburgh University Press, 1963), p. 81; and Daftary, *op. cit.*

[8] Watt, *op. cit.*

conflict with the Bāṭinites and other schismatic groups, were not only powerful challenges to al-Ghazālī and his contemporaries as viewed in the context of the promising and more hopeful atmosphere that prevailed under the Seljuks, but also functioned as stimulants for serious thinking about politics and socio-political reform. It should be remembered in this connection that at least one of al-Ghazālī's political discourses, namely *Faḍā'iḥ al-Bāṭiniyyah* (The Scandals of the Bāṭinites) was written not long after the assassination of Niẓām al-Mulk and at the behest of the young Caliph al-Mustaẓhir.[9] Appropriately dedicated to al-Mustaẓhir,[10] the book has come to be known as *al-Mustaẓhiri*, after the said Caliph. Another one of al-Ghazālī's works, i.e. *Naṣīḥat al-Mulūk* (Counsel for Kings),[11] was addressed to Sultan Muḥammad Ibn Malik Shāh. In addition, al-Ghazālī wrote a number of letters to various rulers and top administrators in the Seljuk Sultanate.[12] A review of this category of al-Ghazālī's writings clearly shows that he was a greatly esteemed personality whose opinions were eagerly sought and respectfully received by the high and mighty as well as others of his age and that he was an untiring campaigner for good governance. He was particularly anxious to see such values as justice, integrity, efficiency, clemency and transparency carefully and consistently observed and demonstrated in both the performance of public duties and in

---

[9] Abū Hamid al-Ghazālī, *Faḍā'iḥ al-Bāṭiniyyah*, pp. 4-6.

[10] Ibid.

[11] Al-Ghazālī, *Al-Tibr al-Masbūk fī Naṣīḥat al-Mulūk* (Beirut: Dar al-Kutub al-'Ilmiyyah, 1988). For English translation, see F.R.C. Bagley, *Book of Counsel for Kings* (Oxford, 1964). Hereafter cited as *Al-Tibr*.

[12] Cf. Abdul Qayyum, *Letters of al-Ghazālī* (Lahore: Islamic Publications Ltd., 1976). This is a selective translation (from Farsi) of some twenty letters with a general introduction. An edited and annotated Arabic translation consisting of thirty two letters and six other pieces has been published: see Dr Nūr al-Dīn 'Ali, ed., *Faḍā'il al-Anām min Rasā'il Ḥujjat al-Islām* (Tunis, 1972).

the personal conduct of rulers and administrators.

II. The Importance and Legitimacy of the State

By contrast with, for example, the Najdite faction of the Kharijites in the Islamic tradition and the anarchists in the modern Western tradition—both of whom considered the state an undesirable and superfluous imposition—al-Ghazālī was firmly convinced that the state (a term which he virtually identifies with politics and statesmanship in general) is a vitally important and necessary institution for human society indeed, a precondition without which social existence would be impossible and civilized living unthinkable. In this respect al-Ghazālī's position is not unlike that of most political thinkers, Western or Muslim. But his reasoning, in many ways was parallel to that of other thinkers in the two traditions, and yet in other ways, quite distinct.

The drastic and dire consequences of the absence or nonexistence of sovereign and effective public authorities, al-Ghazālī points out, can be clearly seen and comprehended by observing what actually happens when offices of state fall vacant whether as a result of civil strife or the natural death of incumbents. "For should such conditions persist without another sovereign or dominant person taking effective control," al-Ghazālī continues, "chaos would set in; killing and death spread; famine prevail; livestock perish; industries cease to function; whatever achievements may have been previously made would then turn into utter loss and grief; none of those who manage to survive would be able to concentrate on either worship or the pursuit of knowledge; while most would simply perish in consequence of continued strife and civil conflict."[13]

---

[13] Al-Ghazālī, *al-Iqtiṣād fi'l-i'tiqād* (The Golden Mean in Belief) (Beirut: Dār al-Kutub al-'Ilmiyyah, 1983), p. 148. All translations provided in this paper are by the present writer.

It is worth noting the remarkable similarity between al-Ghazālī's portrayal of the subject under consideration and that given by Thomas Hobbes some five centuries later (1588-1679). Describing the condition of men in the absence of sovereign authority as one "where every man is enemy to every man," Hobbes further states: "In such condition there is no place for Industry; because the fruit thereof is uncertain: and consequently no Culture of the Earth; no Navigation, nor use of the commodities that may be imported by Sea; no commodious building; no instruments of moving and removing such things as require much force; no knowledge of the face of the earth; no account of time; no arts; no letters; no society; and which is worst of all, continual fear, and danger of violent death; And the life of man, solitary, poor, nasty, brutish and short."[14]

The similarity between the two men's positions paralleled and echoed the troubled conditions, different in many respects though they were, in which they happened to live. In fact, Hobbes explicitly states in the final paragraph of *Leviathan*, that the writing of his masterpiece was "occasioned by the disorders of the present time"—an obvious reference, *inter alia*, to the civil war in England and the far from peaceful conditions on the continent which were among the most important factors that shaped both his personality and his outlook.[15] Although many details of his work were evidently inspired by observation and personal experience, his methodology is based on a number of hypotheses and assumptions about human nature that are largely modeled on

---

[14] Thomas Hobbes, *Leviathan* (London, 1651), Chapter XIII.

[15] Hobbes was born prematurely—reportedly on his mother's having heard of the imminent attack of the Spanish Armada in 1588. It is related that her subsequent comment on the occasion was that "Hobbes and fear were born twins." A remarkably prudent man who managed to survive the tumultuous events of his time and lived on until he was 91 years of age, Hobbes described himself as a diffident person—which he was evidently not.

the deductive method of geometry on the one hand, and extrapolations from Galileo's theory of motion on the other. These constructs are basically and predominantly hypothetical and abstract in nature.[16] In contrast, however, al-Ghazālī's analysis is rooted in a deep understanding and clear appreciation of historical events that actually happened during the period of strife preceding the coming of the Seljuks in the course of his own life time, as well as during earlier phases of Islamic history.

He clearly and succinctly states that "observation of times of civil strife"[17] (*mushāhadātu awqāt al-fitan*), stands as witness for the indispensability of established state authority for securing the safety of persons and property (*al-amnu 'alā al-anfusi wa 'l-amwāli lā yantazimu illā bi Sultanin muṭā'a*).[18]

For al-Ghazālī, therefore, it is an uncontestable fact—attested by observation—that the state (*al-Sultan*) and its attendant function of politics (*al-siyāsah*: management of public affairs)[19] are indispensable if only for preventing civil strife and maintaining law and order, thereby making it possible for society to thrive and civilization to flourish. Considering the various forms of activity in which men engage themselves in society, al-Ghazālī identifies three categories of industry or professions: *basic* (without which life cannot be sustained); *secondary* (which service

---

[16] Cf. C.B. Macpherson's introduction to the Penguin edition of Hobbes' *Leviathan* (London, 1985) p. 16 *FF*.

[17] Al-Ghazālī, *al-Iqtiṣād fī'l-'I'tiqād*, p. 148.

[18] Ibid.

[19] Al-Ghazālī also uses the term *siyāsah* with reference to the management and control of self, household, neighbourhood and township. In justification of this broad usage, he asks: "how can a person who is not capable of managing and controlling himself and his own desires be entrusted with the management and control of the affairs of others?" Cf. *Mīzān*, pp. 231-232. It is however with the narrower or more specialized sense of the term that we are concerned here.

the former); and *tertiary* or supplementary.[20] Of all these he says, the most "honourable" and important are the basic: (*wa ashrafu hādhihī al-ṣinā'āt uṣūluhā*), i.e. agriculture, building, clothing, and politics.[21] Among these, the most "honourable" and therefore most important of all is politics; for life on earth is unsustainable without it (*ashrafu hādhihī al-ṣinā'āti al-siyāsāt idh la qawāma li'l-'ālami illā bihī*).[22] This is so he says, not only on account of the prevention of civil strife via the maintenance of law and order and proper management of public affairs by state agents as already mentioned, but also because it is through the guidance and leadership that rulers and statesmen provide [or should provide] that society is held together and its interests served (*bi'l-ta'lifi wa'l istiṣlāḥ'*).[23] For al-Ghazālī therefore, political leadership is the most demanding profession of all because it requires a greater degree of competence and ability than that of any other profession: *tastad'ī hādhihī al-ṣinā'ātu min al-kamāli fī man yatakaffalu bihī ma lā yastad'ihi sā'iru al-ṣinā'āt.*

Clearly therefore, the state and politics for al-Ghazālī are of the utmost importance for human life on earth.

But al-Ghazālī was firmly convinced that politics and the state are, above all, indispensable for infinitely more important reasons

---

[20] Al-Ghazālī, *Iḥyā' 'Ulūm al-Dīn* (Istanbul: Dar Tamal, 1985), vol. I, pp. 22 23 and *Mīzān al-'Amal* ed., Dr. Sulayman Dunya (Cairo: Dār al-Ma'ārif, 1964), pp. 328-329. It should perhaps be pointed out in this connection that, for al-Ghazālī, scholarship or education (*al-ta'līm*) is, by far, the most honorable and fundamental of all pursuits: *'aṣl al-'uṣūl wa 'ashraf al-'amal.* But he does not include it among the professions or industries as indicated above. Cf. *Mīzān*, p. 328 and *Iḥyā'*, vol. I, pp. 21-22. Elsewhere however, he says that it is, in certain respects, a profession; in others, a form of worship, and, in yet other respects, a vicegerency for God on earth. Cf *Mīzān*, p. 330.

[21] *Iḥyā'*, vol. 1, p. 22 and *Mīzān*, *loc. cit.*

[22] *Mīzān*, p. 329; also *Iḥyā'*, *loc. cit.*

[23] Ibid, vol. 1, p. 22.

besides these. The latter arise in connection with the fact, as he saw it, that human beings are everywhere and forever engaged in the pursuit of happiness: ... *al-sa'ādatu ... maṭlūbu al-awaking wa 'l ākhirīn.*[24] Though they (especially Muslims) are expected and fully entitled to seek happiness and enjoy the good things of life—physical, intellectual, artistic and otherwise[25]—human beings endowed with reason and intelligence as they are, cannot fail to realize, he says, that life on earth is fragile and transient and that true happiness and everlasting bliss can hopefully be attained only in the Hereafter.[26] By creating and maintaining the physical conditions in which individuals and society as a whole are encouraged and supported by the wise and appropriate guidance given by rulers, the *'ulamā'* can pursue their various objectives ethically with due consideration for the social and spiritual precepts of the faith. The state provides the greatest service that it is capable of delivering: i.e. helping people, individually and collectively, to lead decent, enjoyable and responsible lives here on earth, thereby simultaneously seeking with the Grace of the Merciful and Compassionate Lord, eternal bliss and everlasting happiness in the Hereafter. For, as al-Ghazālī repeatedly tells us, religious and worldly affairs are complementary and absolutely inseparable. Thus, partly paraphrasing a saying of the Prophet, al-Ghazālī says that this world is like a farm that we till and cultivate with a view to harvest the fruits thereof in the Hereafter. Otherwise faith and the virtues with which it seeks to adorn the soul would remain barren and incomplete unless buttressed and facilitated by a good life here on earth: *al-dunyā mazra'atu al-ākhirah, wa la yatimmu al-dīnu illā bi 'l-dunyā*. It is for this reason that it has been said, he continues, that faith and the state

[24] *Op. cit.*, p. 21.

[25] *Mīzān*, p. 179.

[26] Ibid., pp. 294-304 and *Iḥyā'* (*Kitāb al-ḥalāl wa al-ḥarām*), vol. II, book 5, p. 21; cf. *Faḍā'iḥ 'al-Bāṭiniyyah*, p. 205.

are twins: *al-dīnu wa 'l-Sultan taw 'amān.* Religion is the foundation of properly established societies while the state is the protector thereof, and that which is without this properly laid foundation is doomed to collapse, while at the same time that which is not well guarded is bound to dissipate and be lost: *al-dīnu 'ussun wa 'l-Sultanu ḥāris, wa mā lā aṣla lahā famahdūm, wa mā lā ḥārisa lahā Faḍā'i'.*[27]

For al-Ghazālī therefore, the importance and legitimacy of the state and hence of politics, ultimately derives—not merely from its rationally or pragmatically proven utility in saving humans from the perils of chaos and anarchy by maintaining law and order and thus making social existence possible etc, but from providing infinitely more valuable opportunities and guidance for individuals and society to lead spiritually and ethically, as well as physically, good and wholesome lives. For in this way, people would not only have the possibility of enjoying full and meaningful lives during their sojourn on earth, but would hopefully and much more importantly, attain salvation and bliss everlasting in the Hereafter.

Consistent with this, al-Ghazālī then goes on to say that the obligation incumbent on Muslims to institute or appoint an imām (or caliph, or ruler) is not, as the Mu'tazilites for example had argued, dictated by reason as distinct from faith, but is derived from the *Sharī'ah*: *lā yanbaghī an taẓunna anna wujūba [naṣb al-imām] ma 'khūdhun min al-'aql [b'al] inna al-wujūba yū'khadhu min al-Shar'a.*[28]

Once the *Sharī'ah* is thus clearly seen and unequivocally recognized as the fount of legitimacy and the basis on which Islamic government stands, however, there can be no objection to

---

[27] *Al-Iqtiṣād, op. cit.*, pp. 148-149; *Iḥyā'*, vol. I, p. 30; *Mīzān*, p. 372 and *Faḍā'iḥ al- Bāṭiniyyah*, p. 205.

[28] *Al-Iqtiṣād*, p. 147.

the rational consideration of the uses and advantages of instituting an imām or caliph: for the objectives of the *Sharī'ah* (*maqāṣid al-Sharī'ah*) do, of course, include on the one hand, the promotion of policies and actions that are beneficial to humankind, and on the other, the removal or eradication of others that are harmful or destructive.[29]

In accordance with this approach, al-Ghazālī then indicates his dissatisfaction with the manner in which some scholars have tended to argue for the establishment of caliphs on the basis of *ijmā'* (or consensus) without further comment or explanation. Instead he says that it is necessary to investigate and clearly state the rationale on the basis of which *ijmā'* itself stands. Al-Ghazālī's enquiry in this regard leads him to argue: first that the establishment of the faith (or Islamic order: *niẓām al-islām*) was certainly the prime concern or objective of the Prophet; and secondly that the realization of that objective would be inconceivable in the absence of an imam (or leader) whose orders and directives are obeyed and followed by one and all. In other words, he concludes, *niẓām al-dīn*, i.e., the Islamic order or system cannot be realized except through the establishment of a properly constituted and effective worldly system or order: *inna niẓāma al-dīnī lā yaḥṣulu illā bi niẓāmi al-dunyā*.[30]

To this, al-Ghazālī points out that some may object by saying that the reverse should be the case. In other words that faith and the world should be considered contradictory and mutually exclusive. But this, al-Ghazālī argues, is a misconception based on gross misunderstanding of the nature of both the faith (Islam) and the world.

For while it is undoubtedly true that indulgence in worldly pleasures and the pursuit of luxurious life styles are certainly

---

[29] Ibid.

[30] Ibid, pp. 147-148.

destructive for the soul and corrosive to ethical sensibilities, a morally measured and responsible or moderate involvement in worldly affairs vis-a-vis having enough of the good things of life to meet basic human needs are, in fact, preconditions without which neither the good life in general, nor spiritual refinement and moral fulfillment in particular, can be attained.[31] More specifically the argument continues, the establishment of "*niẓām al-dīn*" or Islamic order, is contingent upon the acquisition of knowledge and on worship in its various forms and facets. But neither of these can be accomplished in the absence of physical life, good health, or adequate provisions for the satisfaction of such basic needs as all humans have for food, shelter and clothing in conditions of peace and security. A person who has to spend all his time and energy defending his life against hostile forces in order to secure the wherewithal for physical survival, would surely not be able either to seek knowledge or engage in worship and the performance of good deeds: the two indispensable prerequisites of attaining salvation and eternal bliss in the Hereafter. It should therefore, be clear that the establishment of a well organized worldly system, complete with a properly constituted and effective *imāmate* (or government) that at the very least keeps law and order as well as gives a modicum of appropriate guidance, is a necessary *precondition* for the existence and development of a healthy spiritual and moral (specifically Islamic) order. In al-Ghazālī's own succinct words: *...niẓāmu al-dunyā...sharṭun ...li niẓāmi al-dīn.*[32]

But al-Ghazālī is not contented merely to demonstrate the correctness of his position and the coherence of his argument. Taking the battle to the opponents' camp, so to speak, he

[31] Ibid, p. 148.

[32] Ibid. Also, *Faḍā'iḥ al-Bāṭiniyyah* (henceforth: *al-Mustaẓhirī*), pp. 196-200.

vigorously assails those ignoramus (*al-juhhāl*)[33] who mistakenly think that in order to be a truly good Muslim one must renounce the world on the assumption that it is all contaminated with evil and *ḥarām* (i.e. unlawful) things and actions. Describing this attitude as a most harmful *bid'ah* (i.e. accretion),[34] al-Ghazālī proceeds to expose its weaknesses and contradictions in several ways and at some length. Suffice it to note here, that he is strongly of the opinion that a true *zāhid* (i.e; ascetic, or very devout person) is not necessarily one who is bereft of wealth, but one who is not obsessed by, or excessively preoccupied with wealth, even if he happened to be the richest person on earth. Citing numerous passages from the Holy Qur'an, alongside several sayings of the Prophet, furthermore, al-Ghazālī grants that there are indeed good and evil forces in the world, as well as many grey areas between the two. With sufficient knowledge and good common sense however, it should be quite possible for a conscientious Muslim who is capable of work to navigate his or her way through life in a manner perfectly consistent with dignity and moral integrity. Indeed, the argument continues, hard work for the purpose of securing honest earnings with a view to satisfying the legitimate needs and ambitions of oneself and one's dependents, including, parents,—is not merely permissible. In the light of both Qur'anic precepts and Prophetic teachings rather it is a highly commendable form of worship, or even of *jihād*, the assured reward for which is Godly blessings and heavenly bliss.[35]

Winding up the whole argument, al-Ghazālī says that the state is necessary and indispensable for social life and worldly order. These, in turn, are necessary and indispensable for healthy spiritual and moral life. And, for him, as we have seen, religion encompasses the socio-economic, political and cultural, as well as

---

[33] *Iḥyā'*, vol. 2, book 5, p. 20 *FF*.

[34] Ibid.

[35] *Iḥyā'*, vol. I, book 4, p. 168 *FF*, and vol. II, books, pp. 21-137.

the spiritual and moral aspects of life viewed as necessary and indispensable for the attainment of salvation and eternal bliss in the Hereafter.[36] This constitutes true happiness[37] and is the ultimate objective of the *Sharī'ah*; indeed' of all prophetic missions. The state and politics are of pivotal importance throughout, and it is from their central role in both this world and with regard to the Hereafter that they derive their legitimacy and ultimate significance.

III. Principles and Institutions of Government

It should be clear from what has been said above, that the *Sharī'ah*, for al-Ghazālī, was the fount of legitimacy for all actions of the *ummah* and constituted the basis on which governmental, as well as other, institutions stood.[38] It is indicative of the great importance which he attached to the *Sharī'ah* in general and to *uṣūl al-fiqh* (principles of jurisprudence) in particular, that although he was, of course, fully cognizant of the masterly contributions which had already been made to the subject by al-Shāfi'ī and Imām al-Ḥaramayn, among others, and despite the fact that he had himself discussed it in several of his earlier works, al-Ghazālī dedicated some of the last years of his life to the writing of a comprehensive and highly systematic book on the subject: namely *al-Mustaṣfā min 'Ilm al-Uṣūl.*[39] Subsequently described by Ibn Khaldūn as one of the best four books ever written on *uṣūl al-fiqh*,[40] al-Mustaṣfā, alongside its counterparts, came to be widely

---

[36] *Al-Iqtiṣād*, p. 149.

[37] *Mīzān*, p. 305 and *Iḥyā'*, vol. 1, p. 21.

[38] *Iḥyā'*, vol. 1, p. 9 *FF.*

[39] See, for example, Dr Muhammad Sulaiman al-Ashqar's edition, published in two volumes, by Mu'assasat al-Risālah, Beirut, 1997.

[40] 'Abd al-Raḥmān Ibn Khaldūn: *Tārīkh Ibn Khaldūn, al-Muqaddimah* (Beirut: Dār al-Kutub al-'ilmiyyah, 1992), p. 487. Also, Franz Rosenthal's English translation of *The Muqaddimah* (New York: Bollington Foundation,

regarded *inter alia* as a veritable manual in the light of which *mujtahids* throughout the ages, could rationally and consistently with the teachings and principles enshrined in the Qur'an and the *Sunnah*, produce appropriate *aḥkām* (i.e. rulings and judgements) to fit the needs and requirements of Muslim societies in different and changing circumstances.

One of the greatest challenges which al-Ghazālī had to face in his own day and age was the fact that the caliphate was no longer what it used to be or should have been. For while caliphs as the custodians of the *Sharī'ah*, continued to enjoy a certain essentially moral or theoretical authority, real power in the sense of ability to take effective decisions in matters of public policy and that the said decisions were implemented, was wielded not by caliphs but by Seljuk Sultans and their aides, whether military or civilian. The caliphs, for their part, were often far from being ideally qualified in terms of learning, character and general ability for the important office of the leadership entrusted to them. Meanwhile the Bāṭinites, opposed to Seljuk Sultans and 'Abbasid caliphs alike, continued to fight both not only militarily but also politically and ideologically.

Apart from having to rebut the ideological and political onslaught of the Bāṭinites, al-Ghazālī and his contemporaries had to contend with the even more serious and difficult question—or cluster of questions—of how to reconcile the situation arising from the feebleness of the caliphs on the one hand, and the domination of both the caliphs and the *ummah* by the Seljuk Sultans and war lords on the other, with the precepts and principles of the *Sharī'ah*. Given this situation, was there any way in which the *Sharī'ah* could still remain the fount of legitimacy for both the society and state? Or, had the *Shar'ī* legitimacy in fact been lost in the existing set up and was the *ummah*, in

---

1957), vol. 3, pp. 28-29.

consequence, living in sin?

If such questions were deeply troubling for all politically conscious Muslims at the time (which they undoubtedly were), they must have been much more unsettling for those individuals who were endowed with highly sensitive souls and minds, of whom al-Ghazālī was the most prominent example.

But there were other troubling questions besides. Among the most pressing of these were several that arose in connection with the manner in which *Sultans*, *walīs*, and lesser functionaries and administrators who managed public affairs were in many instances far removed from the high standards of justice, efficiency and transparency stipulated by the *Sharī'ah*. And furthermore, as if to render an already difficult situation more complex, the *'ulamā'* who as the professional interpreters and expositors of the *Sharī'ah*, were supposed to be models of integrity and champions of reform, were also themselves often corrupt self-seeking individuals.[41]

Al-Ghazālī tackled the first set of questions (concerning caliphs and *Sultans*) by first of all, recognizing the situation for what it actually was: an obvious and painfully flawed condition which only tenuously reflected the values and principles of the *Sharī'ah*. In terms of *uṣūl al-fiqh*, al-Ghazālī, not surprisingly, considered it an anomalous or extraordinary situation in which necessity rendered legitimate and acceptable judgements and practices which would otherwise be regarded as illegitimate and unacceptable: *al-ḍarūrāt tubīḥu al-maḥẓūrāt.*[42] Short of revolution, which, like Hobbes, al-Ghazālī would not entertain for fear that it would almost certainly unleash unpredictable and uncontrollable forces of destruction that would undermine the entire fabric of both society and the state, the situation was simply

[41] *Iḥyā'*, vol. II, book 7, pp. 92-93.

[42] *Al-Iqtiṣād*, p. 151.

not capable of admitting or making possible a neat or perfect solution. Only a contrived series of partial reforms and compromises could be realistically considered.

In theory, al-Ghazālī pointed out, the accession to the caliphate could be affected through any of three possible ways, namely: designation by the Prophet; designation by a reigning caliph; or through selection by a militarily and politically dominant person or group of persons to whom obedience is rendered by the majority of the populace.[43] (It is a remarkable fact-perhaps reflective of the desperately contentious circumstances in which he lived-that al-Ghazālī did not even mention *shūrā*, whereby rulers would be chosen by the ruled as a fourth, theoretically possible, way).

In practice however, al-Ghazālī: boldly, though perhaps with a tinge of controlled sadness, stated: *al-wilāyatu al-ān lā tatba'u illā al-shawkah: fa man bāya'ahu sāḥibu 'l-shawkah fa huwa al-khalīfah*[44] "... accession [to the caliphate] nowadays is entirely dependent upon military might; for that person [from among the Abbasids] to whom allegiance is professed by the holder of military might, is caliph".

As if engaged in a desperate search for some way whereby a veneer of legitimacy could be shed upon the above described procedures and processes, al-Ghazālī then goes on to say that: "provided the independent wielder of military might in question professes allegiance to the caliph [and demonstrates his allegiance] by seeing to it that the caliph's name is mentioned in the *khuṭbah* [in congregations for Friday and 'Id prayers] and on the coinage, the said [war lord] should be recognized as a [legitimate] *Sultans* whose orders and judgements are to be

---

[43] Ibid, pp. 149-150.

[44] *Iḥyā'*, vol. II, book 5, p. 110 and *al-Mustaẓhirī*, pp. 176-177.

followed and implemented throughout the realm..."[45] ... *wa man istabadda bi 'l-shawkah wa huwa muṭī'un li 'l-khalīfah fī al al-khuṭbah wa 'l sikkah, fa huwa Sultanun nāfidhu 'l-ḥukm wa 'l-qaḍā' fī aqṭār al-arḍ, wilāyatun nāfidhata 'l aḥkām.*

In this way the danger of the *ummah* being plunged into sin is averted, for the *Sultans* who has effective control of power, is recognized as a legitimate (if clearly dominant) partner of the caliph, in the management of the affairs of the *ummah.*

But it was not only in military prowess and political power that caliphs or would-be-caliphs in those days were deficient. For, apart from having been born 'Abbasid, thereby fulfilling one of the conditions which were then regarded as essential qualifications for assuming the caliphate (i.e., Qurayshite descent), the other required qualifications included the basic one of being educated at least to the level of mufti or *mujtahid*, and were—according to al-Ghazālī himself—totally missing.[46]

Just as the lack of military might and political power could be compensated for by recognizing loyal *Sultans* as partners with caliphs in the management of public affairs in the above indicated manner, their lack of knowledge and proper education however, al-Ghazālī argues, could be made up for by arranging for caliphs, who were at the very least expected to be conscientious and reasonably intelligent men,[47] to seek appropriate guidance and welcome good advice given by competent God-fearing scholars or *'ulamā'.*[48]

By virtue of his being an expert in politics and conflict resolution, al-Ghazālī says the *'ālim* (scholar-jurist) should be the

---

[45] *Iḥyā', loc. cit.*

[46] *Al-Iqtiṣād*, p. 151; *Al-Mustaẓhirī*, pp. 192-194.

[47] *Al-Mustaẓhirī*, pp. 185-186.

[48] *Iḥyā'*, vol. 2, book 7, pp. 68-93.

Sultan's tutor and guide in the management and control of public affairs: *al-faqīhu huwa al-'ālimu bi qānūni 'l siyāsah wa ṭarīqi al-tawaṣṣut bayna 'l-khalq idhā tanāza'ū bi ḥukm al-shahawāt, fa kāna al-faqīhu mu'allim al-Sultan wa murshidahu ilā ṭarīqi siyāsati 'l khalqi wa ḍabṭihim liyantazima bi istiqāmatihim umūruhum fi'd-dunyā.*[49]

With the three principal institutions in the caliphate (i.e., *Sultans*, caliphs and *'ulamā'*) thus complementing each other and hopefully acting in concert, the integrity of the *ummah* would be secured and the legitimacy of the body politic sustained.

As if to disarm potential doubters and critics in advance of any possible attack, al-Ghazālī then hastens to add that the alternative (of, for example, withdrawing recognition of legitimacy from such *Sultans* and caliphs as have been described above) would be the collapse of the entire edifice of legality and of legal transactions. This would undermine all judicial and administrative appointments and decisions; as well as all marriages and testimonials; indeed, the whole system of rights and obligations that, under the *Sharī'ah*, are due not only to men and women here on earth, but also, and infinitely more importantly, to the Lord above. The *ummah* in its entirety would be irredeemably plunged into sin.[50] Which would be better, al-Ghazālī then rhetorically asks: to accept as legitimate an admittedly imperfect caliphate and thus safeguard the integrity of the social order and the validity of official appointments, judicial decisions, marital contracts, etc.?—or risk the collapse of the entire social order simply because of the non-availability of persons who are fully qualified for the caliphate as ideally

[49] *Iḥyā'*, vol. 1, book 1, p. 30.

[50] *Al-Iqtiṣād*, p. 151; *Al-Mustaẓhirī*, pp. 169-170, and *Iḥyā'*, vol. I, book 2, p.10.

conceived?[51]

In any case, al-Ghazālī points out that obeying rulers and giving them loyal support and assistance even though, as humans, they cannot but be imperfect, are religious duties which, as such cannot be lightly shirked or put aside by any (equally human and imperfect) person who would consider himself or herself truly Muslim.[52]

Al-Ghazālī's argument aimed inter alia at bridging the gap between the ideal and the real in the socio-political situation of his time and was, to say the least, clearly original. None of his predecessors, including the brilliant al-Mawardī and al-Juwaynī, had either faced the problem or attempted to resolve its inherent tensions and contradictions the way al-Ghazālī did. Not surprisingly, therefore, his thesis and the generally persuasive arguments which underpinned it have met with wide acceptance, not only among his own contemporaries, but also among succeeding generations of Sunni Muslims around the world.

As might have been expected however, the Bāṭinites and the Shī'ah in general, were not similarly impressed. Al-Ghazālī, for his part, was certainly not interested in winning them over to his point of view. His primary objective as far as the Shī'ah in general and the Bāṭinites in particular were concerned was, rather, to rebut their arguments and demonstrate the incoherence of their views (especially those of the *Ta'līmiyyah* of his time: *Bāṭiniyyat hādhā al-'aṣr'*, as he described them),[53] regarding the Sunni caliphate in general, and that of the young 'Abbasid caliph, al-Mustaẓhir, in particular. The book, *Faḍā'iḥ al-Bāṭiniyyah / Al-Mustaẓhirī*, which al-Ghazālī wrote to that end, is a highly

---

[51] *Al-Iqtiṣād*, p. 151; *Al-Mustaẓhirī*, pp. 191-194.

[52] *Al-Mustaẓhirī*, pp. 3-4 and 190, also *Al-Iqtiṣād*, p. 150, and *Iḥyā'*, vol. 2, book 5, p.110.

[53] *Al-Mustaẓhirī*, p.17.

systematic and fairly detailed refutation of a wide range of Shī'ī and, especially, Ismā'ilite beliefs and positions: theological, juridical, and political.

We need not explore al-Ghazālī's arguments in this connection in any detail here. Suffice it to note that, beginning with an exposition of Bāṭinite esotericism and how it necessarily leads to the undermining of faith *and Sharī'ah (ibṭāl al-Sharāi' [wa] al-insilākh 'an qawā'id al-dīn)* as well as thinking (*ra'y*) and reasoning (*taṣarruf al-'uqūl*),[54] al-Ghazālī then proceeds to reject as preposterous and totally unfounded, the fundamental claim commonly held by Bāṭinites and all Shī'ites that Imam 'Ali and his progeny after him had been designated successors by the Prophet. His argument in this respect is twofold. Al-Ghazālī first points out that it is simply inconceivable that the Companions (totally devoted to the Prophet and proverbially keen on watching, memorizing and propagating his every utterance or action as they were) could have conspired—and unanimously so—to conceal or deny knowledge of anything pertaining to the Prophet or the faith however small or apparently insignificant, let alone one of such obvious gravity and importance as the question of the leadership of the *ummah.* Had he designated anyone to succeed him everybody would have surely known and testified accordingly. Assuming, for the sake of the argument, that the impossible did somehow happen, and that the document containing the alleged designation was conspiratorially hidden or destroyed, why, al-Ghazālī then asks, did neither Imam 'Ali himself nor any of his supporters at the time, seeing that the validity of his succession to the caliphate was challenged by adversaries against whom he had to fight a series of prolonged and bitter battles, not produce, or even mention either the supposed document or the alleged

[54] Ibid, pp. 11-17.

designation.[55]

Devoid of true faith *(siḥḥat al-'aqīdah wa salāmat al-dīn)* as well as of any evidence to substantiate his claim to the imamate or caliphate therefore, Al-Ghazālī concludes, there are no basis whatsoever for considering the Bāṭinite's nominee or claimant for the imamate as anything other than inadmissible and totally unacceptable.[56]

Recapitulating on the arguments which he had earlier marshaled in support of his main thesis, al-Ghazālī then reasserts his position that the 'Abbasid caliphate in general and that of the incumbent caliph, al-Mustaẓhir in particular, were alone legitimate and valid. In that context, al-Ghazālī then introduces another and interesting new principle: namely, the majority rule, or in his own words, *al-tarjīḥ bi 'l-kathrah.* Using language which is familiar enough in the context of modern debates and discussions about the merits and limitations of democracy and democratic procedures, al-Ghazālī says that since it is virtually impossible for all concerned in any given situation where a potentially divisive issue is being considered to come to a unanimously agreed position, it is imperative that all should abide by the opinion of the majority: ... *fa innahum law ikhtalafū* ... *wajaba al-tarjīḥ bi 'l-kathrah.*[57] On that count too, al-Ghazālī maintains, the Bāṭinites who constituted no more than a small fraction of the body politic, had no right or claim for the leadership of the *ummah.* By contrast, the 'Abbasids (including al-Mustaẓhir), because they were recognized by the overwhelming majority of the populace, including all outstanding scholars and *'ulamā'* as well as those who enjoyed military might and political power, were indeed the legitimate imams or caliphs to whom

---

[55] Ibid, pp. 132-140 and p. 174.

[56] Ibid, pp. 172-173.

[57] Ibid, p. 175.

obedience was therefore religiously and morally owed by one and all.[58]

To the Bāṭinite inspired jibe that the obedience owed by the *Sultans* and war lords to the caliph was not infrequently conspicuous by its absence, al-Ghazālī's response was twofold. Al-Ghazālī begins by asserting that, for the Seljuk Sultans and warlords, obedience to the caliph was indeed a matter of faith and principle which they would ardently defend with all their might against any enemy or challenger: that they would in fact regard defending the 'Abbasid caliphate in this way as *jihād fī sabīl Allāh.*[59] The fact that they did sometimes behave contrary to the caliph's wishes or directives did not amount to a negation of the loyalty which they sincerely owed him in principle. The same, al-Ghazālī argues, is in fact true with regard to the obedience owed by any servant to his master or even by men of faith to God. Sincere commitment to the principle cannot fairly be denied merely because practice sometimes happens to be inconsistent with the principle in question.

As was usual with him, al-Ghazālī then carries the battle into the court of the adversaries. Why do those Bāṭinites who hasten to raise this kind of question, not think of Imām 'Ali's experience with his supposedly loyal supporters (shī'a) who so frequently let him down in both word and deed that almost all his speeches echo his disappointment and bitter complaints about their treacherous disobedience to himself? If the failure of so many of Imām 'Alī's supporters to be true to him could not lead us to saying that there were all disloyal, why should it be said that occasionally similar conduct on the part of some of the Seljuk Sultans and warlords be regarded as tantamount to withdrawal of loyalty and obedience

[58] Ibid, pp. 174-177.

[59] Ibid, p. 183.

from 'Abbasid caliphs?[60] For al-Ghazālī, therefore, the validity of the majority principle (*al-tarjīḥ bi 'l-kathrah*), with all its aforementioned corollaries, remains intact.

Reconstructing the juridical and political basis of the 'Abbasid caliphate at a time when power had already passed from the hands of the caliphs to those of the Seljuk Sultans and war lords, and defending the thus refurbished caliphate against the ideological onslaught of the Bāṭinites and others, were two major objectives for the realization of which al-Ghazālī, as we have seen, had ardently struggled and not without a considerable measure of success.

But al-Ghazālī was also anxious to see that the actual performance of the caliphate and its constituent organs in the day-to-day management and administration of the affairs of the *ummah* were, as far as possible, in conformity with the high standards of good governance, including integrity, clemency, justice, efficiency, transparency etc., which are enshrined in the *Sharī'ah*.

Being a most distinguished thinker and a highly influential reform-minded teacher and public personality but not a ruler or administrator himself, al-Ghazālī's chosen method for the realization of his objective in this regard was, naturally, the written and / or spoken word of advice.[61] Al-Ghazālī was indeed a

---

[60] Ibid, pp. 183-184.

[61] It is almost certain that in choosing this method, al-Ghazālī had the famous *ḥadīth* in mind: *al-dīn al-naṣīḥah*: meaning that [good] advice [sincerely given to rulers, groups, individuals or to the *ummah* at large] is [of the essence of] faith. As such advice is a form of worship (*'ibādah*) or, depending on circumstances, even of *jihād*—a most commendable form of action.

prolific and untiring source of such advice; including admonition, encouragement, warning, etc. as appropriate, and which he directed to *Sultans*, judges, *walīs* and *'ulamā'*, as well as to the caliph and members of the public at large: sometimes in the form of books and pamphlets; some others as letters and epistles of various kinds and length. Consistently with his afore-mentioned views, especially in connection with the importance and legitimacy of the state, al-Ghazālī was constantly concerned with the attainment of excellence in thought and action. This was not only for its own sake or as a necessary precondition for the realization of the good life here on earth (which, as we have seen, he greatly valued and appreciated) but, also, and much more importantly as a prerequisite, God-willing, for salvation and the attainment of eternal bliss in the Hereafter. For al-Ghazālī, the spiritual and ethical aspects of the human experience continue to be the uppermost considerations in political and social thought and action.

This is particularly clear in the advice contained in the tenth and final chapter of *Faḍā'iḥ al-Bāṭiniyyah*, which al-Ghazālī gives to the young caliph al-Mustaẓhir. Not insignificantly in the circumstances, the thirty pages of this chapter only formally and proverbially touch on matters relating to power, politics and administration. It more directly and effectively focuses instead, as its very title clearly indicates,[62] on the need for the caliph, if his tenure as such is to continue for long, to concentrate on the deepening of his faith, the refinement of his spiritual sensibilities, and the acquisition and development of a number of ethical and moral qualities in his character. Among the qualities and attributes on which special emphasis is placed are piety, righteousness, self-restraint, justice, clemency, integrity, courtesy,

---

[62] *Al-Mustaẓhirī*, pp. 195-225. The title of the said chapter is *Fī'l waẓā'i fi'l dīniyyati allatī bi'l mūwaẓabati 'alayhā yadūmu istiḥqaqu al-imāmah.*

kindness, love of learning and wisdom, the veneration of *'ulamā'*, and the respectful consideration of the latter's advice.

Traditionally regarded in Muslim societies as *warathatu 'l anbiyā'* (i.e., heirs to the prophets) the *'ulamā'* and certainly those of them who, for al-Ghazālī, were truly worthy of the designation, were not merely purveyors of knowledge and information, or occupants of various posts and offices; but also, as custodians of the *Sharī'ah*, they were, leaders of society and tutors of rulers and statesmen. Naturally therefore, al-Ghazālī, was most anxious to see the *'ulamā'* shoulder the heavy and important responsibilities entrusted to them by both society and the state, with requisite competence and integrity.

Extraordinarily insightful and perceptive and, at the same time, endowed with exceptionally powerful analytical abilities as well as system-building skills, al-Ghazālī has in fact enriched the human heritage with a wide range of theories, concepts, and tools of analysis that, taken together, encompass the human experience in its entirety. It goes without saying that giving an adequate idea about his views on learning and educational processes for instance, or with regard to the ways and means whereby moral integrity may be built-up, or cognitive abilities and academic competence enhanced, are all beyond our present concerns.

Suffice it to note that as far as the basic ingredients of what he regarded as the necessary and appropriate education of truly qualified *'ulamā'* were concerned, al-Ghazālī was strongly of the opinion that both the rational and religious sciences should be included. Those who claim that revelation is on its own sufficient and accordingly insist on the exclusion of rational sciences, al-Ghazālī says, are ignorant while those, on the other hand, who maintain that reason and the rational sciences are enough and would therefore have us do without the light and guidance of the Qur'an and the *Sunnah*, are arrogant and misguided. The two together, i.e reason and revelation, al-Ghazālī argues, are in fact necessary and complement each other.[63]

An encyclopaedist by nature[64] and conviction, and a passionate believer in the inter-disciplinary approach to learning, al-Ghazālī in fact insists that serious scholars and would be real *'ulamā'* should endeavour, wherever and whenever possible, to learn enough of each science in existence to be able, at the very least, to understand and appreciate the methods and objectives of the science or the sciences in question; for all sciences, al-Ghazālī states, are closely interconnected and complement each other. Therefore, if life is too short for one to master all sciences, one should at least take a whiff of each: *...inna al-'ulamā kullahā muta'āwinatun mutarābiṭatun ba'ḍuhā bi ba'ḍ...[fa] idhā lam yattasi'a al-'umūr li jamī'il-'ulūm ...fayaktafī bi shammatin min kulli 'ilm.*[65]

The same integrative outlook on life and knowledge is also evident in al-Ghazālī's way of considering the old debate between the *fuqahā'* (who favour the legalistic or juridical approach, whereby considerable emphasis is put on *aḥkām* i.e. rules and regulations) on the one hand, and the *mutaṣawwifah* or *ṣūfīs* (who attach greater importance to spirituality and the moral dimension of life and religious thought and practice, while perhaps neglecting *fiqh*) on the other. Al-Ghazālī, as may be expected, is strongly critical of the 'radicals' or 'exclusivists' on both sides and resolves the tension by demonstrating the importance and complementarity of the two approaches.[66]

It goes without saying that, for al-Ghazālī, knowledge in all its

---

[63] *Iḥyā'*, vol. II, book 8, p. 30.

[64] Al-Ghazālī himself eloquently testifies to this in the first few pages of his remarkable intellectual autobiography, *al-Munqidh min al-Ḍalal.*

[65] *Mīzān*, pp. 348-350.

[66] *Iḥyā'*, vol. 1, book 1, pp. 24-70 and vol. 2, book 8, pp. 31-35.

forms and aspects (excepting only such spurious or pseudo sciences as magic and astrology which he describes as either useless or harmful)[67] is of the utmost value and importance.

In the last analysis however, al-Ghazālī repeatedly says that what is really important (both for life here on earth and most certainly in the Hereafter) is not knowledge or learning or scholarship *per se*, however well conceived or brilliantly demonstrated they may be. What is ultimately important and of infinitely durable value is actual conduct or behaviour: what we do with our lives and knowledge rather than what we know, think, or say.

It was mainly in this connection that al-Ghazālī was grieved to find that most of the *'ulamā'* of his time had failed. *'ulamā' al-sū'* (or evil scholars) as he dubbed them, al-Ghazālī bitterly complains, had all too frequently failed individually by becoming demonstrably arrogant, avaricious, egoistic, and downright hypocritical. They also failed, collectively: first, by not fulfilling their duties as responsible leaders and constructive critics of society, thus commanding right and forbidding wrong as they should always do; and secondly, by becoming seekers after power, wealth and position, who, as such, and in order to attain their unworthy aims, allowed themselves to become sycophants, flatterers, and boon-friends of kings and *Sultans* instead of giving them much needed honest counsel and advice.[68] Al-Ghazālī sums up the whole tragic situation by saying that when the *'ulamā'* succumb to such worldly temptations as love of wealth and power they become corrupt. Thus snared and seduced by the glitter of worldly pleasures they are no longer able to fulfill their prescribed duty of commanding right and forbidding wrong, even among the criminal dredges and fall-outs of society, let alone kings and

---

[67] *Iḥyā'*, vol. 1, book 1, pp. 49-53 and 65.

[68] *Iḥyā'*, vol. 2, book 7, pp. 92-93.

dignitaries. These in turn abandon themselves to [still greater] corruption. Following the example of their kings and rulers, the people at large then proceed along [the same slippery slope].[69]

This brings us to the third principal institution in the caliphate after the caliph and the *'ulamā'*, namely the *Sultans* and kings.

The Seljuk Sultans and kings were, of course, the effective rulers of the caliphate. Not surprisingly therefore, al-Ghazālī directed a lot of his attention and advice (including his book, *Naṣīḥat al-Mulūk* (Counsel for Kings) and the many letters and shorter messages which were subsequently collected and published as *Faḍā'il al-Anām min Rasā'il Ḥujjatu'l-Islām*), to the said rulers and their wide range of assistants, including *wazīrs*, *qāḍīs*, top administrators, and other dignitaries.

The dominant themes of all these writings are the need for those in charge of the affairs of the *ummah* to maintain law and order, uphold justice, and thus make it possible for the people—with the guidance of their rulers and the *'ulamā'*—to pursue the good life in conditions of peace and tranquility.

In trying to attain these objectives and thus, hopefully, salvation and eternal bliss in the life to come, al-Ghazālī repeatedly points out that the rulers and the ruled must abide by the *Sharī'ah* and be guided by the good example of the Prophet and those who have devoutly followed him, while also learning from the experiences and wisdom of other peoples and nations whenever these are found to be consistent with the teachings and principles of Islam.

---

[69] Al-Ghazālī's actual words are: *fasādu al-ra'iyyah bi fasādi 'l-mulūk; wa fasādu 'l- mulūk bi fasādi 'l-'ulamā'; wa fasādu 'l-'ulamā' bistīla'i ḥubbi 'l-māli wa 'l-jāh; wa man istawlā 'alayhi ḥubbu 'l-dunyā lam yaqdir 'ala'l-ḥisbati 'alā' l-'arādhil fa kayfa 'alā'l-mulūk wa 'l-akābīr*. Ibid.

Thus bearing in mind that a king or a *Sultans*—as the ancient saying goes al-Ghazālī notes—is like the shadow of God on earth: the people must not only desist from rebellion and insurrection; they should actively follow and obey, even love their kings and *Sultans*.[70]

Sultans, on the other hand, should realize that governance (*wilāyah*) is a great bounty (*ni'mah*) which is conditionally conferred by God on a select few. If it is wisely and justly used, it will certainly yield great pleasure and everlasting bliss. Contrariwise, if it is abused and misplaced, it will inevitably precipitate boundless misery and unhappiness without end.[71]

The principal key to the happiness of both the rulers and the ruled-on earth and in the life to come-is justice. If the realm is justly ruled, the people will prosper and the country will be tranquil and peaceful. Injustice, on the other hand, will breed resentment among the people and bring about the destruction of the land.[72]

It is important to remember furthermore, that in trying to establish justice in the realm, it is not enough, al-Ghazālī points out, that the *Sultans* himself be just and avoid wrongdoing; he should also ensure that his aids and assistants are likewise upright and just.[73] To achieve that objective, the *Sultans* should observe and supervise the conduct of his aids and *walīs* as carefully as he would the conduct of his family and household.[74] Special care should be taken in making appointments to the judiciary. Only persons of integrity and good character, as well as appropriate academic or professional qualifications, should be appointed *qāḍīs*

---

[70] *Al-Tibr*, p. 43.

[71] Ibid, p. 14.

[72] Ibid, p. 44.

[73] Ibid, p. 22.

[74] Ibid.

because they will be entrusted with the direct application of the *Sharī'ah*.[75]

Wazīrs should be perspicacious, honest and particularly capable in the management of public affairs. Occasional and minor slips on the *wazīr's* part should be graciously forgiven by the *Sultan*. As the *Sultan's* right hand man the *wazīr* should be treated as a confidant, consulted in all matters of state and protected from invidious reporting by jealous rivals. Should it be decided that his services are no longer needed, his [legitimately earned] wealth or property should not be coveted or confiscated.[76]

Since justice is best known through the *Sharī'ah*[77] the *Sultans* should always seek the company of the *'ulamā'* and carefully listen to their advice. In so engaging himself however the *Sultans* should be careful not to fall in the clutches of *'ulamā' al-sū'* (or evil scholars) who, through flattery, trickery and sycophancy, would only want to secure certain *ḥarām* (i.e. illegitimate) benefits for themselves. The true (or *bona fide*) *'ālim*, al-Ghazālī points out to the *Sultan*, is he who does not long for your bounty and would not hesitate to give genuine and dispassionate opinion or advice [come what may].[78]

In order to make absolutely sure that justice is upheld and the authority of the state and all those who are in charge of public affairs is respected and held in awe, al-Ghazālī advises the *Sultan* to make himself a good example for others. He should carefully observe the values, rules and principles of the faith, and in addition to being just, strong and decisive, should endeavour to adorn himself with such qualities as self restraint, modesty,

---

[75] Letter to the *wazīr* Fakhr al-Mulk: no 6 in *Faḍā'il al-anām*, p. 65.

[76] *Al-Tibr*, pp. 83-84.

[77] Al-*Mustaẓhiri*, p. 205.

[78] *Al-Tibr*, pp. 18-19.

clemency and affability.[79] If he absolutely cannot help being attracted to such things as drinking alcohol, hunting and playing chess, the *Sultans* should be careful not to allow these to distract him from attending to his duties, both religious and political. There should be a time for everything al-Ghazālī says.[80] No less realistically and interestingly, al-Ghazālī concludes his *Naṣīḥat al-Mulūk* with two chapters on the fairer sex and how they should be sensitively, perhaps passionately but always ethically and responsibly treated—especially by those, such as *Sultans* and *wazīrs*, who are in charge of public affairs and the destiny of the *ummah*.[81]

IV. Some Concluding Remarks: The Contemporary Relevance of al-Ghazālī's Political Thought

Al-Ghazālī departed this world some nine hundred years ago. His thought and ideas, theological, philosophical, ethical, political and otherwise however, have continued to attract, fascinate, inspire and sometimes enrage many thinking people, Muslim and non-Muslim alike, for almost a millennium now. And they are likely to continue to do so for as long as thinking men and women exist.

This has been the case, to some extent, because the nature of knowledge, its pursuit and the process of thinking itself-all

---

[79] Ibid, p. 9. *FF*.

[80] Ibid, p. 65.

[81] *Al-Tibr*, pp. 122-131. It should be mentioned in this connection that the authenticity of the second half of *Naṣīḥat al-Mulūk* has been questioned by some scholars. See the entries on al-Ghazālī by Bowering and Pourjavady in the *Encyclopaedia Iranica*, vol. X and Patricia Crone (1987). The majority of Muslim and Western scholars however remain convinced that the whole text is the authentic work of al-Ghazālī. For a clear review of the subject see Nik Roskiman Abdul Samad, Al-Ghazel on *Administrative Ethics With Special Reference To His Naṣīḥah al-Mulūk* (Kuala Lumpur, Malaysia: ISTAC, 2003), pp. 39-44.

subjects of perennial and universal importance-have been pivotal to the life and thought of al-Ghazālī and he had many brilliant and enlightening things to say about each of them. Living at a time when the creation of 'a knowledge-based society' has become a universally cherished ambition of humanity-even though the concept may have been variously understood and only partially realized so far-all those who are in any way seriously concerned with the subject today would, therefore, naturally want to consult al-Ghazālī and perhaps others who, like him, may have, to a greater or lesser extent, enriched the human heritage across cultural and linguistic boundaries.

The value of his integrative approach to knowledge and the human experience in general should also be a matter of considerable interest and appreciation for the many across the world today who are increasingly distressed by the prevalent and growing state of post modern fragmentation in general and, especially, those who contemplate or have to bear the consequences of the rapidly growing separation, and in many cases the now well established divorce, between ethics and morality on the one hand, and politics along with a whole series of social functions and activities, including education and business, as well as numerous applications or misapplications of modern scientific research on the other.

Al-Ghazālī's specifically political thought as we have seen was highly original and, perhaps even more importantly, characterized *inter alia* by an unflinching realism which, far from the cynicism normally associated with the term in much of our contemporary political discourse, was, however, firmly rooted in spiritual and ethical values and beliefs. The particular historical context in which al-Ghazālī developed his social and political thought has of course disappeared a long time ago. But the strong bond which he creatively forged between spiritual teachings and ethical values and the difficult realities of the situation in existence at the time remains. And this without the cynicism we nowadays generally assume is an unavoidable, almost necessary, consequence or attendant feature of realism. This latter stands as a ray of light, which shining across the centuries, lights up and dissipates the darkness we often fight against today.

Another major theme in al-Ghazālī's political thought that is more easily and perhaps less contentiously seen and recognized as relevant today, is his constant and unwavering concern with good governance—including such vitally important ingredients as justice, clemency, transparency and integrity.

Closely related to good governance and its various constituent elements in al-Ghazālī's social and political thought are his views regarding the role of the 'intelligentsia' i.e: scholars and the better educated generally, both in society and the political system. Unlike, for example, Marx in the modern Western tradition, al-Ghazālī did not assign a revolutionary role to the intelligentsia: and this for the simple reason that he did not see revolution as either an emancipatory or constructive process. Perhaps more like Edmund Burke and Thomas Hobbes, al-Ghazālī saw revolutions as basically destructive and therefore morally unjustifiable forms of behaviour. As befits a deeply conscious Muslim, however, al-Ghazālī was fully committed to the cause of constant struggle for reform and renewal (*al-iṣlāḥ wa 'l-tajdīd*). In this context he felt that it was wrong and irresponsible for members of the intelligentsia to content themselves with being mere technicians and faceless bureaucrats. Over and beyond careers, security of tenure and job satisfaction, etc., scholars in particular and the better educated classes in general, al-Ghazālī strongly believed, should be leaders and supporters of social reform and unwavering practitioners of constructive criticism in the political arena. In traditional Islamic terminology, they should have the moral courage and sense of responsibility to be constantly engaged in and committed to *al-amr bi 'l-ma'rūf wa 'l-nahy 'ani'l-munkar*:

i.e., commanding right and forbidding wrong. And in order to be able to fulfill their duties in this respect consistently and with sincerity, these would be reformers of society and the state, in accordance with the teachings and principles of the faith, had to begin by reforming their own ways in both thought and conduct. Politics, morality, thought and action are thus closely related to each other in al-Ghazālī's integrative system and worldview.

One more point needs to be mentioned before bringing these few remarks to an end. It is about the majority-rule, or *al-tarjīḥ bi 'l-kathrah.* We have seen how al-Ghazālī had imaginatively and skillfully introduced this concept as a means of resolving tensions when communities are split over divisive or controversial issues. It would be easy, but demonstrably unjustifiable, to jump from there (as some have done) to the conclusion that al-Ghazālī should therefore be regarded as a precursor of modern democratic thought.

Fortunately, our appreciation of al-Ghazālī's genius and brilliant contributions to social and political thought—some aspects of which have been briefly indicated above—does not have to depend on such far fetched claims.

Abu Ḥāmid Al-Ghazālī on the Formation and Development of Economic, Social and Political Life

Sabri Orman

Introduction

A keen interest in economic phenomena is part and parcel of the intellectual legacy of Abū Ḥāmid al-Ghazālī (1058-1111 C.E). This interest is a logical extension of his main concern which can be briefly expressed as moral guidance for the attainment of happiness formulated as an all-encompassing life-program. Thus, the treatment of economic matters in al-Ghazālī's agenda is part of a larger and more ambitious programme.

For Al-Ghazālī the ultimate objective of man in this life is to know and love Allah (God) and to show obedience to Him (*'Ilm*, (*ḥāl*, and *'amal*). But, in order to attain that goal one must first survive, and this can only be achieved by providing for one's basic needs. This leads, *inter alia*, to economic activity. But, economic activity involves moral risks, and such risks can be avoided only by a sound knowledge of the true nature of economic activity. For, to him, one cannot behave properly without proper knowledge. (Theory comes first: *'Ilm*, *ḥāl*, and then *'amal*). With a view to help his reader in this regard, al-Ghazālī undertakes a thorough examination of economic life as it is, followed by the formulation of legal and ethical structures that are intended to guard the moral safety of economic subjects.

In the light of the above considerations, it would not be wrong to characterize al-Ghazālī's approach to economic life as primarily analytical, and, secondarily, normative. It is however important to note that al-Ghazālī regards the analytical and normative approaches as complementary rather than alternative methods. The present paper will focus on the outcome of al-Ghazālī's analytical approach to economic phenomena, especially on the formation and development of economic, social and political life as treated in his magnum opus, *Iḥyā' 'Ulūm al-Dīn*.

I. Starting Points-Man and the Objective World

In trying to explain the emergence of economic life al-Ghazālī starts from two points: the nature of man and his natural environment that we prefer to call "the objective World" or "the World as it is."[1]

Man and his nature play a central role in al-Ghazālī's various analyses.[2] The same applies to his treatment of the formation of economic, social and political life, and it constitutes one of his starting points in this regard. "Man is in need of three things", says al-Ghazālī, "food, clothing and shelter", adding that food is

---

[1] For an analysis of al-Ghazālī's two-dimensional conception of the World as subjective and objective, see, Sabri Orman, *Gazali 'nin Iktisat Felsefesi* (Economic Philosophy of al-Ghazālī), (Istanbul: Insan Yayinlari, 1984), pp. 81-85.

[2] A concise treatment of al-Ghazālī's anthropology and its implications for moral and economic life can be found in Ibid., pp. 69-81.

needed for nutrition, sustenance, and survival; that clothing is needed for protection against hot and cold weather; and that shelter (or dwelling) is needed, in addition to the protection it provides against heat and cold, for protection of one's family and material belongings (*amwāl*) against other harmful external forces.[3]

Al-Ghazālī's second point of departure is the natural or material environment in the sense of "the objective World" as mentioned above. He defines what we prefer to call "the objective World" and what he himself calls "the World as it is" or "the World in itself" (*al-dunyā fi nafsihā*) as follows: "The World consists of the stock of existing objects or substances (*a'yān mawjūdah*) that are useful for human beings and with their betterment and improvement (*iṣlāḥ*) human beings are engaged."[4] This definition contains three basic elements:

1. Available or existing substances,
2. Utility of these substances, and
3. Human engagement with the betterment and improvement of the same.

Al-Ghazālī warns that sometimes the world may seem to be made of only one of these elements, but that in fact it covers all of them.

Starting with the first of the three above mentioned elements, he maintains that the world is made of the earth and all the objects that it contains, and that these objects comprise minerals, plants and animals (*ḥayawān*).

In regard to the utility of these materials for human beings, he

[3] Abū Ḥāmid al-Ghazālī, *Iḥyā' 'Ulūm al-Dīn*, Vol. Ill, (Beirut: Dār al-Ma'rifah, n.d.); p. 225.

[4] Al-Ghazālī, *Iḥyā'*, III, p. 224.

says that the earth functions as a bed or cradle, a place in which to stay, a residence. The other objects, on the other hand, serve to meet the needs of humans for food, drink, dressing and marriage. Plants are sought for nutrition and medical reasons—to be used as medicine. Minerals are sought to produce tools and kitchen utensils, to be used as money, and to serve a wide range of other purposes.

Animals fall into two basic categories: human beings, and non-human, or "animals" in the narrower and more usual sense of the word. In the last sense, animals are primarily used for nutrition, and as beasts of burden.

As for human beings, there is demand either for their bodies or for their hearts. The human body is needed either for work and employment or for pleasure and enjoyment. Human hearts, on the other hand, are wanted in order to acquire a place in, to be revered and extolled by, and in short to obtain what al-Ghazālī designates as *jāh*. And this, i.e *jāh*, he defines as the power to rule over the hearts of people.[5]

Al-Ghazālī, considers the third and the last elements of the foregoing definitions, that is Man's engagement with existing objects, again on the basis of the same distinction between the heart or spirit (*qalb*), on the one hand, and the body, on the other.

He identifies two types of relations between Man and these (material) objects or substances. One of them is the relationship between the human heart and the above-mentioned objects, and the other is the relationship between the human body and the same objects.

Making these things the object of one's love or desire, constitutes an example of the former, and al-Ghazālī conceptualizes it as *al-dunyā al-bāṭinah* (internal or subjective

---

[5] Ibid., p. 224.

world). This psychological tie with the material world, in his opinion, is the major source of most of the moral problems experienced by man such as jealousy, hatred, arrogance, boastfulness, flattery, hypocrisy, greed, and love of being praised. Bodily ties or relations with the material world, on the other hand, manifest themselves in human efforts towards changing the available objects so as to suit one's own or others' needs, and are designated *al-dunyā al-ẓāhirah* (the external or objective world) in al-Ghazālī's terminology. All sorts of arts, crafts, and trades are the outcomes of this last type of relationship.[6]

II. The Emergence of Economic Life

We have seen in the first stage of al-Ghazālī's analysis that man has basic needs that have to be satisfied in order for him to be able to survive, and that, on the other hand, his natural environment contains objects or resources that are capable of being used for the satisfaction of these needs. And in the last paragraph we learnt about al-Ghazālī's ideas regarding the types of relations between man and his natural environment. We thus have at hand the basic or necessary theoretical equipment in the light of which we can proceed to discuss his ideas about the beginning and formation of economic life.

What happens next in such a situation is obvious: humans would start looking for the satisfaction of their various needs and desires. But, unlike animals, what they need in terms of food, shelter and clothing are not available ready-made, because God has not created them so as to dispense with human work and effort. The case with animals is just the opposite, because He created their means of need-satisfaction ready-made. So, plants feed animals without a need for cooking; heat and cold do not affect their bodies as they do humans, so they can do without

---

[6] Ibid.

dwellings, and since their fur and skins serve well the same purpose they also can do without clothing.[7] By contrast, humans have to work in order to improve (*iṣlāḥ*) the available objects so as to fit or satisfy their needs.

But, is this possible? Al-Ghazālī's answer to this question is in the affirmative. In his opinion, the stock of all things in existence (*al-mawjūdāt*) can be classified into three groups in terms of their being amenable to change, improvement or *iṣlāḥ*.

1. Those that are beyond any change whatsoever;
2. Those that are open to change but beyond the reach of human beings; and
3. Those that are open to change within the reach of human beings.

As an illustration of the first group he mentions the nature and attributes of God; of the second the angels, the heavens, the mountains, and the seas; and of the third the earth and its elements, and the other things it contains, such as minerals, plants and animals.[8]

The natural environment is both in need of and capable of improvement, and as a consequence human work and effort toward need-satisfaction from the same environment is both necessary and sufficient.

Setting out to work for need fulfillment from the natural environment is nothing but the beginning of economic life.

III. Division of Labour and Social Life

Just as the anthropological characteristics of mankind required the initiation of economic life and activity, they also served as the

[7] Ibid., p. 225.
[8] Ibid., p. 281.

cause and motive force of the emergence and development of division of labour and of societal life. Al-Ghazālī discusses the division of labour before his treatment of the beginning and formation of social life, and then considers it among the causes that lead to the subsequent development of social life.[9]

Al-Ghazālī treats the division of labour as a logical consequence or reflection of human needs. According to him, the fact that humans have to work for the satisfaction of their needs necessarily leads to the development of five crafts. These are the roots and origins of all other crafts, and can be listed as follows: agriculture or farming (*filāḥah*), herdsmanship or animal husbandry (*ri'āyah*), hunting or gathering (*iqtināṣ*), weaving (*ḥiyākah*), and construction (*binā'*).

Construction takes care of the need for shelter and lodging; weaving and the related crafts such as spinning and tailoring, take care of clothing; agriculture and herdsmanship do the same in regard to food. Al-Ghazālī points out that by hunting or gathering (*iqtināṣ*) he means collecting and appropriating every thing that is available naturally, without any involvement on behalf of human work and labour, like animals, herbs, grass, wood and minerals, and he adds that it, in fact, covers many other crafts and occupations.

As can be seen al-Ghazālī's "five basic crafts" are nothing but the inevitable results of "three basic human needs".

Abu Ḥāmid carries on the same line of reasoning by saying that these five crafts, in turn, require three more crafts. The underlying logic is that the execution of the said crafts is, as a prerequisite, dependent on the availability of some tools and instruments (*adāwat wa ālāt*). Tools, on the other hand, are made either of plants (wood), or of minerals (iron, lead and the like), or

[9] Ibid., p. 226.

of leather. As a result there arise "tool making" crafts and craftsmen, such as carpentry, smithcraft, and leathercraft. Here by carpentry, smithcraft and leathercraft is meant all types of productive work and activity related to wood, iron and other metals, as well as hides, leather and their derivatives, respectively. He goes on to say that those mentioned so far are only "mother crafts", and that. there are many other derivative crafts, but that he is concerned here only with genres rather than with units.

After this preliminary introduction to the division of labour, which is to be elaborated later on, Al-Ghazālī proceeds to an explanation of the formation of social life. He establishes his construction again on the basis of human nature. In other words, his explanation of social life is also anthropological in nature. In his opinion, humans are created in such a way that they cannot live and survive in isolation from one another. In other words, individual human beings are not self-sufficient, and are dependent on others for their survival, i.e., they are social beings. Al-Ghazālī mentions two reasons for this:

1. Preservation of human race. This requires procreation, and this in turn cannot come about without a union and association between members of the two sexes.

2. Need for cooperation in regards to provision of basic needs and child raising or education. Understandably, sexual association leads inevitably to child production, and an individual alone cannot undertake the tasks of both child rearing and of provision of basic needs such as food, shelter and clothing.[10]

---

[10] For the information conveyed in this section so far, see, *Iḥyā'*, III, pp. 225-226. (al-Ghazālī's emphasis on child rearing and child education as a constituent element of social life indicates the differences of development between children and young animals. It will be remembered that a similar distinction between humans and animals was made earlier on).

Notice that al-Ghazālī is trying to explain the need for social life on the basis of the need for family, the smallest social unit. He thinks that living in a house together with children and spouses is feasible only within the framework of "a larger group" where everybody undertakes a different craft. "How can a solitary individual perform farming", he asks, "while he is in need of tools, and tools are in need of a carpenter and an ironsmith, and they in their turn are in need of bread, and bread is in need of a miller and a baker?" After subjecting clothing as another example to a similar line of reasoning, he concludes: "That is why it has not been possible for individual human beings to live alone, and there emerged the need for (social or) communal life (*ijtimā'*).[11]

He then goes on to say that if people tried to lead communal life in an open space they would be vulnerable to such harmful factors as heat, cold, rain, theft and robbery. For that reason they would have inevitably felt the need for strong buildings and houses where each household would stay with their respective tools, utensils and furniture. Al-Ghazālī then takes one more step, and attempts an explanation of the development of villages and towns:

> Houses may very well provide protection against heat, cold and rain, and against theft and similar disturbing acts from neighbors. But, sometimes houses are attacked by a group of robbers from outside the camp. This leads households to back each other and to cooperate, and to seek protection by building walls that surround all houses. Thus, there emerged villages and towns (*al-bilād*) that are an outcome of this necessity.[12]

[11] *Iḥyā'*, III, p. 226.
[12] Ibid.

IV. The State and the Social Division of Labour

Al-Ghazālī explains the emergence, formation and development of the state as a necessary consequence of social life. Once materialized, social or communal life produces a network of human relations. One natural result of these relations is a variety of conflicts and disagreements. Furthermore, there are people in need of protection in a society. Conflicts have to be resolved and the needy should be taken care of. Efforts spent in this direction lead to the establishment of various institutions—a process that once started, develops in an ever growing way, one development breeding another. The result is the emergence of a variety of institutions, and the resultant institutions need to be coordinated so that they will be able to serve their original purposes, and not lead to conflict and disorder. The need for such coordination, constitutes the *raison d'etre* of a central authority, in al-Ghazālī's words a *malik* or an *amīr*, i.e. a public authority or a state.

It will be recalled that al-Ghazālī's explanation of the formation of social life was an extension of his ideas on the requirements of family life. The same applies to his theory of the state. In his view, once humans started living in houses and towns, there arose conflicts between them. The explanation is that, for example, in family life, on the one hand, husbands try to establish some sort of dominant authority (*riyāsah wa wilāyah*) over wives, and on the other hand, parents try another version of the same (*wilāyah*) on children, who are weak and dependant on them. But, unlike animals, domination over rational beings (*'āqil*) can provoke opposition or rebellion. Animals do not have the same ability to oppose, even when they are treated unjustly, while a wife is able to oppose her husband, and children are able to oppose their parents.[13]

---

[13] Ibid.

On the other hand, for the purposes of mutual need fulfillment, inhabitants of towns and cities enter into various relations with each other, which can, in turn, lead to renewed conflicts. Thus, left to themselves, they will eventually start fighting, which may ultimately lead to their destruction. For example, herdsmen and farmers inevitably go into conflict while trying to appropriate pastures, land and water as these are not sufficient to meet the needs of everybody.

Furthermore, there are those who for reasons such as illness, disability and old age are not able to work in order to earn their livelihood. If such people are left to themselves they will perish, and if they are left to the care and attention of everybody nobody will care.

Al-Ghazālī maintains that the said developments of social life (*ijtimā'*), necessarily leads to the emergence of crafts or occupations (*ṣinā'āt*). One of these is the profession of surveying or cadastre (*misāḥah*) which serves the purpose of surveying land so that it may be distributed in a fair and just way. Another craft or profession is the military art that serves to defend and protect the group or country against outside attacks and robbery. Still another is the art of arbitration and conflict resolution. Among the many socially necessary crafts is the need for a proper knowledge of the law (*fiqh*), which serves to resolve conflicts. Al-Ghazālī regards all these as "indispensible political affairs", and he is of opinion that they can be undertaken only by specialists with professional qualifications. But, if the said professionals are to occupy themselves with mastering and practicing their respective professions, they cannot engage in other occupation which requires yet other skills. For any society to survive and prosper therefore a wide range of skills and professions need to be evolved and practiced by master craftsmen and specialists all of whom will have to be paid for their services.

Thus arises the need for taxation (*al-kharāj*). The need for taxation in turn breeds the need for some other occupations, such as tax assessors (*'ummāl*), tax collectors (*jubāt*), and treasurers (*khuzzān*).[14]

As can be seen, what al-Ghazālī calls "political affairs" (*al-umūr al-siyāsiyyah*) are introduced as social needs or consequences thereof. It is primarily in order to coordinate the activities of the various socially necessary professions along with the activities of groups and individuals that the state arises. For Al-Ghazālī therefore the state is a socially necessary structure. If the affairs and activities undertaken by different groups of peoples who are not properly coordinated and integrated (*lā tajma'uhum rābiṭah*) the social order would collapse; chaos and disorder would prevail. The top manager of the whole show for Al-Ghazālī is the sovereign (*malik*) or the commander (*amīr*). What al-Ghazālī means by the terms *malik* and *amīr* is simply the state. In line with the conventions of his time he symbolizes the state by the figure on top of it.

He lists the functions of *malik* or *amīr* in the following manner: to make assignments on the basis of merit; to observe equity in the imposition and distribution of taxes; to decide on matters of war and the deployment of soldiers; and to appoint officers of high rank, and others.[15]

Finally, al-Ghazālī tries to depict the social scene under a fully-fledged state. In his opinion in such a state of affairs people are divided into three major groups or classes according to the tasks they perform, reflecting the social division of labour.

1. Those who are engaged in farming, animal husbandry and other productive crafts and trades.

---

[14] For al-Ghazālī's ideas mentioned so far, see, *Iḥyā'*, III, p. 226.

[15] *Iḥyā'*, III, pp. 226-221.

2. Those who undertake defense of the country, the military.
3. Those who mediate between the first two groups by taking from one and giving to the other.[16]

It seems that the first group or class consists of those segments of society that are engaged in basic economic activities. We have seen earlier that they in turn branch out among themselves into various vocational groups. The status of the second group is obvious enough. The third group covers all those who are employed by the state with the exception of the military.

Al-Ghazālī's foregoing taxonomy may very well be viewed as a picture of a class structure. But, considering his emphasis on the functional aspects of the components of the said taxonomy we prefer to call it "the social division of labour."

V. Exchange, Money, Markets and Trade

Al-Ghazālī examines what we are going to deal with under the present heading after his examination of the state and social division of labour. But, this should not be taken to imply a historical or chronological ordering of the two. For he examines the division oflabour, which is not quite meaningful without exchange, before and as a preliminary to his treatment of the state. What is more, it will be recalled, he explains the need for the establishment of the state on the basis of the earlier need for resolving conflicts that arise among people who had already implemented a division of labour, and entered into a network of relations.

The order employed by al-Ghazālī in this regard can be construed as a matter of convenience in presentation. It seems as if, after a brief introduction, he prefers to cut short and postpone his analysis of economic life in order to resume it in greater detail

[16] Ibid., p. 227.

later on-after having made a brief introduction to the basic structures and institutions of social life of which economic life is also a part, thus having prepared a more convenient ground for his treatment of the exchange mechanism.

a. Exchange, Commerce and Trade, and Markets

He begins his analysis of this topic with the following sentence: "Then this is all about crafts and trades. But, they remain incomplete without *amwāl* and tool, *ālāt.*" This is followed by a definition of the term *māl* (pl. *amwāl*). In al-Ghazālī's terminology *māl* (goods) means all substances (*a'yān*) inside or under the earth and all that is available on it, that are useful to man or can be benefited from (*mā yuntafa' bih*). There is, in his opinion, an order of priority, some sort of hierarchy, among goods. First in order are foodstuffs; then come places of dwelling (houses) and of earning a livelihood such as land, shops and marketplaces; then clothes; then house tools, utensils and furniture, and lastly come tools that make tools (*ālāt al-ālāt*). He does not neglect to add that animals also, in some sense, can be considered as means or instruments. For instance, hounds, cattle and horses serve as instruments for hunting, tilling and riding, respectively.

Al-Ghazālī starts examining the issue of exchange after the aforementioned introduction. His treatment of the subject is both concise and interesting. To quote him, in translation:

> Then from this [the need for goods and tools] there emanates the need for sale (*bay'*), because usually the farmer lives in a place where farming tools are not available, and the ironsmith and the carpenter live in a place where cultivation is not possible. So, the farmer necessarily requires the two, and the two require the fanner. One party has to give what he has available to the

> other party in order to take from that party what he needs, and this takes the form of an exchange (*mu'āwadah*). But, sometimes it may so happen that the carpenter, for instance, may demand (*ṭalab*) food from the fanner in return for his tools, while the farmer is not in need of tools at that time, and does not buy them. It may also happen that the farmer may demand tools from the carpenter in exchange for food while the latter has food at that time, and as a result does not need it. So, interests are hindered. As a consequence there emerges the need for a shop that brings together tools of all types of crafts, whose owner keeps them ready for those who are in need of them. The same applies to houses whose owners buy the com that is brought to them by farmers, and keep it ready for those who may demand it. All these in turn lead to the appearance of marketplaces and storehouses. Thenceforth the farmers unable to find anybody in need of their com will sell it at a lower price to traders, who in anticipation of profit, store it waiting for those who need it. The same applies to all goods and commodities (*al-amti'ah wa 'l-amwāl*).[17]

As it will have been noticed, al-Ghazālī: explains exchange after having dealt with the division of labour rather than treating it in isolation. On the other hand, after dealing with the now well-known problem of the lack of double coincidence in time between the mutual needs of the two parties in barter-trade, he attempts to explain trade, commerce and trade centres. His explanation of the motivation behind the risks taken and the burdens carried by the tradesmen, while trying to play their various roles in the above process, is equally interesting: namely, anticipation of profit.

---

[17] Ibid.

b. Interregional and International Trade

Al-Ghazālī maintains that at this stage of economic development another inevitable process takes place: interregional and international trade, or as he puts it "a frequent coming and going (*taraddud*) between villages, towns and countries". He goes on to say that all tools are not available in every city and all kinds of foodstuff are not available in all villages. In other words no village or town is self-sufficient, and there is some sort of dependency between them. This being the case, some people involve themselves in buying foodstuff from villages, and tools from towns, and then transporting them to other places where they are needed.

This development leads, on the one hand, to the rise of a new group of tradesmen who are engaged in the above mentioned activities and, on the other, to the development of new types of transactions (*mu'āmalah*) and acquisition (*iktisāb*). For instance, the need for transportation causes the development of dealers in this activity. Since goods cannot be carried by humans, animals are used for the purpose, and since owners of goods may not at the same time have in their possession any animals or enough of them, they will be required to transact with animal owners in return for a payment. So comes about a new class of tradesmen (dealers in transportation), a new type of transaction (leasing, or *ijārah*), and a new category of acquisition, hire or rent (*kirā'*).[18]

Al-Ghazālī's analysis of the motivation behind the behaviour of dealers in international trade is worth noting at this juncture. He says that it is basically nothing other than their greed and desire to gather wealth while in fact they simply manage to make parties in a transaction meet. Although it may not be intended by traders and dealers, this activity has some other consequences that

[18] Ibid.

help human affairs in general to remain in good order. In this sense, he says, they toil day and night in long voyages to serve the purposes of others, while their own share of it is to gather wealth that will eventually be consumed, at least in part, by others, such as robbers or unjust rulers. He also believes that their short-sightedness and ignorance, (one could very well say, unconsciously) is somewhat predestined by God to serve as a regulatory force for the stability and order of countries (*niẓāman li 'l-bilād*), and in the interest of people (*maṣlaḥatan li 'l-'ibād*).

> In fact, all mundane affairs are regulated by *ghaflah* (inadvertence, or we may perhaps say, irrationality) and low mindedness (*khissat al-himmah*). Since if humans were rational and high-minded they would keep away (shun or turn away from) mundane affairs (*dunyā*). Then all forms of life would have been paralysed, and if so, then all humans would perish, and of course, *zuhhād* (ascetics) would [themselves] also perish.[19]

c. Money and Monetary Exchange

In the last stage of his analysis of the process of the formation and development of economic, social and political life, Al-Ghazālī attempts to provide an explanation of the institution of money. This way of thinking is in line with historical facts. Indeed money as an institution has been able to come to the fore and acquire an established position, only centuries after the development of trade both local and international. Great advantages enjoyed by clever traders of barter mechanism can be taken to account for the delayed development of monetary exchange.

Al-Ghazālī's exposition of the process of the emergence of money is so condensed that it defies any better rendition. We shall therefore conclude this section by quoting it in translation:

---

[19] Ibid.

Then, because of the need for exchange (*bay'*, literally, sale), there arise the need for currency. Because, how would one know who might want to buy a meal in exchange for a dress and know the equivalent amount of the meal? Furthermore, transactions of this kind are required for a variety of goods, such as a dress to be sold in exchange for a meal, and an animal to be sold in exchange for a dress. Since these are matters that are not proportional to each other, there is a need for a just ruler to mediate between the two parties by fairly adjusting one to the other so that the amount thus specified can be demanded. And since the need for such a mediator is continual, it must be a durable good, and again since the most durable goods are metals, currency is made of gold, silver and copper. This requires minting, engraving and valuation, and this in turn leads to the need for a mint house and money changers (*sayrafi*, goldsmith).[20]

Conclusion

So far we have tried to provide an overview of Abū Ḥāmid al-Ghazālī's analytical ideas pertaining to the formation of economic, social and political life, based on his *magnum opus*, *Iḥyā' 'Ulūm al-Dīn*. Needless to say, the picture obtained here reflects only Al-Ghazālī of *al-Iḥyā'* and this may be subject to modification depending on the availability or discovery of other relevant material in his numerous other works.

As will have been noticed the above discussed ideas do not reflect specific categories of any particular times and places. Rather, problems are tackled in a theoretical world, and from a logical point of view, in isolation from the course of specific historical events or conditions. One can confidently say however

[20] *Iḥyā'*, III, pp. 227-228.

that, within the present framework of analysis, instead of the formation of the first human society or of one specific historical society, Al-Ghazālī has successfully tried to explain the process of the formation and development of any conceivable society. In this sense his ideas can be fairly said to constitute a comprehensive sociological theory of the formative stages of human society in general. This theory, it must be stressed, moves from the premises derived from the anthropological characteristics of the human race, and deduces from these by way of inference a comprehensive, coherent and well-integrated body of economic, social and political structures and institutions.

I think that both the substance and the logical structure of the ideas presented in this paper will appear quite familiar to students of modern literature in economics, social theory and political theory. This is important because, instead of couching al-Ghazālī's thought about the said matters in terms of modern language and concepts, we have tried to convey his ideas in a descriptive manner that closely and faithfully follows his own logic and language and, up to a point also, reflects the intellectual environment in which he lived.

The Ghazalian Origins of Modern Philosophy

Cemil Akdogan**

Introduction

We can trace the origins of modern philosophy back to Abū Ḥamid al-Ghazālī (1058-1111) who preceded and anticipated some of the work achieved by Rene Descartes (1596-1650) and David Hume (1711-1776). Although their frameworks are different, the parallels between al-Ghazālī and Descartes, particularly on the issues of absolute truth, scepticism, dreamlike reality, and the separation of soul from body, are obvious. As for Hume's work on causality which prompted Immanuel Kant (1724-1804) to write his famous *Critique of Pure Reason*, it is fundamentally not more than what al-Ghazālī achieved on the same subject a long time ago.

Al-Ghazālī, insisting upon *tawhid*, the Muslim doctrine of Unity and the omnipotence of God, did not accept the real distinction between primary and secondary qualities, but Galileo

** I am grateful to Prof. Syed Muhammad Naquib al-Attas who read the first draft of this article and graciously steered me away from some mistakes.

Galilei (1564-1642), Rene Descartes and Robert Boyle (1627-1691), the representatives of modern science in the seventeenth century, vehemently defended this distinction and made it the backbone of modern philosophy. With this distinction they "effected a final dualism between matter and spirit in a way which left nature open to the scrutiny and service of secular science, and which set the stage for man being left only with the world on his hands."[1]

To objectify and secularize science and also to clinch the dualism between body and soul, Galileo, Descartes, and Boyle, the seventeenth century philosopher-scientists, made the real distinction between primary and secondary qualities "central to a unified metaphysical and scientific view of the world that [has] dominated"[2] in the West from the seventeenth century onward. Even today scientists and the majority of analytical philosophers continue to support a real distinction between primary and secondary qualities, since primary qualities represent the original properties of matter or the external world, and "the belief in an external world [*qua* world] ... is the basis of all natural science."[3]

The seventeenth century philosopher-scientists believed that primary qualities are the geomeotrical properties of objects such as shape, size, and motion and that they are inseparable from objects, but secondary qualities such as color, taste, warmth, etc. arise in our minds be- cause of the effect of the primary qualities of the insensible parts of objects on our sensory organs. Primary

---

[1] Syed Muhammad Naquib al-Attas, *Islam and Secularism* (Kuala Lumpur: Muslim Youth Movement of Malaysia (ABIM), 1978), p. 33. Hereafter I will refer to the second impression of the same book (Kuala Lumpur: ISTAC, 1993).

[2] Smith, A.D., "Of Primary and Secondary Qualities", *The Philosophical Review*, vol. 99, no. 2, April 1990, p. 221.

[3] Albert Einstein, *Ideas and Opinions*, trans. Sonja Bergmann (New York: Dell Publishing Company, Inc., 1979), 260.

qualities representing the objective reality are the proper subject of science whereas secondary qualities are subjective entities that exist only in the mind. More specifically, primary qualities are related to quantity, mathematics, body, passive objects, objectivity, facts, knowledge, and science, but secondary qualities are related to the soul, perceiving subjects, subjectivity, values, emotion, faith, and religion.

Depending on this real distinction Europeans secularized the study of science and excluded morality and religion from it. As Robert N. Proctor says:

> The exclusion of morals from science in the seventeenth and eighteenth century was defended on the basis of a separation of primary and secondary qualities: desires and passions were subjective, human, additives to the original of nature, distorting our understanding of the true nature of things.[4]

Thus, due to the distinction between primary and secondary qualities, science became the centerpiece of European civilization. Europeans also turned science into a unique product of the West by understanding and practicing it in accordance with this distinction. They duly based reality on mathematization and experimentation. According to them whatever was observable or measurable was real and whatever existed in the human mind was subjective, emotional and unscientific. Since primary qualities are amenable to mathematical treatment and can describe nature in mathematical and observational terms, they concentrated upon them and neglected secondary qualities, i.e., the human mind or subjectivity.

Unless we trace how the real distinction between primary and secondary qualities developed from Descartes until John Locke

---

[4] Robert N. Proctor, *Value-Free Science* (Cambridge, Massachusetts: Harvard University Press, 1991), p. 62.

(1632-1704), we cannot adequately make sense of the development of modern philosophy, and particularly Kant's achievement.

Although Locke's distinction between primary and secondary qualities has been the subject of heated debates since he wrote his famous book, *An Essay Concerning Human Understanding* in 1690, there has not yet been a consistent interpretation of Locke's distinction.

Most of the undergraduate students in the West normally learn about this distinction as a result of reading Locke's *Essay*, but ironically enough and contrary to the popular view, Locke, instead of maintaining the distinction in the sense of Descartes, Galileo and Boyle, demolished it.

In this article I will establish that Locke, as a philosopher, is drastically different in his interpretation of the distinction from Galileo, Descartes and Boyle, the philosopher-scientists and the representatives of the scientific community in the seventeenth century. As we will see, Locke did not inherit the distinction from science or the philosopher-scientists as claimed by the traditional account. On the contrary, he began to dismantle the distinction, but Kant "starting from an incomparably higher standpoint"[5] demolished it consistently and completely once and for all. What is common between Locke and Kant is that both, being the representatives of philosophy, go from the ideas of primary qualities to physical reality.

Al-Ghazālī

In his *Deliverance from Error* al-Ghazālī wanted to find out the absolute truth. To that extent he went through a period of

---

[5] Arthur Schopenhauer, *The World as Will and Representation*, trans. E. F. Payne (New York: Dover Publications, 1969), 418.

personal scepticism during which he even doubted the truth of sense-data, logic and mathematics. He also compared conscious states such as wakefulness or sense data to the state of dreaming. Later, he once again began to believe in logic, mathematics and self evident ideas. As we know, these features also exist in Descartes's philosophy. The main difference between them is that al-Ghazālī works within the framework of Islamic theology in which there is "no problem of God", whereas Descartes begins with the problem of God and places his emphasis upon the human mind or secular philosophy.

In order to find out absolute truth al-Ghazālī gave up the authority in matters of faith temporarily:

> The thirst for grasping the real meaning of things was indeed my habit and want from my early years ... As a result, the fetters of servile conformism fell away from me, and inherited beliefs lost their hold on me, when I was still quite young. For I saw that the children of Christians always grew up embracing Christianity, and the children of Jews always grew up adhering to Judaism, and the children of Muslims always grew up following the religion of Islam. I also heard the tradition related from the Apostle of God—God's blessing and peace be upon him!—in which he said: "Every infant is born endowed with the *fitra*: then his parents make him Jew or Christian or Magian. Consequently, I felt an inner urge to seek the true meaning of the original *fitra*, and the true meaning of the beliefs arising through slavish aping of parents and teachers. I wanted to sift out these uncritical beliefs, the beginnings of which are suggestions imposed from without, since there are differences of opinion in the discernment of those that are true from those that are false. So I began by saying to myself: "What I seek is knowledge of the true meaning of things. Of necessity, therefore, I must inquire into just what

the true meaning of knowledge is."[6]

If authority is not trustable[7], then is it possible to believe in sense perception and necessary truths that seem to be self-evident? al-Ghazālī responded to this inquiry as follows:

> I ... scrutinized all my cognitions and found myself devoid of any knowledge ... except in the case of sense-data and self-evident truths. So I said: "Now that despair has befallen me, the only hope I have of acquiring an insight into obscure matters is to start from things that are perfectly clear, namely sense-data and the self-evident truths ... With great earnestness, therefore, I began to reflect on my sense-data to see if I could make myself doubt them. This protracted effort to induce doubt finally brought me to the point where my soul would not allow me to admit safety from error even in the case of my sense-data. Rather it began to be open to doubt about them.[8]

So to distinguish absolute truth from falsity al-Ghazālī even doubted the reliability of sense data and self-evident truths. In order to show that sense data or the things we clearly perceive such as our wakefulness may be deceitful he offered the example

---

[6] Trans. Richard Joseph McCarthy, S. J., Freed*om and Fulfillment: An Annotated Translation of al-Ghazālī's al-Munqidh min al-Ḍalāl and Other Relevant Works of al-Ghazālī* (Boston, Twayne Publishers, 1980), p. 63.

[7] A.I. Sabra makes the same claim for *al-kalam*: "*Al-kalam*, whether that of the Mu'tazila or of the later, 'orthodox' Ash'arites, declares itself against the passive acceptance of authority in matters of faith, an attitude which it calls by the name of *taqlīd* (the imitation or unquestioning following of authority), and which it seeks, expressly and as a matter of principle, to replace by a state of knowledge (*'ilm*) rooted in reason (*'aql*)." See his article, "Science and Philosophy in Medieval Islamic Theology", in *Zeitschrift fur Geschichte der Arabisch-Islamischen Wissenschaften*, Band 9, 1995, p. 9.

[8] Trans. Richard Joseph McCarthy, S. J., *Freedom and Fulfillment: An Annotated Translation of al-Ghazālī's al-Munqidh min al-Ḍalāl and Other Relevant Works of al-Ghazālī*, p. 64.

of dreams:

> sense-data reinforced their difficulty by an appeal to dreaming, saying: "Don't you see that when you are asleep you believe certain things and imagine certain circumstances and believe they are fixed and lasting and entertain no doubts about that being their status? Then you wake up and know that all your imaginings and beliefs were groundless and unsubstantial.[9]

Surely, sense data sometimes deceive us. For instance, when we look at a star we see it as big as a coin. But actually it is bigger than even the whole earth itself. How do we know this? Of course, through our intellect (the reason-judge), i.e., geometrical calculations.[10] Then how about mathematical and logical truths? Can we trust them? According to al-Ghazālī we cannot trust them either, since they may also deceive us:

> Perhaps ... I can rely only on those rational data which belong to the category of primary truths, such as our asserting that 'Ten is more than three,' and 'One and the same thing cannot be simultaneously affirmed and denied,' and 'One and the same thing cannot be incipient and eternal, existent and nonexistent, necessary and impossible.' Then sense-data spoke up: "What assurance have you that your reliance on rational data is not like your reliance on sense-data? Indeed, you used to have confidence in me. Then the reason-judge came along and gave me the lie. But were it not for the reason-judge, you would still accept me as true. So there may be, beyond the perception of reason, another judge. And if the latter revealed itself, it would give the lie to the judgements of reason, just as the reason-judge revealed itself and gave the lie to the judgements of sense. The mere fact of the

[9] Ibid.

[10] Ibid., p. 65.

> nonappearance of that further perception does not prove the impossibility of its existence."[11]

After God cured al-Ghazālī of scepticism, which had lasted about two months, he once again began to believe in "the self-evident data of reason and relied on them with safety and certainty."[12]

Al-Ghazālī also distinguished between body and soul in his *Al-Risālatu al-Laduniyya* not in order to arrive at a dualism as suggested by Fazlur Rahman and others but to place humanity outside and above nature. According to him the soul of human beings directly originates from God Himself and that is why it is immaterial, immortal, special, unique and different from the body or the rest of natural creation itself. As a result, man is no longer a passive part of the natural order as stipulated by many religions and ancient philosophies, but a vicegerent on earth.

In al-Ghazālī's view "God Most High created man from two different things, one of them the body, which is subject to generation and corruption, composite, made up of parts, earthly, whose nature cannot be complete except by means of something else, and that other is the soul, which is substantial, simple, enlightened, comprehending, acting, moving, giving completion to instruments and bodies."[13]

Thus he made soul pivotal to his metaphysics and distinguished it from body.[14] Without soul the body is not complete and cannot function. As al-Ghazālī states:

> The body is subject to dissolution as it was subject to being

[11] Ibid., p. 65.

[12] Ibid., p. 66.

[13] Al-Ghazālī, *Al-Risālatu Al-Laduniyya*, Part II, trans. Margaret Smith, in the *Journal of the Royal Asiatic Society*, 1938, p. 193.

[14] To distinguish between two things is not necessarily a dualism.

> compounded of matter and form, which is set forth in the books. And from verses and traditions and intellectual proofs, we have come to know that the spirit [the soul] is a simple substance, perfect, having life in itself, and from it is derived what makes the body sound or what corrupts it.[15]

Thus Al-Ghazālī ended the hold of ancient philosophy by freeing the human soul from its material attachments and making it originate from God.[16] So, long before Descartes and other modern philosophers[17] he revolutionized metaphysics on the basis

---

[15] Al-Ghazālī, Al-*Risālatu Al-Ladunniya*, pp. 197-198.

[16] As we know, the soul was part of cosmos in Greek philosophy. It was made up of delicate materials such as pure water, pure air, pure fire or light atoms and was like an inner engine which moved things, be they inanimate objects or human beings. Even Plato placed the soul between the perfect ideas and the sensory world and made it part of the world. As for Aristotle it is the form which is not separable from body or matter. In other words the soul cannot exist independently of the body and thus in the Islamic world Farabi, Ibn Sina and lbn Rushd; who were Aristotelians could not satisfactorily explain the immortality, of human souls. Furthermore, they all accepted that the active intellect which is immortal did not belong to particular individuals, but rather to the whole human species. Thus according to Greek and Islamic philosophers the soul either originated from matter or was part of the world or body.

[17] Descartes and some other modern philosophers such as Kant also insisted that human beings are unique and that they are not animals, but they did so in a secular context. Stuart G. Shanker explains this point with regard to Descartes as follows; "Descartes ... [repudiates] the orthodox doctrine of the 'Great Chain of Being'. He is insisting that there is a hiatus between animals and man that cannot be filled by any 'missing links'. The body may be a machine (which was itself a heretical view), but man, by his abilities to reason, to speak a language, to direct his actions and to be conscious of his cognitions, is categorically not an animal. There is no hint in the *Discourse* that any of these attributes can be possessed in degrees ... When Aristotle tells us that 'Man is by nature a political animal', or Seneca that 'Man is a reasoning animal', the emphasis is on animal: one analyses man as an animal species (see the opening chapter of Aristotle's Metaphysics). But all

of the Qur'an:

> God related the spirit sometimes to Himself and sometimes to His command and sometimes to His glory for He said: "I breathed into him of My Spirit," and He said also: "Say, the Spirit (proceedeth) at the command of my Lord." Also He said: "And We breathed into him of Our spirit." Now God, Most High is too glorious to attach unto Himself a body or an accident, because of their lowliness and their liability to change and their swift dissolution and corruption.[18]

Al-Ghazālī defined the soul as a "perfect, simple substance which is concerned solely with remembering and studying and reflection and discrimination and careful consideration."[19] and made it a different and independent substance. It is no longer a subtle matter or a collection of atoms or an accident.[20] Although the body is inanimate, mortal, and imperfect, the soul is alive, immortal and perfect.[21] More importantly, the souls created by God in a special way are the only direct links between God and man.

For al-Ghazālī, "man is both soul and body, he is at once a physical being and a spirit, and his soul governs his body."[22] This

---

this is changed in the Discourse of Descartes. See, Stuart G. Shanker ed. *Philosophy of Science, Logic and Mathematics in the Twentieth Century* (London: Routledge, 1996), p. 316. Descartes discusses the differences between human beings and animals at the end of Part V of his *Discourse*.

[18] Al-Ghazālī, *Al-Risalatu Al-Laduniyya*, Part II, p., 197.

[19] Ibid., p. 194.

[20] Ibid., pp. 196-197.

[21] Ibid., p. 197.

[22] Syed Muhammad Naquib al-Attas, *Islam and Secularism*, p. 69. On this point al-Ghazālī is crystal clear: Man is "composed of an outward shape, called the body, and an inward entity called ... soul ... which uses all the other faculties as its instruments and servants." Al-Ghazālī, *The Alchemy of Happiness*, trans. Claud Field (London: The Octagon Press, 1980), pp. 18-19.

dual nature of man does not necessarily imply a dualism since, in his view, soul and body are two different aspects of the same entity, i.e., man. Furthermore, there; is an interaction between them, i.e., "soul is a spiritual principle which having life in itself vitalizes the body and controls it and regulates it. The body is the instrument and vehicle of the soul."[23]

But Descartes, as the representative of seventeenth century philosopher-scientists, emphasized the real distinction between soul (secondary qualities) and body (primary qualities) and made them independent and complete substances. That is why, if not he, at least his followers (Cartesians) tried to "cut all connection between ... [soul and body in order] to establish a rigorous parallelism between them [through] a divine mechanism. "[24]

Al-Ghazālī instead of accepting such a real distinction, simply distinguished soul from body and made them interdependent. "The human soul, though independent of the body, yet requires the body in this physical world"[25] to govern it, to perceive things, and to interpret "the worlds of sense and sensible experience, of images, and of intelligible forms or ideas."[26]

Although al-Ghazālī did not accept the real distinction between soul and body, Fazlur Rahman wrongly claimed that al-Ghazālī's distinction between body and soul results in a dualism:

> There is hardly a passage in the Qur'an that says that man is composed of two separate, let alone disparate, substances, the body and the soul (even though later

[23] Ed. M. M. Sharif, *A History of Muslim Philosophy*, 2 volumes (Wiesbaden: Otto Hartassowitz, 1963), p. 620.

[24] Henry Bergson, *Creative Evolution* (Mineola, New York: Dover Publications, Inc., 1998), p. 350.

[25] Syed Muhammad Naquib al-Attas, *Prolegomena to the Metaphysics of Islam* (Kuala Lumpur: ISTAC, 1995), 165.

[26] Ibid., p. 171.

> orthodox Islam, particularly after al-Ghazālī and largely through his influence, came to accept it). The term *nafs*, frequently employed by the Qur'an and often translated as "soul," simply means "person" or "self", and such phrases as *al-nafs al-mutma'inna* and *al-nafs al-lawwama* (usually translated as "the satisfied soul" and "the blaming soul") are best understood as states, aspects, dispositions, or tendencies of the human personality. These may well be regarded as "mental" (as distinguished from "physical") in nature, provided the "mind" is not construed as a separate substance.[27]

But the Qur'an surely falsifies what Fazlur Rahman claims, since at least in four chapters (surahs) of the Qur'an (surah 15: ayat 28-29; surah 23: ayat 12-14; surah 32: ayat 7-9; surah 38: ayat 71-72) it is clearly shown that "man has a dual nature, he is both soul and body, he is at once physical being and spirit."[28] For instance, the surah Al-Mu'minun (23: 12-14) points out that man is created out of many distinct materials such as blood, bones and flesh and that God unified those materials with soul:

> Man We did create from a quintessence of clay; Then We placed him as a drop of sperm in a place of rest, firmly fixed; Then We made the sperm into a clot of congealed blood; then of that clot We made a lump; then We made out of that lump bones and clothed the bones with flesh; then We developed out of it another creature. So blessed be God, the Best to create.[29]

To be more specific, after fashioning man from clay God blew into him his spirit:

---

[27] Fazlur Rahman, *Major Themes of the Qur'an* (Kuala Lumpur: Islamic Book Trust, 1999), second edition, p. 17.

[28] Syed Muhammad Naquib al-Attas, *Islam and Secularism*, p. 139 and p. 55.

[29] Ibid., p. 55.

Behold, thy Lord said
To the angels: "I am
About to create man
From clay:"
"When I have fashioned him And breathed
Into him of My spirit,
Fall ye down in prostration Unto him."[30]

"In this text He [God] states that the body is ascribed to clay, but that the spirit is ascribed to the Lord of the Worlds."[31] So, body and soul are different and separate entities. As the Qur'an makes it clear soul or spirit is breathed into the body of man by God, and surely it is not the same thing with the physical body. In the words of al-Ghazālī, "God Most High is too glorious to attach unto Himself a body or accident, because of their lowliness and their liability to change and their swift dissolution and corruption."[32] Moreover, "it is by means of soul that man is the Lord of creation as it is by means of soul that man acquires the knowledge of God and His attributes and by no other organs of the body. It is by means of soul that man can go to the nearness of God and make efforts to realize Him. So soul is the king of the body and its different organs are its servants to carry out its orders and commands."[33]

But strangely enough, Fazlur Rahman does not accept that

[30] Surah 38: ayat 71-72. See *The Holy Qur'an*, trans. *Mushaf Al-Madinah An-Nabawiyah*, Rev. and edit. The Presidency of lslamic Researches, Ifta, Call and Guidance, King Fahd Holy Qur'an Printing Complex, 1389.

[31] Al-Ghazālī on Disciplining the soul. *Kitab Riyadat al-Nafs and on Breaking the Two Desires. Kitab Kasr al-Shahwatayn. Books XXII and XXIII of the Religious Sciences. Ihya' Ulūm al-Dīn*, trans.T. J. Winter (Cambridge, UK: The Islamic Texts Society, 1995), 17.

[32] Al-Ghazālī, Al-*Risalatu Al-Laduniyya*, Part II, p. 197.

[33] Imam al-Ghazali's *Ihya Ulum-id-din*, trans. Maulana Fazlul Karim (New Delhi: Kitab Bhavan, 1982), vol. III, p. 1.

"man is composed of two separate substances, the body and the soul."[34] As we can surmise, being an exaggerated Unitarian, he fears that if we accept two separate substances in man, this will automatically lead us to the acceptance of a radical mind-body dualism.[35] But this is sheer nonsense! As al-Ghazālī says,

> It is true that in the preliminary observation it is difficult to know many as one, but it is possible to explain them. The same thing becomes many things from one consideration and becomes one from another consideration. Body, life [soul], hands, feet, bones etc. if looked at separately become many things of the same man and if looked from another angle becomes one man composed of many things. There are many persons who see the same one man but do not think of his different organs at that time.[36]

Furthermore, *nafs* indeed means soul or self[37] or something spiritual, and it cannot be equated with the physical person or body. As we know, self is abstract and invisible whereas person denotes something physical and visible. Therefore, Fazlur Rahman, the exaggerated unitarian, is wrong when he identifies nafs with both person and self in order to avoid accepting nafs or soul as a separate substance. He explicates this point further:

> The term *nafs*, which later in Islamic philosophy and Sufism came to mean soul as a substance separate from the body, in the Qur'an means mostly "himself" or "herself" and, in the plural, "themselves"; while in some contexts it means the "person" or the "inner person," i.e., the living reality of man-but not separate from or exclusive of the

[34] Fazlur Rahman, *Major Themes of the Qur'an*, p. 17.

[35] Ibid., p. 17 and 112.

[36] Imam al-Ghazali's *Ihya Ulum-id-din*, trans. Maulana Fazlul Karim, vol. IV, 238-239.

[37] Syed Muhammad Naquib al-Attas, *Prolegomena to the Metaphysics of Islam*, p. 144.

> body. In fact, it is body with a certain life-and-intelligence center that constitutes the inner identity or personality of man.[38]

In the second sentence of this quotation "it" cannot mean "the term *nafs*", but "*nafs*" itself. Fazlur Rahman unjustifiably equates *nafs* with body which has "a certain life-and-intelligence center" in order to keep *tawhid*, in the exaggerated sense, intact. Although he is aware that *nafs* is mental or spiritual,[39] he does not want to accept it as a separate substance. But by making soul part of the body or solely dependent on it, he unwittingly exalts body rather than soul. Of course, such a stand is against the spirit of the Qur'an according to which soul, belonging to the invisible realm, is more important than the body and man is composed of two separate substances, namely the body and the soul. Furthermore, according to Islam the soul existed long before the body[40] and will continue to exist even after the death of the body.

Al-Ghazālī knows that the dual nature of man or the multiple organs of man or opposing attitudes do not necessarily involve dualism or pluralism. That is why he sincerely thinks that to apply the concept of '*tawhid*' to some concrete and opposing situations

---

[38] Fazlur Rahman, *Major themes of the Qur'an*, p. 112.

[39] Fazlur Rahman clearly says "that *al-nafs al-mutma'inna and al-nafs al-lawwama* (usually translated as "the satisfied soul" and "the blaming soul") are best understood as states, aspects, dispositions, or tendencies of the the human personality. These may well be, regarded as "mental" (as distinguished from "physical") in nature, provided the "mind" is not construed as a separate substance.!" (Fazlur Rahman, *Major Themes of the Qur'an*, 17). Also, "the inner person" or "the living reality of man" refers to something spiritual, but according to Fazlur Rahman it is "not separate from or exclusive of the body. In fact, it is body with a certain life-and-intelligence center that constitutes the inner identity or personality of man." Ibid., 112.

[40] Syed Muhammad Naquib al-Attas, *Prolegomena to the Metaphysics of Islam*, pp. 171-172.

or things is not meaningful and practical. As he says in a letter he wrote to Shihab-ul-Islam:

> Any attempt at serious discussion of *Tawhid* or "The one Reality as opposed to many" is practically foredoomed to failure; because it involves the impossible task of bringing together two attitudes [or two things such as soul and body] which are not only diametrically opposed to each other, but have no common basis of discourse, and each of which resolutely closes the door upon anything like genuine inquiry and examination. One cannot achieve *Tawhid* by simply saying that Allah is One. That such introversion is not an easy thing, that it involves a habit of concentration and attention against which flesh and spirit alike rebel is known to all the mystics who have tried to attain to it.[41]

Al-Ghazālī also defended *kalam* atomism in order to reinforce *tawhid* and the omnipotence of God. The goal of *kalam* atomism is to affirm the omnipotence and absolute freedom of God, whose sovereign will creates and controls all events. This control is permanent and ever-lasting,[42] but "noneternal, being originated in new yet similar guises in discrete durations of existence for as long as He wills."[43]

Although al-Ghazālī believed that the physical reality, i.e., the light of the sun, heavenly bodies, the earth and whatever exists between them consists of atoms, he did not support the real distinction between primary and secondary qualities. As a matter of fact there is no room in Islamic or *kalam* atomism for such a

---

[41] *Letters of Al-Ghazzali*, trans. Abdul Qayyum (New Delhi: Kitab Bhavan, 1992), p. 51.

[42] Bernard Pullman, *The Atom in the History of Human Thought* (Oxford: Oxford University Press, 1998), p. 107.

[43] Syed Muhammad Naquib al-Attas, *Prolegomena to the Metaphysics of Islam*, 13. About discontinuity of creation, also see, Ibid., pp. 139-140.

distinction, since both primary and secondary qualities have the same status. According to al-Ghazālī's or *kalām* atomism primary qualities as well as secondary qualities are part of or accidents of individual atoms. More specifically, in *kalām* atomism "atoms have the primary attributes [qualities] of size, which is a minimal unit, and shape, which is a cube, but they do not have the primary attribute of motion and secondary attributes [qualities] are the result of accidents which inhere in atoms and have a real, not phenomenal, existence."[44]

Al-Ghazālī on the Problem of Causality

In order to affirm God's omnipotence al-Ghazālī attacked the necessary connection between external events, thus preceding Hume's work on the concept of causality.

In al-Ghazālī's view, God causes everything, therefore there is no room for secondary causation. In order to explain this point further al-Ghazālī asserted that:

> The connection between what is habitually believed to be a cause and what is habitually believed to be an effect is not necessary, according to us. But [with] any two things, where "this" is not "that" and "that" is not "this," and where neither the affirmation of the one entails the affirmation of the other nor the negation of the one entails negation of the other, it is not a necessity of the existence of the one that the other should exist, and it is not a necessity of the nonexistence of the one that the other should not exist-for example, the quenching of thirst and drinking, satiety and eating, burning and contact with fire, light and the appearance of the sun, death and decapitation, healing and the drinking of medicine, the purging of the bowels and the

[44] Alnoor Dhanani, *The Physical Theory of Kalam* (Leiden: E. J. Brill, 1994), 192.

> using of a purgative, and so on to [include] all [that is] observable among connected things in medicine, astronomy, arts, and crafts. Their connection is due to the prior decree of God, who creates them side by side, not to its being necessary in itself, incapable of separation. On the contrary, it is within [divine] power to create satiety without eating, to create death without decapitation, to continue life after decapitation, and so on to all connected things. The philosophers denied the possibility of [this] and claimed it to be impossible.[45]

According to al-Ghazālī the relationship or connection between a cause and an effect is not necessary. Two things or events follow one another, but one does not affect the other in any way, since both things are passive and inanimate. For instance, fire does not actually burn a piece of cotton, but God does. According to al-Ghazālī "fire, which is inanimate, has no action. For what proof is there that it is an agent? They [the philosophers] have no proof other than observing the occurrence of the burning at the [juncture of] contact with the fire. Observation, however, [only] shows the occurrence [of burning] at [the time of the contact with the fire], but does not show the occurrence [of burning] by [the fire] and that there is no other cause for it"[46]

Al-Ghazālī further states that "the continuous habit of [the] occurrence [of burning] repeatedly, one time after another, fixes unshakably in our minds the belief in [its] occurrence according to past habit.[47] If we use Kant's terminology, here al-Ghazālī claims that "the understanding [i.e., our intellect] ... derive[s] its laws from nature [i.e., experience]."[48] In other words, our mind or

[45] Al-Ghazālī, *The Incoherence of the Philosophers*, trans. Michael E. Marmura (Provo, Utah: Brigham Young University Press, 1997), 170.

[46] Ibid., p. 171.

[47] Ibid., p. 174.

[48] Immanuel Kant, *Prolegomena to Any Future Metaphysics*, trans. Lewis

intellect does not impose laws upon nature.

Descartes: His Scepticism and Dualism

Descartes, the first architect of modern philosophy, followed the method of al-Ghazālī, but he placed emphasis on philosophy or human reason, rather than theology:

> I have always thought that two issues-namely, God and the soul-are chief among those that ought to be demonstrated with the aid of philosophy rather than theology.[49]

Like al-Ghazālī, Descartes also rejected authority or custom and relied solely on his own reasoning:

> I considered how one and the same man with the very same mind, were he brought up from infancy among the French or the Germans, would become different from what he would be had he always lived among the Chinese or the cannibals. Thus it is more custom and example that persuades us than any certain knowledge; and yet the majority opinion is worthless as a proof of truths that are at all difficult to discover, since it is much more likely that one man would have found them than a whole multitude of people. Hence I could not choose anyone whose opinions seemed to me should be preferred over those of the others, and I found myself, as it were, constrained to try to guide myself on my own.[50]

After establishing his self-responsibility in finding the absolute truth, Descartes also doubted the reliability of senses on the ground that they sometimes deceive us. For instance, to

---

White Beck (Indianapolis and New York: Bobbs-Merrill, 1950), p. 67.

[49] Rene Descartes, *Discourse on Method and Meditations on First Philosophy*, fourth edition, trans. Donald A. Cress (Indianapolis: Hackett Publishing Company, 1998), p. 47.

[50] Ibid., 9.

misjudge things is possible if they are far away or not clearly perceptible. But how about the things that we clearly perceive such as our wakefulness or the fire in front of which we are sitting? Descartes argues that we can even be wrong about them. To prove this point he uses dreams as al-Ghazālī had done a long time before:

> How often does my evening slumber persuade me of such ordinary things as these: that I am here, clothed in my dressing gown, seated next to the fireplace when in fact I am lying undressed in bed! But right now my eyes are certainly wide awake when I gaze upon this sheet of paper. This head which I am shaking is not heavy with sleep. I extend this hand consciously and deliberately, and I feel it. Such things would not be so distinct for someone who is asleep. As if I did not recall having been deceived on other occasions even by similar thoughts in my dreams! As I consider these matters more carefully, I see so plainly that there are no definitive signs by which to distinguish being awake from being asleep. As a result, I am becoming quite dizzy, and this dizziness nearly convinces me that I am asleep.[51]

Then he doubted necessary truths by raising the following question:

> Since I judge that others sometimes make mistakes in matters that they believe they know most perfectly, may I not, in like fashion, be deceived every time I add two and three or count the sides of a square, or perform an even simpler operation, if that can be imagined?[52]

However, Descartes's scepticism lasted only for a short while. In order to begin with a new slate he first demonstrated the

[51] Ibid., p. 60.

[52] Ibid., p. 61.

existence of his mind or consciousness to his satisfaction. Although he could doubt everything, he could not doubt that he was doubting or thinking. In this manner he arrived at his "first and most certain" proposition: *I think,* therefore I am:

> While rejecting all those things which we can somehow doubt, and even imagining them to be false, we can indeed easily suppose that there is no God, no heaven, no material bodies; and even that we ourselves have no hands, or feet, in short, no body; yet we do not on that account suppose that we, who are thinking such things, are nothing: for it is contradictory for us to believe that that which thinks, at the very time when it is thinking, does not exist. And, accordingly, this knowledge, I think, therefore I am, is the first and most certain to be acquired by and present itself to anyone who is philosophizing in correct order.[53]

Thus he made the existence of his consciousness or mind the cornerstone of his philosophy. His next step was to prove the existence of both God and physical reality. Descartes himself tells us how he proceeded:

> I took the being or the existence of ... mind as the first Principle. From this I very clearly deduced the following: that there is a God who is the author of everything which is in the world; and who, being the source of all truth, did not make our understanding of a nature such that it could be mistaken in the judgment it makes of things of which it has a very clear and very distinct perception. Those are all the Principles which I use concerning immaterial or Metaphysical things. And from those Principles, I very clearly deduce the Principles of corporeal or Physical things; namely, that there are bodies extended in length, width, and depth, which have diverse figures and are

[53] Rene Descartes, *Principles of Philosophy*, trans. Valentine Rodger Miller and Reese P. Miller, (Dordrecht: Reidel, 1983), Article 7, Part 1, p. 5.

> moved in diverse ways. There, in short, are all the Principles from I which deduce the truth of other things.[54]

Although Descartes tried to prove the existence of God by depending on the idea of a perfect being in his mind, he was not successful in this attempt. We know today, thanks to Kant's work, that the existence of God can neither be proven nor disproven through rational means. Prof. Syed Muhammad Naquib al-Attas explains admirably:

> Descartes established the existence of the self, the existence of the individual creature, man, to himself by means of empirical intuition; this does not necessarily establish the existence of objects outside of thought. In the case of the existence of God, the more impossibly complicated it became, seeing that unlike man He is not subject to empirical intuition. Now what is more problematic about the existence of God is that since His being in thought, His Essence, cannot be known, and since His Being is identical with His Existence, it follows that His Existence also cannot be known. His existence can be known only if the identity of His Being and His Existence can be demonstrated rationally, which is not possible to accomplish. At least up till the present time the idea that God's existence can rationally be demonstrated is only a matter of faith.[55]

Descartes's "system was ideally suited to the needs of 17th century science. It left a place for God and thereby averted the charge that dropping spirit and taking everything as matter must make atheists; and it separated mind and matter, so that [natural sciences] could forget what impresses the mind so forcibly: [secondary] qualities, meanings, and purposes. Those things were in the mind and not in matter, which is entirely neutral stuff. Such

---

[54] Ibid., from the "Letter from the Author", xxii.

[55] Syed Muhammad Naquib al-Attas, *Islam and Secularism*, p. 11.

is the view of the [scientist] in the lab today."[56]

According to Descartes extension in length, width, and depth constitutes the nature of body or matter whereas thought constitutes the nature of soul. Thus, like al-Ghazālī, Descartes also separated the human soul from the body and assigned similar attributes to the soul:

> By the word "thought", I understand all those things which occur in us while we are conscious, insofar as the consciousness of them is in us. And so not only understanding, willing, and imagining, but also sensing, are here the same as thinking.[57]

The soul is alive, active, and immaterial whereas the body or matter is inanimate, passive, and material. The soul is spiritual and does not occupy a space, but the body does. In other words, the soul cannot be touched or felt physically, because it is not material. Philosophically speaking, it has no extension, and in this respect it is similar to God. That is why Descartes divorced soul from body by making it a thinking substance that does not perish even after the death of the body:

> I knew that I was a substance the whole essence or nature of which is simply to think, and which, in order to exist, has no need of any place nor depends on any material thing. Thus this "I", that is to say, the soul through which I am what I am, is entirely distinct from the body and is even easier to know than the body, and even if there were no body at all, it would not cease to be all that it is.[58]

As we can gather from this quotation, soul and body are two

---

[56] Jacques Barzun, *From Dawn to Decadence* (New York: Harper Collins Publishers, 2000), p. 200.

[57] Rene Descartes, *Principles of Philosophy*, Article 9, Part 1, p. 5.

[58] Rene Descartes, *Discourse on Method and Meditations on First Philosophy*, p. 19.

distinct, complete and independent substances. The soul is not a body and it can exist as it is without having a body. In other words, the soul is not a body and the body is not a soul:

> We clearly perceive that extension, or figure, or local motion (or any similar thing which must be attributed to a body) does not belong to our nature, but only the faculty of thinking, which is therefore known prior to and more certainly than any corporeal things.[59]

Moreover, the soul and the body do not interact, since they are distinct and independent. So, according to Descartes, man is a pair of things and lives two parallel lives in two different and parallel worlds.

Because of this radical dualism of Descartes the soul does not govern the body,[60] since the immaterial soul can in no way affect the material body. "It then becomes very difficult to account for the evident facts of psycho-physical interaction Cartesians such as Geulincx, who are generally known as 'occasionalists', refused to admit that two heterogeneous types of substances can act on one another. When interaction apparently takes place, what really occurs is that on the occasion of a psychic event God causes the corresponding physical event, or conversely."[61]

Thus it is crystal clear that "Descartes's universe is bifurcated. And at its center stands neither the Earth nor the Sun, but the

---

[59] Rene Descartes, *Principles of Philosophy*, Article 8, Part I, p. 5.

[60] To please theologians "Descartes himself asserted that the mind can and does act on the body: but his theory of interaction was felt to be one of the least satisfactory features of his system." Furthermore, "on Descartes' principles it would appear to be very difficult to maintain that there is any intrinsic relationship between the two factors [i.e., soul and body]". Frederick Copleston, S. J., *A History of Philosophy*, vol. IV, 12 and 120.

[61] Frederick Copleston, S. J., *A History of Philosophy*, vol. IV (New York; Image Books, 1994), p. 12.

mind of the individual, responding to the world around it."[62]

With this dualism of Descartes, the roller coaster of modern philosophy began its journey, swinging between idealism and realism until Kant stopped it temporarily.

Hume on Causality

If we disregard their frameworks, al-Ghazālī's and David Hume's views on causality are similar. As Eugene A. Myers writes:

> Al-Ghazzali held that events are brought about by the will of God rather than by external causes. He therefore denied the principle of causality. This view was adopted by the English thinker David Hume (1711-1776), who defined the relationship of cause and effect as the result of recollections rather than of principle, emphasizing that even though one event follows another, the first is not a priori the cause of the second. While al Ghazzali referred the ultimate ground to God, Hume referred the ultimate ground to recollections. The similarity of al Ghazzali's and Hume's thinking on this subject prompted Ernest Renan, the eminent French historian, to remind his readers, "Hume has said [about the causal nexus] nothing more than al Ghazzali had already said."[63]

David Hume, who is a sceptic, evaluates cause-effect relationship after the fashion of al-Ghazālī, but he does it in a secular context. If two events are conjoined, we call one event cause and the other event effect. Although we can experientially detect no link between them, after observing them together

---

[62] Stuart G. Shanker, "Descartes' Legacy: the mechanist / vitalist debates" in *Philosophy of Science, Logic and Mathematics in the Twentieth Century* (London: Routledge, 1996), p. 316.

[63] Eugene A: Myers, *Arabic Thought and the Western World* (New York: Frederick Ungar Publishing Co., 1964), p. 40.

several or more times we feel in our mind that those events are necessarily connected with one another. In the words of Hume:

> When one particular species of event has always, in all instances, been conjoined with another we call the one object Cause; the other, Effect. We suppose that there is some connexion between them; some power in the one, by which it infallibly produces the other, and operates with the greatest certainty and strongest necessity. It appears, then, that this idea of a necessary connexion among events arises from a number of similar instances which occur of the constant conjunction of these events. But there is nothing in a number of instances, different from every single instance, which is supposed to be exactly similar; except only, that after a repetition of similar instances, the mind is carried by habit, upon the appearance of one event, to expect its usual attendant, and to believe that it will exist. This connexion, therefore, which we feel in the mind, this customary transition of the imagination from one object to its usual attendant, is the sentiment or impression from which we form the idea of power or necessary connexion.[64]

For both al-Ghazālī and Hume the law of causality or the cause-effect relationship originates from our experiences and is linked by psychological habit. In other words, our mind acquires the conception of causality after being affected by the habitual succession of events in time. In the words of Hume, "... reason alone can never give rise to any original idea and that reason, as distinguished from experience, can never make us conclude, that a cause or productive quality is absolutely requisite to every beginning of existence."[65] Kant reiterates how Hume dealt with

[64] David Hume, *An Enquiry Concerning Human Understanding*, ed. Antony Flew (La Salle: Illinois, 1988), p. 114.

[65] David Hume, *A Treatise of Human Nature*, ed. L. A. Selby-Bigg, 1888, second ed. rev. by P. H. Nidditch (Oxford: Clarendon, 1978), p. 157.

the problem of causality in the preface of his book, *Prolegomena to Any Future Metaphysics*:

> Hume started chiefly from a single but important concept in metaphysics, namely, that of the connection of cause and effect. He challenged reason, which pretends to have given birth to this concept of herself, to answer him by what right she thinks anything could be so constituted that if that thing be posited, something else also must necessarily be posited; for this is the meaning of the concept of cause. He demonstrated irrefutably that it was perfectly impossible for reason to think a priori and by means of concepts such a combination, for it implies necessity. We cannot at all see why, in consequence of the existence of one thing, another must necessarily exist or how the concept of such a combination can arise a priori. Hence he inferred that reason was altogether deluded with reference to this concept, which she erroneously considered as one of her own children, whereas in reality it was nothing but a bastard of imagination, impregnated by experience, which subsumed certain representations under the law of association and mistook a subjective necessity (habit) for an objective necessity arising from insight. Hence, he inferred that reason had no power to think such combinations, even in general, because her concepts would then be purely fictitious and all her pretended a priori cognitions nothing but common experiences marked with a false stamp.[66]

Kant wrote his famous *Critique of Pure Reason* to resolve Hume's problem of causality in its widest implication[67] and "found that the concept of the connection of cause and effect was by no means the only concept by which the understanding thinks

---

[66] Immanuel Kant, *Prolegomena to Any Future Metaphysics*, pp. 5-6.
[67] Ibid., p. 9.

the connection of things a priori, but rather metaphysics consist altogether of such concepts."[68] Those a priori concepts such as substance, causality, time, space and quantity impose order on our experiences.

The Distinction between Primary and Secondary Qualities

With the distinction between primary and secondary qualities the seventeenth century philosopher-scientists rebelled against Aristotelianism and stripped animism from nature in order to rule and subdue it with no compunctions.

Aristotle had accepted secondary qualities as original properties of things, but in the seventeenth century the majority of philosophers claimed that colors, smells, pain, tastes, etc. do not exist in physical objects, but only in our minds. Proctor confirms this point:

> Few among the ancients would ever have said that the color, taste, or smell of a thing was incidental to its nature, or that such qualities were in 'us' but not in the things themselves. [69]

The distinction between primary and secondary qualities also turned the organic and purposeful world of Aristotle into a mechanical, inert, devalorized, secularized, or disenchanted "cosmos is everywhere the same and devoid of purpose."[70] Prof. Syed Muhammad Naquib al-Attas tells us aptly:

> By the 'disenchantment' of nature ... [the Western philosopher-scientists] mean the freeing of nature from its religious overtones; and this involves the dispelling of animistic spirits and gods and magic from the natural

[68] Ibid., p. 8.
[69] Robert N. Proctor, *Value-Free Science*, p. 56.
[70] Ibid., p. 7.

> world, separating it from God and distinguishing man from it, so that man may no longer regard nature as a divine entity, which thus allows him to act freely upon nature, to make use of it according to his needs and plans.[71]

Moreover, Aristotle's approach towards nature was qualitative and common sensical, but Descartes, Galileo and Boyle made nature passive, mechanical, mathematical, and scientific. By concentrating upon primary qualities, which represent the geometrical features of nature, they mathematicized nature and thus dealt the severest blow to Aristotelianism.

The separation of nature from both mind and God in order to understand and manipulate it in the sense of Francis Bacon resulted in the dichotomy between subjectivity and objectivity. According to Francis Bacon scientists must approach nature with a blank mind (*tabula rasa*) and eliminate values or idols in their minds. The goal of doing this is "to separate the original of nature from the additives of human perception, to capture the true essence of things".[72] Thus in order to become objective and value-free, science had to deal with primary qualities that are the fundamental characteristics of matter and ignore secondary qualities that are subjective. As a result of this approach modern philosopher-scientists generally viewed nature as consisting of matter in motion and as a machine working according to mechanical principles and claimed that the qualities we observe in nature do not actually exist, but arise out of the process of perception.

In Galileo, Descartes and Boyle primary qualities are original properties of matter whereas secondary qualities are relations or powers to produce ideas in our mind. Such relations are dependent on, but not reducible to primary qualities. Locke on

---

[71] Syed Muhammad Naquib al-Attas, *Islam and Secularism*, p. 18.

[72] Robert N. Proctor, *Value-Free Science*, 54.

the other hand claims that both primary and secondary qualities are ideas or powers. Finally, Kant fully eradicated primary qualities as the original properties of matter, thus turning matter into an unknown entity or the thing-in-itself. In other words, he made matter or world our mind's representation.

Galileo

Galileo succinctly proposed his understanding of the distinction between primary and secondary qualities in Assayer in 1623. To him primary qualities are properties of matter. An object or substance always has a size, shape, motion, place, and number. In no way can we separate these properties from the substance:

> I say that whenever I conceive any material or corporeal substance, I immediately feel the need to think of it as bounded, and as having this or that shape; as being large or small in relation to other things, and in some specific place at any given time; as being in motion or rest; as touching or not touching some other body; and as being one in number, or few, or many. From these conditions I cannot separate such a substance by any stretch of my imagination.[73]

Although primary qualities belong to objects, secondary qualities reside only in the human mind. In the words of Galileo "a multitude of minute particles having certain shapes and moving with certain velocities penetrate our sensory organs by their extreme subtlety"[74] and cause in us secondary qualities such as heat, colors, tastes, titillation, and others.

It is only after an interaction between our mind and the minute particles that we can have secondary qualities. Therefore,

---

[73] Stillman Drake, *Discoveries and Opinions of Galileo* (New York: Doubleday Anchor Books, 1957), p. 274.

[74] Ibid., p. 277.

Galileo does not accept secondary qualities as the independent properties or free creations of mind. Although he specifically does not use the term "relation", he is aware that secondary qualities can be ascribed solely neither to body nor to mind. But the end product such as redness and sweetness is formed in our mind and has no resemblance whatsoever to its cause, that is, "a multitude of minute particles".

According to Galileo, without sensory organs secondary qualities cannot exist:

> To excite in us tastes, odors, and sounds I believe that nothing is required in external bodies except shapes, numbers, and slow or rapid movements. I think that if ears, tongues, and noses were removed, shapes and numbers and motions would remain, but not odors or tastes or sounds[75]

If we annihilate living or perceiving creatures, secondary qualities will surely vanish, but whether we annihilate living beings or not, primary qualities will remain intact, because they belong to inanimate objects:

> A piece of paper or feather drawn lightly over any part of our bodies performs intrinsically the same operations of moving and touching, but by touching the eye, the nose, or the upper lip it excites in us an almost intolerable titillation, even though elsewhere it is scarcely felt. This titillation belongs entirely to us and not to the feather; if the live and sensitive body were removed it would remain no more than a mere word. If the ears, the tongues, and noses were removed, shapes and numbers and motions would remain, but not odors or tastes or sounds. The latter, I believe, are nothing more than names when separated from living things, just as tickling and titillation are nothing but names

[75] Ibid., pp. 276-277.

in the absence of such things as noses and armpits.[76]

This is why for Galileo primary qualities are objective and mathematical, but secondary qualities are unscientific, unreliable and subject to the distortions of our sensory organs. In other words, primary qualities give us the essence of reality, whereas secondary qualities represent only appearances.

To mathematicize or quantify nature Galileo made primary qualities the sole subject of science, since according to him the language of nature is mathematical.

Descartes

Descartes, being not only a philosopher but also a scientist, followed Galileo's distinction of primary and secondary qualities. According to him primary qualities are nothing else but properties of objects. However, he mostly uses the term "mode" instead of the term "property".[77] In Descartes's view there are two distinct and lesser substances, namely, mind and body, and these two substances have their own properties, or modes. For instance, understanding, imagining, recollecting, and willing are properties of mind, but primary qualities such as figure, situation, motion, etc. are properties of body.

Secondary qualities such as pain, colors, tastes, etc. are just a result of the interaction between body and mind. Therefore, again, they can neither be ascribed to the mind nor to the body:

> I do not recognize more than two principal kinds of things: one is intellectual or cogitative things, that is, things pertaining to the mind or thinking substance; and the other, material things, or things pertaining to extended

---

[76] Ibid., pp. 275-277.

[77] Rene Descartes, *Principles of Philosophy*, Articles 64 and 65, Part 1, pp. 29-30.

> substance or body. Perception, volition, and all modes of perceiving and willing pertain to thinking substance; while size (or extension in length, width, and depth), figure, motion, situation, divisibility of its parts, and such, pertain to extended substance. However, we also experience in ourselves certain other things which should be attributed neither solely to the mind nor solely to the body, and which, as I shall show later in the proper place, originate from the close and profound union of our mind with the body: specifically, the appetites of hunger, thirst, etc.; and similarly the emotions or passions of the soul (which do not consist solely in thought), for example, the emotions of anger, merriment, sadness, love, etc.; and finally all sensations, such as pain, pleasure, light and colour, sounds, odors, tastes, heat, hardness, and the other tactile qualities.[78]

Although Descartes does not also employ the term "relation", he demonstrates more clearly than Galileo that secondary qualities are just relations between the body and the mind. Without the effect of the interaction between the body and the mind there can exist no secondary qualities, since they are not properties of the mind or body alone.

Descartes also brings the minute particles of matter into the picture as the causal basis of our ideas of secondary qualities. Then, how can these minute particles produce something entirely different such as our ideas of secondary qualities in mind? According to Descartes these minute particles have power to excite our nerves in order to cause in us ideas of secondary qualities.[79] So he coined the term "power" in order to establish secondary qualities as relations.

---

[78] Ibid., pp. 21-22.

[79] Ibid., part IV, principle 198, 281-282.

Boyle

Although Boyle followed both Galileo and Descartes with regard to the distinction between primary and secondary qualities, he was the only person who expounded the distinction much more explicitly than Galileo and Descartes by utilizing the new term "power" concerning secondary qualities, and by coining the basic terms of the distinction, namely, "primary qualities" and "secondary qualities". He also used the term "relation" for the first time.[80]

Being a scientist, Boyle accepted that only geometrical or quantifiable properties, i.e., primary qualities, belong to sensible objects and not secondary qualities such as colors, sounds, smells, etc. To elucidate the distinction between primary and secondary qualities he presents his famous key-lock analogy and uses the term "power":

> When Tubal-Cain or whoever else were the Smith, that invented Locks and Keyes, had made his first Lock, (for we may Reasonably suppose him to have made that before the Key, though the Comparison may be made use of without that Supposition), that was only a Piece of Iron, contrived into such a Shape; and when afterwards he made a Key to that Lock, that also in itself considered was nothing but a Piece of Iron of such Determinate Figure but in regard that these two pieces of Iron might now be applied to one another after a Certain manner, and that there was a Congruity betwixt the Wards of the Lock and those of the Key, the Lock and the Key did each of them now obtain a new Capacity, and it became a main part of the Notion and Description Lock or Unlock by that other Piece of Iron we call a Key, and it was looked upon as a Peculty and Power

[80] Robert Boyle, *The Origin of Forms and Qualities*, Oxford, printed by H. Hall, Printer to the University, 1667, pp. 28-29.

> in the Key, that it was Fitted to Open and Shut the Lock, and yet by these new Attributes, there was not added any Real or Physical Entity either to the Lock or to the Key, each of them remaining indeed nothing but the same piece of Iron, just so shaped as it was before.[81]

A piece of iron, either a key or a lock, has a certain shape, a certain size, and other primary qualities. Thus, Boyle identifies primary qualities as the properties of matter or sensibly objects and strictly separates them from powers. As for secondary qualities, they are powers or the relations between sensible objects and sensory organs and are analogical to the relation between the key and the lock. The key has the capacity or power to turn the lock, and the lock has the power to be turned by the key. For instance if the lock is altered, then the key will lose its power to turn the lock. Notice that when the other object, the lock is altered, the key loses its own power. To relate the key-lock example to secondary qualities, Boyle establishes a connection between sensory organs and insensible or microscopic primary qualities.[82] If the insensible primary qualities of an object have the capacity or power to fit into the sensory organs, then this relationship results in our mind as a secondary quality such as redness or sweetness.

Alterations in the sensory organs will cause changes in the perception of sensible objects. Secondary qualities are then powers or capacities of sensible objects to produce ideas in us. Therefore, we should not identify secondary qualities with the properties of matter itself, i.e., primary qualities.

To be more specific, Boyle wants to say that secondary qualities depend, on or are explained by, but not identified with, the minute particles of matter itself. In other words, power is

---

[81] Ibid., pp. 11-12.

[82] Ibid., p. 13.

explained by, but not identified with, the minute particles of matter as they are part of the inanimate nature. Boyle writes:

> I say not, that there are no other accidents in Bodies than Colours, Odours, and the like; for I have already taught, that there are simpler and more primitive Affections of Matter, from which these Secondary Qualities, if I may call them, do depend.[83]

Even in the following passage Boyle's new analogy does not identify poisoning or secondary qualities with the properties of matter:

> Though the powers of Poisons be not only looked upon as real Qualities, but are reckoned among the Abstruest ones; yet this Deleterious Faculty, which is supposed to be a Peculiar and Superadded Entity in the beaten Glass, is really nothing distinct from the Glass itself, (which though a Concrete made up of those innocent Ingredients, Salt and Ashes, is yet a hard and Stiffe Body,) as it is furnished with that determinate Bignesse and Figure of Parts, which have been acquired by Comminuition.[84]

Here the power of poison or poisoning is not "a Peculiar Superadded Entity in the beaten glass", but is dependent on the matter itself, namely the beaten glass. Boyle is once more explaining secondary qualities by means of the primary qualities. In this instance, the power is none other than the capacity of glass to affect our body, since right after this passage Boyle tries to show the relation between the membranes of stomachs of animals and human beings and the beaten glass with its primary qualities such as sharp corners, a certain size, etc.

When the membranes are strong and glass parts are quite

---

[83] Ibid., p. 29.

[84] Ibid., p. 16.

small, like powder, then the beaten glass will not be able to cut the veins and the membranes of the stomach and cause a bleeding in those tissues. But when the beaten glass fits the membranes like a key's fitting a lock, i.e., when the glass parts are big enough and the membranes are weak, then the relation between the membranes of the stomach and the beaten glass will result in the power of poisoning.[85]

In the following passage Boyle once again metaphorically evaluates secondary qualities as relations between bodies:

> That the Muliplicity of Qualities, that are sometimes to be met with in the same Natural Bodies, needs not make men reject the Opinion we have been proposing, by persuading them, that so many Differing Attributes, as may be sometimes found in one and the same Natural Body, cannot proceed from the bare Texture and other Mechanical Affections of its Matter. For we must consider each Body, not bare as it is in itself an entire and distinct portion of Matter, but as it is a Part of the Universe, and consequently placed among a great number and Variety of other Bodies, upon which it may act, and by which it may be acted on in many waies, (or upon many Accounts), each of which Men are wont to fancy as a distinct Power or Quality in the Body, by which those Actions, or those Passions are produced.[86]

So far we have seen that Galileo, Descartes, and Boyle all identify primary qualities with properties of matter and secondary qualities with relation.

[85] Ibid., pp. 16-17.
[86] Ibid., p. 18.

Locke

A long and deep rooted tradition in the history of philosophy claims that Locke faithfully followed Galileo's, Descartes's and Boyle's distinction between primary and secondary qualities. As David M. Armstrong writes:

> According to Locke, and here he is following Galileo, Descartes, and Boyle, physical objects themselves have only the properties of extension, figure, motion, solidity and number ... Following Boyle, Locke calls these the primary qualities of objects.[87]

Amazingly enough, in this ongoing debate, instead of assessing Locke on his own merits, almost everybody implicitly or explicitly assumed that Locke's distinction is the same as Boyle's. Therefore, to clarify Locke's position, they have constantly referred back to Boyle. Even in 1999 Kenneth Clatterbaugh reconfirms that this tradition is still alive:

> It is standard among Locke scholars to take Boyle as Locke's inspiration for his view of matter and his distinction between primary and secondary qualities.[88]

However, to use Boyle as the proper source for understanding Locke's distinction has not necessarily been advantageous and correct, and yet, to date, almost no one has been able to free himself from this traditional account.

An implication of the traditional view is that philosophy, with Locke, acquired the distinction from science and maintained it intact. For example John Herman Randall, Jr. writes in his book, *The Career of Philosophy*:

---

[87] *Berkeley's Philosophical Writings*, ed. David M. Armstrong (London, 1965), p. 13.

[88] Kenneth Clatterbaugh, *The Causation Debate in Modern Philosophy, 1637-1739* (London: Routledge, 1999), p. 183.

> The real basis of this distinction, in Locke as in the science upon which he drew, that primary qualities lend themselves to mathematical treatment, while secondary qualities do not.[89]

But Locke did not copy the scientific account of the distinction from Boyle. While primary qualities are more significant than secondary qualities in Boyle, Locke for the first time put both primary and secondary qualities on the same footing, by defining both sorts of qualities in the same way, viz. as powers to produce ideas in us.

Locke's definition of a quality is as follows: "The Power to produce any Idea in our mind, I call Quality of the Subject wherein that power is."[90] Concerning this definition, he does not make any distinction between the idea of primary qualities and the idea of secondary qualities. Power, then, is applicable to both primary and secondary qualities, and it produces in us any idea.

After making the distinction between idea and quality Locke gives an example to further explain his definition. A snowball has the power to produce in us the ideas of white, cold, and round. Locke calls "the Powers to produce [these] Ideas in us, as they are in the Snow-ball"[91] qualities. Notice that roundness is a primary quality, and a power in the snowball produces in us the idea of roundness. Thus primary qualities are also powers.

Locke does not identify primary qualities of sensible objects with properties of matter or body. He only says that the ideas of extension, figure, number and motion of sensible objects are all caused by the properties of insensible particles. In other words,

---

[89] John Herman Randall, Jr., *The Career of Philosophy* (London, 1966), vol. 1, p. 607.

[90] John Locke, *An Essay Concerning Human Understanding*, ed. Peter H. Nidditch (Oxford: Clarendon, 1975), p. 134.

[91] Ibid.

the primary qualities of insensible particles produce in us the ideas of macroscopic or sensible primary qualities. Indeed, as Locke himself says:

> Extension, Figure, Number, and Motion of Bodies of an observable bigness, may be perceived at a distance by the sight, 'tis evident some singly imperceptible Bodies must come from them to the Eyes, and thereby convey to the Brain some Motion, which produces these ideas which we have of them to the eyes, and thereby convey to the brain some motion, which produces these Ideas, which we have of them in us.[92]

Immediately after this, Locke continues:

> After the same manner, that the Ideas of these original Qualities are produced in us, we may conceive, that the Ideas of secondary Qualities are also produced, viz. by the operation of insensible particles on our Senses.[93]

Notice especially the adverb "also" which clearly signals that both ideas of primary qualities and ideas of secondary qualities are produced by the operation of insensible particles on our senses. However, contrary to Locke, Boyle did not explain macroscopic primary qualities by means of insensible particles, but rather accepted them as intrinsic or original properties of matter itself.

In Locke's view secondary qualities, without exception, are produced by the primary qualities of insensible particles. Although we cannot feel or perceive the insensible particles, they cause in us our ideas of secondary qualities. As Locke says:

> Qualities, which in truth are nothing in the Objects themselves, but Powers to produce various Sensations in us by their primary Qualities, i.e., by the Bulk, Figure, Texture,

---

[92] Ibid., p. 136.

[93] Ibid.

> and Motion of their insensible parts, as Colours, Sounds, Tastes, etc. These I call secondary Qualities.[94]

Yet Locke inconsistently and without much thought wrote that sensible primary qualities do really belong to physical objects:

> Take a grain of Wheat, divide it into two parts, each part has still Solidity, Extension, Figure, and Mobility; divide it again, and it retains still the same qualities; and so divide it on, till the parts become insensible, they must retain still each of them all those qualities.[95]

Locke further added that "the Ideas of Primary Qualities of Bodies, are Resemblances of them, and their Patterns do really exist in the Bodies themselves; but the Ideas, produced in us by these Secondary Qualities, have no resemblance of them at all. There is nothing like our Ideas, existing in the Bodies themselves."[96]

For Locke primary qualities of body consist of solidity, extension, figure, and mobility of the insensible particles and they cause in us the ideas of sensible primary qualities. Since Locke's sensible primary qualities are on a par with secondary qualities on a causal basis, his evaluation of primary qualities is rather different than those of Galileo, Descartes and Boyle. Therefore, he cannot maintain consistently that sensible primary qualities are intrinsic properties of matter, because if we had microscopic eyes we would perceive collections of billions of small particles instead of a figure such as roundness and the roundness that we perceive in our mind would not be identical or a representation of what really belongs to the object. Consequently, there cannot be any resemblance between the ideas of primary qualities and their patterns in bodies. Thus Locke cannot defend in any way the

---

[94] Ibid., p. 135.

[95] Ibid.

[96] Ibid., p. 137.

distinction between primary and secondary qualities.

Furthermore, Locke equates both primary and secondary qualities, since he is primarily interested in human knowledge or ideas in mind and as ideas both primary and secondary qualities are on a par, i.e., they are just ideas. Also, the causal basis for both kinds of ideas is the same, namely the operation of insensible particles on our senses. Moreover, external objects neither touch our sensory organs nor our minds, since they are always at a distance from us. Then how can we perceive their primary qualities such as extension and figure? As Locke says, we can perceive them only through an impulse or rather through the motion of their insensible particles. Notice that we can never perceive the insensible particles due to their smallness and invisibility. Then how do we know that they have their original, primary or irreducible qualities such as solidity, extension, figure, and mobility and that these qualities are inseparable from matter and indestructable? As we will see later, Kant, being aware of this inconsistency in Locke, demonstrated that even the primary qualities of insensible particles do not belong to matter.

Kant and His Importance in Modern Philosophy

Kant is the supreme philosopher in modern philosophy, since he banished the last traces of the ancient worldview from modern philosophy and was able to tie the loose ends existing thereafter particularly in the Humean and Lockean systems from his own standpoint. With Kant's approval, Carol Arnold Wilmans summarizes Kant's achievement in the following passage:

> Ancient philosophers were quite mistaken in the role they assigned man in the world, since they considered him a machine within it, entirely dependent on the world or on external things and circumstances, and so made him an all but passive part of the world. Now the critique of reason

> has appeared and assigned man a thoroughly active existence in the world. Man himself is the original maker of all his representations and concepts, and ought to be the sole author of all his actions.[97]

Indeed, with Kant modern philosophy reached its pinnacle. What Kant really achieved is not a synthesis or a compromise between realism and idealism, but the formulation of an original philosophy which rejects those alternatives effectively. If we forget about his fixed categories of the mind, his philosophy still remains valid not only for the present but also for the future. The Berkeleian and post-Kantian philosophy, particularly from Fichte until Hegel, is in trouble, because it deliberately cuts off all its ties with reality or things-in-themselves. Of course, in this approach "knowledge gives birth to itself and is capable of affording its own justification."[98]

It is not really a surprise that after Kant the West once again succumbed to dualism with the positivism of the nineteenth century and the logical positivism or the analytical philosophy of the twentieth century at one end and with the speculative or absolute idealism of the eighteenth and nineteenth centuries and the postmodernism of the twentieth century at the other end. As a matter of fact, "the West has been an endless series of opposites"[99]

---

[97] Immanuel Kant, *The Conflict of the Faculties*, ed. Mary J. Gregor (Lincoln and London: University of Nebraska Press, 1979), p. 129.

[98] John Dewey, *The Influence of Darwin on Philosophy and Other Essays* (Armherst, New York: Prometheus Books, 1997), p. 297.

[99] Jacques Barzun, *From Dawn to Decadence*, xiii. I have heard this idea many times from Prof. Syed Muhammad Naquib al-Attas in his Saturday Night Lectures since 1994. He also suggests in his book *Prolegomena to the Metaphysics of Islam* that Europe has always swung from one extreme to another. In his own words: "Dualism abides in all aspects of Westem life and philosophy: the speculative, the social, the political, the cultural-just as it pervades with equal inexorableness the Western religion." (*Prolegomena*

or dualisms not only in philosophy, but also in other fields as well.

Kant and the Problem of Causality

Hume awakened Kant from his dogmatic slumber and "gave [his] investigations in the field of speculative philosophy a quite new direction."[100] Kant realized that the concept of causality "was not derived from [nature or] experience, as Hume had attempted to derive [it], but sprang from pure understanding."[101] In Kant's view not only causality but also other concepts such as time and space are known by us a priori. So our understanding with its a priori concepts "does not derive its laws from, but prescribes them to, nature."[102] With this view "Kant made a decisive advance over all previous philosophers in giving up the idea that any description of the world [is] simply a copy of the world."[103] In other words, the human mind no longer passively reflects reality as a mirror does. Thus Kant achieved the greatest revolution in philosophy or a Copernican revolution. Karl Popper summarizes this point rather well:

> We must give up the view that we are passive observers, waiting for nature to impress its regularity upon us. Instead we must adopt the view that in digesting our sense-data we actively impress the order and the laws of our intellect upon them. Our cosmos bears the imprint of our minds ... Copernicus deprived man of his central position in the physical universe. Kant's Copernican Revolution takes the sting out of this. He shows us not only that our location in the physical universe is irrelevant, but also that in a sense our universe may well be said to turn about us; for it is we

---

to the Metaphysics of Islam, 86).

[100] Immanuel Kant, *Prolegomena to Any Future Metaphysics*, p. 8.

[101] Ibid.

[102] Ibid., p. 67.

[103] Hilary Putnam, *Pragmatism* (Oxford: Blackwell, 1995), p. 30.

> who produce, at least in part, the order we find in it; it is we who create our knowledge of it. We are discoverers: and discovery is a creative art.[104]

Surely, in acquiring knowledge we both need our active mind or *a priori* concepts as well as sense data. As Kant tells us:

> Without sensibility no object would be given to us, and without understanding none would be thought. Thoughts without content are empty, intuitions without concepts are blind. It is thus just as necessary to make the mind's concepts sensible (i.e., to add an object to them in intuition) as it is to make its intuitions understandable (i.e., to bring them under concepts). Further, these two faculties or capacities cannot exchange their functions. The understanding is not capable of intuiting anything, and the senses are not capable of thinking anything. Only from their unification can cognition arise.[105]

Thus Kant deftly rejected both realism and idealism by saying that "thoughts without content are empty, intuitions without concepts are blind". As a matter of fact, "the whole course of [philosophy] since Kant's time has tended to justify this remark. The sensationalist [realist] and the rationalist have worked themselves out. Pretty much all students [of philosophy] are

---

[104] Karl R. Popper, *Conjectures and Refutations: The Growth of Scientific Knowledge* (London: Routledge and Kegan Paul, 1972), fourth ed., pp. 180-181. According to Islam and al-Ghazālī: the soul of man is also active and creative. As Prof. Syed Muhammad Naquib al-Attas writes: "The soul is not something passive; it is creative, and through perception, imagination and intelligence it participates in the 'creation' and interpretation of the worlds of sense and sensible experience, of images, and of intelligible forms or ideas." Syed Muhammad Naquib al-Attas, *Prolegomena to the Metaphysics of* Islam, p. 171.

[105] Immanuel Kant, *Critique of Pure Reason*, trans, and edit. Paul Guyer and Allen W. Wood (Cambridge: Cambridge University Press, 1998), Part II, B 76, pp. 193-194.

convinced that we can reduce knowledge neither to a set of associated sensations, nor yet to a purely rational system of relations of thought. Knowledge is judgement, and judgement requires both a material of sense perception and an ordering, regulating principle, reason; so much seems certain"[106] and inevitable.

How did Kant demolish the distinction between primary and secondary qualities?

Kant distinguished between the thing-in-itself and the phenomenon. With such a distinction he once and for all annihilated primary qualities as the real properties of things-in-themselves. Since things are always perceived through the mind, we cannot know objects or their real properties as they are in themselves. Thus, according to Kant both primary and secondary qualities are phenomena, existing only in the mind:

> Long before Locke's time, but assuredly since him, it has been generally assumed and granted without detriment to the actual existence of external things that many of their predicates may be said to belong, not to the things in themselves, but to their appearances, and to have no proper existence outside our representation. Heat, color, and taste for instance, are of this kind. Now, if I go farther and, for weighty reasons, rank as mere appearances, the remaining qualities of bodies also, which are called primary—such as extension, place, and, in general, space, with all that which belongs to it (impenetrability or materiality, shape, etc.)—no one in the least can adduce the reason of its being inadmissable. As little as the man who admits colors not to be properties of the object in itself, but only as modifications of the sense of sight, should on that account

[106] John Dewey, *The Influence of Darwin on Philosophy and Other Essays*, 297.

> be called an idealist, so little can my thesis be named idealistic merely because I find that more, nay, all the properties which constitute the intuition of a body belong merely to its appearance. The existence of the thing that appears is thereby not destroyed, as in genuine idealism, but it is only shown that we cannot possibly know it by the senses as it is in itself.[107]

Here Kant recapitulates what he essentially did. Descartes, Galileo, Boyle and Locke had associated secondary qualities to appearances without rejecting the existence of external things. What Kant achieved in his system is to accept primary qualities to be appearances as well. No longer primary qualities belong to external things or matter. Since they are conditioned by the categories of space, time and causality, they are the product of our brain functions. Thus they are not related to experience or the outside world at all and are more ideal than secondary qualities which are dependent on our sensory organs. As Schopenhauer says:

> [The] Lockean distinction, which was easy to find, and keeps only to the surface of things, was, so to speak, merely a youthful prelude to the Kantian. Thus, starting from an incomparably higher standpoint, Kant explains all that Locke had admitted as qualitates primariae, that is, as qualities of the thing-in-itself, as also belonging merely to its phenomenon in our faculty of perception or apprehension, and this just because the conditions of this faculty, namely space, time, and causality, are known by us a priori. Thus Locke had abstracted from the thing-in-itself the share that the sense-organs have in its phenomenon; but Kant further abstracted the share of the brain-functions (although not under this name). In this way the distinction between the phenomenon and the thing-in-itself obtained

---

[107] Immanuel Kant, *Prolegomena to Any Future Metaphysics*, pp. 36-37.

> an infinitely greater significance, and a very much deeper meaning.[108]

Locke had made the primary qualities of insensible particles the original qualities of matter, but according to Kant they do not belong to matter, since "we cannot possibly know [matter or its properties] by the senses as it is in itself."[109]

If primary qualities are also appearances in our mind and have no resemblance to external things, then do external things or objects really exist? Kant's answer to this question is a resounding yes, because he never cuts off his ties with the external things. What he claims is that external things and the mind interact closely and as a result we have those appearances which have no resemblance to things-in-themselves. If so, can we know what-the things-in-themselves are? According to Kant we can never know what those things really are in themselves. They are unknowable by us, since our knowledge is limited by phenomena or appearances. Furthermore, as Kant tells us, he is not really an idealist. He is neither a realist nor an idealist, because in his understanding the mind and the things-in-themselves are inseparable from one another. Arthur Schopenhauer explains how this close interaction between the mind and the object determines the world of appearances or the phenomenal world:

> The phenomenal world is conditioned just as much by the subject as by the object, and by isolating the most universal forms of its phenomenon, i.e., of the representation, he [Kant] demonstrated that we know these forms and survey them according to their whole constitutional nature not only by starting from the object, but just as well by starting from the subject, since they are really the limit between object and subject and are common to both. He [Kant]

---

[108] Arthur Schopenhauer, *The World as Will and Representation*, p. 418.

[109] Immanuel Kant, *Prolegomena to Any Future Metaphysics*, p. 37.

> concluded that, by pursuing this limit, we do not penetrate into the inner nature of the object or the subject, and consequently that we never know the essential nature of the world, namely the-thing-in itself.[110]

Conclusion

As we have seen, al-Ghazālī's scope of vision is such that he not only anticipated the main ideas of Descartes, the father of the modern philosophy, but also preceded Hume's work on causality which in turn inspired Kant, the supreme philosopher, to achieve the greatest revolution in modern philosophy by relinquishing the correspondence theory of truth.

Even the famous post-positivist philosophers of the twentieth century such as Karl Popper, Thomas Kuhn, Imre Lakatos, Paul Feyerabend, Hilary Putnam and Richard Rorty are all Neo-Kantians, since they also do not accept the correspondence theory of truth. Thus al-Ghazālī's legacy is not only relevant to modern philosophy, but also to the contemporary philosophy of science.

Furthermore, al-Ghazālī did not endorse the real distinction between primary and secondary qualities because of his belief in the unity of God and *kalām* atomism. But in the seventeenth century the majority of Western philosophers accepted that primary qualities are the original properties of physical objects and those secondary qualities such as colors, smells, tastes, etc. are simply ideas in our mind. Finally, Locke and Kant, as the representatives of philosophy, successfully ended this scientific, artificial and deceptive distinction by making primary qualities ideas as well.

Although Locke inconsistently supposed that the primary

---

[110] Arthur Schopenhauer, *The World as Will and Representation*, pp. 421-422.

qualities of insensible particles are the original qualities of matter, Kant once and for all dismissed primary qualities as the real properties of things-in-themselves due to his distinction between the thing-in-itself and the phenomenon. Since things are always perceived through the mind, we cannot know objects or their real properties as they are in themselves. As Prof. al-Attas nicely sums up, "in the act of perception, the perceiver perceives the form of the external object; that is, an image or representation of the external reality, and not the reality itself."[111]

[111] Syed Muhammad Naquib al-Attas, *Prolegomena to the Metaphysics of Islam*, p. 150

Al-Ghazālī's "Spiritual Crisis" Reconsidered

Mustafa Mahmoud Abu-Sway

There have been many and, not-infrequently, sceptical speculations about the reality and motivation behind al-Ghazālī's unexpected abandonment of his distinguished professorial position at the *Niẓāmiyyah* college[1] and his departure from Baghdad. It is the aim of this paper to examine some of these speculations in an attempt to establish the veracity and the nature of what has become known in modern literature as the "spiritual crisis"[2] of al-Ghazālī. It should be emphasized at the outset however that the scope of this paper is limited to certain works, which, for the most part, seek to suggest alternative explanations that are quite different from what al-Ghazālī himself has stated with regard to his "conversion" to *taṣawwuf* and renunciation of

[1] Niẓām al-Mulk built a college that was named after him in each city in Iraq and Khurāsān. These include Baghdad, Balkh, Nishapur, Hirāt, Aṣfahan, Al-Baṣrah, Marw, Ṭabaristān, and Al-Mūṣil. Tāj al-Dīn al-Subkī, *Ṭabaqāt al-Shāfi'yyah al-Kubrā* (Cairo: 'Isā al-Bābi al-Halabī & Co., 1964), 4: 314.

[2] Cf. 'Abd al-Amīr al-A'sam, al-*Faylasūf al-Ghazālī* (Beirut: Dar al-Andalus, 1981), 42; Al-Sharbāṣī, 34; 'Abd al-Raḥmān Dimashqiyyah, *Abū Ḥāmid al-Ghazālī wa'l- Taṣawwuf* (Riyad: Dar Ṭibah, 1988), 43.

the world.

After the death of al-Juwaynī in 478 A.H. / 1085 C.E.,[3] his most prominent student, al-Ghazālī went to the Camp (*Al-Mu'askar*) to see vizier *Niẓām al-Mulk*, whose court was a meeting place for scholars. There, he debated with other scholars on various subjects and won their respect. About six years later at *Al-Mu'askar*, *Niẓām al-Mulk* assigned al-Ghazālī to teach at the *Niẓāmiyyah* of Baghdad, where he lectured between 484 A.H / 1091 CE. and 488 A.H. / 1095 CE.[4] This position won him prestige, wealth, and "respect that even princes, kings, and viziers could not match."[5] Al-Ghazālī, according to the Ḥanbalite scholar, Ibn al-Jawzī (d. 597 A.H. / 1200 C.E.), who studied at the hands of al-Ghazālī's student, the *Maliki* judge Ibn al-'Arabī, came to Baghdad directly from *Aṣfahan* where the Camp must have been located.[6]

At the *Niẓāmiyyah*, several hundred students attended al-Ghazālī's lectures. In due course, several of these students became famous scholars, judges, and a few became lecturers at the *Niẓāmiyyah* of Baghdad itself.[7] Also, according to Ibn al-Jawzī's

---

[3] 'Abd al-Malik [Imam al-Ḥaramayn] lbn 'Abd Allah [Al-Shaikh Abū Muhammad] lbn Yusuf. He was the teacher par excellence at the time.

[4] Al-Subkī, 6: 196-197.

[5] Al-Zubaydı, *Itḥāf al-Sādah al-Muttaqīn bi Sharḥ Asrār Iḥyā' 'Ulūm al-Dīn* (Beirut: Dar Iḥyā' al-Turāth al-'Arabī), 1: 7.

[6] lbn al-Jawzī, *al-Muntaẓam fī Tārīkh al-Mulūk wa 'l-Umam* (Hayderabad: Da'irat al-Ma'ārif al-'Uthmāniyyah, 1939), 9: 55.

[7] They include: judge Abū Naṣr al-Khamqarī (d. 544 A.H / 1149 C.E.); Abū Bakr lbn al-Arabī al-Mālikī (d. 545 A.H. / 1150 C.E.), who was quoted frequently in criticism of al-Ghazālī:; Abū 'Abdullāh Shāfi' lbn 'Abd al-Rashīd al-Jīlī al-Shāfi'ī (d. 541 A.H. / 1146 C.E.), whose lectures were attended by lbn al-Jawzī; Abū Manṣūr Sa'd lbn Muḥammad al-Bazzār (d. 539 A.H. / 1144 C.E.), who taught at the Niẓamiyyah; Imam Abū al-Fatḥ Aḥmad lbn 'Ali lbn Burhān (d. 518 A.H. / 1124 C.E.), who taught at the Niẓāmiyyah for a short period: and Abū 'Abdullah lbn Tūmart, founder of

al-Muntaẓam fi Tārīkh al-Mulūk wa'l-Umam, scholars such as lbn 'Aqil and Abu al-Khaṭṭāb, among the heads of the Ḥanbalite school of jurisprudence, attended his lectures and incorporated them in their writings.[8]

The ending (on his own initiative) of al-Ghazālī's career at the *Niẓāmiyyah* of Baghdad was unexpected. He discussed the reason for the relinquishment of his position in his autobiographical work, *Deliverance from Error* (*al-Munqidh min al-Ḍalāl*), in the section on *taṣawwuf*. The aim of this book was to explain his lifetime preoccupation with, and quest for, knowledge of certitude (*'Ilm al-yaqīn*), an occupation which required him to study and scrutinize the ideas of various groups and schools of thought of his time, culminating in his declaration of *taṣawwuf* as the only path that quenched his epistemological thirst through direct experience of the divine. After discussing the methods of the *Mutakallimūn*, the philosophers and the Bāṭinites respectively, al-Ghazālī chose the method of the Sufis as the right method for the attainment of true knowledge.[9] His rejection of the three aforementioned groups was not for the same reason. He concluded that the philosophers were non-believers; the Bāṭinites he described as being like empty shells except for some Pythagorean notions, and while he cherished the *Mutakallimūn* as guardians of faith, he believed that their method fell short of achieving his goal. Indeed,

---

the Al-Muwaḥḥidūn state in Al-Maghrib, among many others. Al-Sharbāṣī made a mistake in listing Abū Ḥāmid al-Isfarāyīnī (d. 406 A.H. / 1015 C.E.), who was one of the heads of the Shāfi'ites, among the students of al-Ghazālī. See Aḥmad al-Sharbāṣī, Al-Ghazālī: (Beirut: Dār al-Jīl, 1975), 32.

[8] Al-Sharbāṣī, 31.

[9] It is my understanding that, in *al-Munqidh*, the Bāṭinites represent the deviationist groups that attempt to change the Sharī'ah from within, and the philosophers represent the Muslim thinkers whose worldview is influenced by Western thought. Almost nine hundred years after al-Ghazālī, both phenomena remain in their essence the same.

in the last few lines of *al-Munqidh*, he declares that his objective was to criticise the philosophers and the Bāṭinites; he did not mention the *Mutakallimūn* in that context.

In order to fully understand and appreciate the Sufi path to knowledge al-Ghazālī found that he had to fulfil a major prerequisite-namely the abandonment of all worldly attachments. Al-Ghazālī concluded that, in order for him to do so, he had to "shun fame, money and to run away from obstacles."[10] He made it clear that any deed which had not been done entirely for the sake of Allah,[11] was an obstacle to proper understanding and salvation. Al-Ghazālī scrutinized his activities, including teaching, and decided that his motivation in undertaking them was not fully and only for the sake of Allah.[12] In order to free himself from the shackles of worldly temptations al-Ghazālī engaged himself in prolonged and profound self scrutiny. Of this he said:

> For nearly six months beginning with Rajab, 488 A.H. [July, 1095 C.E.], I was continuously tossed about between the attractions of worldly desires and the impulses towards eternal life. In that month the matter ceased to be one of choice and became one of compulsion. [Allah impeded my tongue][13] so that I was prevented from lecturing. One particular day I would make an effort to lecture in order to gratify the hearts of my following, but my tongue would not utter a single word nor could I accomplish anything at

---

[10] Al-Ghazālī, *al-Munqidh min al-Ḍalāl*, eds. Jamīl Ṣalība and Kāmil 'Aiyyād (N.p. Dār al-Andalus, 1981), 134.

[11] I used the word "Allah" instead of "God" because the latter has various connotations, in different religions and cultures, that might not represent the Islamic concept.

[12] Al-Ghazālī, *al-Munqidh*, 134.

[13] Originally translated as "God caused my tongue to dry". See Arthur Hayman and James J. Walsh, eds. *Philosophy in the Middle Ages* (Indianapolis: Hackett Publishing Co., 1987), 277.

all.[14]

The fact that al-Ghazālī could not speak caused him grief, which eventually affected his ability to digest food. Soon his health deteriorated and physicians gave up any hope of helping him to recover saying that his problem was an affair of the heart which they simply could not solve. Realizing his profoundly serious and worsening situation, al-Ghazālī then "sought refuge with Allah who made it easy for his heart to turn away from position and wealth, from children and friends."[15] He distributed his wealth, retaining only as much as would be sufficient for the necessary sustenance of himself and that of his children. In public, he declared that he was going on pilgrimage to Makkah, though, in fact, he was planning to go to *al-Shām*.[16] Al-Ghazālī had this plan because he was convinced that the Caliph and the scholars of Baghdad would not understand his position; he was afraid they might prevent him from leaving.[17] He asked his brother Aḥmad to replace him at the *Niẓāmiyyah*,[18] and left Baghdad with the intention of not returning at all.[19]

We need to distinguish at this stage between al-Ghazālī's internal struggle to leave the *Niẓāmiyyah* of Baghdad and his earlier period of skepticism and methodical doubt; this crucial distinction was neglected by many writers on al-Ghazālī. Al-Ghazālī described the nature and length of this period, saying:

> This malady was mysterious and it lasted for nearly two months. During that time I was a skeptic in fact, but not in

---

[14] Hayman and Walsh, 277.

[15] Hayman and Walsh, 278.

[16] Al-Shām usually refers to what later on became known as Greater Syria which includes Jordan, Lebanon, Palestine and Syria. It is also used to indicate the city of Damascus; Al-Ghazālī used it in the latter sense.

[17] Al-Ghazālī, *al-Munqidh*, 137.

[18] Al-Zubaydī, 1: 7.

[19] Al-Ghazālī, *al-Munqidh*, 137.

> utterance and doctrine. At length [Allah] Most High cured me of that sickness. My soul regained its health and equilibrium and once again I accepted the self-evident data of reason and relied on them with safety and certainty. But that was not achieved by constructing a proof or putting together an argument. On the contrary, it was the effect of a light which [Allah] Most High cast into my breast. And that light is the key to most knowledge.[20]

Nevertheless, the relationship between these two periods is very strong; the end of the period of skepticism brought with it the establishment of divine light as a meta-rational source of knowledge. Its eminent sign, according to al-Ghazālī, is distancing oneself from the affairs of this world in favor of the hereafter, the climax of which, in his case, was abandoning his distinguished professorial position at the *Niẓāmiyyah* and leaving all the worldly affairs of Baghdad as a requirement to tread on the path of the hereafter.

Although al-Ghazālī used clear and simple language in describing the reason why he left the *Niẓāmiyyah*, several scholars and commentators challenged his straightforward account, which he recounted in his *al-Munqidh*, and presented various interpretations of the nature and reason for his departure from Baghdad. Not only was al-Ghazālī's version questioned, but according to Nakamura in *An Approach to Ghazālī's Conversion*, a host of scholars including Carra de Vaux, Samuel M. Zwemer, Margaret Smith and R. J. McCarthy were all skeptical about the contents of *al-Munqidh* as a source material; 'Abd al-Dā'im al-Baqarī adopted an extreme position towards *al-Munqidh* by dismissing it as fictional.[21] 'Umar Farrūkh, echoing al-Baqarī's

[20] Richard J. McCarthy, *Freedom and Fulfillment* (Boston: Twayne Publishers, 1980), 66.

[21] Kojiro Nakamura, "*An Approach to Ghazālī's Conversion*," Orient XXI (1985), 47.

dissonant voice, alluded to the "story of skepticism and certitude" as an artistic play (*masraḥiyyah fanniyyah*).[22]

As for Carra de Vaux, he considered al-Ghazālī's internal struggle before leaving Baghdad real. Yet he considered al-Ghazālī's dialogue with the sensibles an intellectual play.[23] Zakariyya al-Imam objected to Carra de Vaux's latter notion, and expressed his astonishment.[24] I would say that if Carra de Vaux was denying that al-Ghazālī went through skepticism, this would raise more than eyebrows. But if he was referring to the style in which it was written, this statement can be said to contain a grain of truth, for al-Ghazālī never claimed that *al-Munqidh* was a spontaneous outcome of that period. Suffice it to note that *al-Munqidh*, as al-Ghazālī himself stated at the very beginning of this book, was written towards the end of his life when he was more than fifty years old, that is, about fourteen years after his departure from Baghdad.

In addition, the position of Margaret Smith regarding al-Ghazālī's "conversion" reflects her acceptance of the reasons he declared in *al-Munqidh*, he said: "The reasons for the abandonment of his career and for the rejection of all that the world had to offer him—a decision which astonished and perplexed all who heard of it—al-Ghazālī sets forth in his *apologia pro vita sua* [*al-Munqidh*].[25] Thus, we find her statement

---

[22] 'Umar Farrūkh, *Tārīkh al-Fikr al-'Arabī ilā Ayyām Ibn Khaldūn* (Beirut: Dar al-'Ilm Li al-Malayin, 1972), 497. Farrūkh cited al-Baqarī's *I'tirāfāt al-Ghazālī aw kayfa Arrakha al-Ghazālī li Nafsih* in his bibliography; the influence of al-Baqarī on Farrūkh is obvious.

[23] Carra de Vaux, Al-Ghazālī, trans. 'Ādil Z'aytir; (Beirut: Al-Mu'assasah al-'Arabiyyah li al-Dirāsāt wa al-Nashr,1984), 48.

[24] Zakariyya Bashir al-Imam, *al-Falsafah al-Nūrāniyyah al-Qur'āniyyah 'ind al-Ghazālī* (Kuwait: Maktabat al-Falah, 1989), 91.

[25] Margaret Smith, *Al-Ghazālī the Mystic* (Lahore: Hijrah International Publishers, 1983), 23.

inconsistent with Nakamura's above-mentioned account.

In the introduction to *Freedom and Fulfillment*, McCarthy discussed the position of al-Baqarī, in which he relied heavily on *Autour de la sincerite d' Al-Ghazālī*, a useful article by 'Abd al-Jalīl. According to McCarthy, Al-Baqarī stripped *al-Munqidh* of its historical value based on the fact that al-Ghazālī pointed out in *Iḥyā'* (Book XXIV) that lying is not intrinsically wrong and that, indeed, sometimes it is even obligatory. Thus, the main thesis of al-Baqarī is that the structure of *al-Munqidh*, despite reflecting some actual realities, is essentially a lie. McCarthy sided with 'Abd al-Jalīl in stating that "al-Baqarī uses this teaching of Ghazālī, but unfortunately with certain lacunae which seem intentional and which permit him to insinuate as a general principle what Ghazālī did not really claim as such."[26] In addition, McCarthy agreed with 'Abd al-Jalīl that none of al-Baqarī's arguments "authorizes a doubt about Ghazālī's sincerity. The human, intellectual and spiritual value of the *Munqidh* remains firm, though it cannot of itself alone serve as an historical source."[27]

Commenting on the reliability of *al-Munqidh*, Nakamura said that al-Ghazālī's account is "by and large genuine and reliable" and that his two crises are historical facts beyond doubt with no evidence to the contrary.[28] In fact, there are established accounts by many contemporaries of al-Ghazālī who witnessed him going through the various stages and changing his lifestyle in favour of *taṣawwuf* which confirm the description in *al-Munqidh*. One of these reliable accounts is that of 'Abd al-Ghāfir Ibn Ismā'īl al-Khaṭīb al-Fārisī (d. 551 A.H. / 1156 C.E.), who personally visited al-Ghazālī several times before and after he changed his way of life to *taṣawwuf* and he verified the reality of al-Ghazālī's changes

[26] McCarthy, xxvi-xxviii.

[27] McCarthy, xxix.

[28] Nakamura, 29.

before attesting to their truthfulness.[29] He stated that after reaching a rank and reputation which superseded that of the princes and the Caliph, al-Ghazālī turned away from all that in exchange for the path of mysticism and preoccupied himself with the affairs of the hereafter.[30] It is imperative to know that before quoting al-Fārisī's narration,[31] al-Subkī stated in the *Tabaqāt* that he was "trustworthy [*thiqah*], contemporary [i.e., of al-Ghazālī] and knowledgeable".[32] The latter statement is a clear indication of the authority of *al-Fārisī*. It should be known that '*thiqah*' in this context is a technical term, which is considered by many scholars of ḥadīth as the highest rank attributed to a Muslim narrator.[33]

Al-Ghazālī's candid description of his innermost feelings, thoughts and physical conditions, which preceded his withdrawal from public teaching, tempted some contemporary scholars to "diagnose" his sickness.[34] These scholars left the realm of philosophy for medicine in their attempt to diagnose and evaluate al-Ghazālī's physical and mental fitness during the period leading to his departure from Baghdad. Although it is not the aim of this paper to define what the job of philosophy is, looking for symptoms in autobiographical works is certainly not philosophy per se. One cannot but criticize such unphilosophical attitudes.

---

[29] Al-Subkī, 2: 208.

[30] Al-Subkī, 4: 206.

[31] For the full text of al-Fārisī's narration, see; Al-Subkī, 4: 203-214.

[32] Al-Subkī, 4: 203.

[33] These scholars include Ibn Abū Ḥātim al-Rāzī, *al-Jarḥ wa'l-Ta'dīl*; Abū Bakr al-Khaṭīb, *al-Kifāyah* and lbn al-Ṣalāh, *'Ulūm al-Ḥadīth. Thabt* and *ḥujjah* are interchangeable with *thiqah*. Al-Dhahabī differed in considering a repetition of *thiqah* or a combination of it with any of the other two as higher; Al-'Irāqī (d. 806 A.H.) agreed with him. See al-'Irāqī, *al-Taqyīd, wa 'l-Īḍāḥ limā Uṭliqa wa Ughliqa min Muqaddimat Ibn al-Ṣalāh* (Beirut: Dar al-Fikr, 1993), 152.

[34] Al-Sharbāṣī, 37.

The most awkward "diagnosis" is that of 'Umar Farrūkh in *Tārīkh al-Fikr al-'Arabī ilā Ayyām Ibn Khaldūn*. After making reference to al-Ghazālī's description, Farrūkh said:

> We undoubtedly declare that al-Ghazālī was sick with *al-kanẓ* or *al-ghanẓ*, a psychological disease which appears, mostly, among those who have extreme religious orientation [*dhawi al-ittijāh al-dīnī al-mutaṭarrif*].[35]

Even if Farrūkh were a physician or a clinical psychologist, which he is not, none of al-Ghazālī's statements warrants the unguarded and decisive terms that he applied in his "diagnoses". To complicate things further, Farrūkh decided, without citing any reference and without attempting to provide any justification, that al-Ghazālī must have been sick for three years prior to the date he stated in *al-Munqidh*.[36] In addition, his statement, which suggests that al-Ghazālī was an extremist, uses language that is alien to Arabic, and which reflects the semantic shift, or rather the adulteration, of contemporary Arabic by modern Western concepts.

Moreover, Farrūkh admitted that available lexicons do not have a clear definition of this disease. Nevertheless, contrary to the latter statement, he came up with a three-page description of *kanẓ*, including its influence on the physical and mental abilities, and the various bodily functions.[37] For comparison, al-Ghazālī's own account of his physical and mental conditions occupied three lines, he said that he reached the point where he could not speak anymore, and that this condition caused him grief, which in turn

---

[35] Farrūkh, 494.

[36] Farrūkh, 493.

[37] For this description, Farrūkh cited: *'Uyūn al-Anbā' fī Ṭabaqāt al-Aṭibbā'*; F. W. Price, ed., *A Text Book for the Practice of Medicine* (London: Oxford Medical Publication, 1947); and W. Mayer-Cross et al., *Clinical Psychology* (London: 1945).

led to loss of appetite and indigestion of food, only to be followed by general weakness.[38] Farrūkh, on the other hand, left the door wide open for the inexperienced reader to accept his long list of *kanẓ* symptoms in *toto*, for he never mentioned which parts of it apply to al-Ghazālī, although I am sure none would include irregular menstruation, which he included in the impact of *kanẓ* on women! This list, which is preceded by a statement describing *kanẓ* as a hereditary disease,[39] includes, but is not restricted to, melancholy, weakened memory, inability to think properly, fear of taking responsibility, being haunted by memories of the past, despair, severe depression, indecisiveness, having frequent illusions, developing inferiority complex, withdrawal from public life, feeling humiliated, insomnia, eating disorders, weakness of sexual desire and blowing minor mistakes out of proportion. Farrūkh, who blew al-Ghazālī's condition out of all proportion, ended his rather lengthy description by stating that, as a result of this disease, the patient would be inclined to become religious and pious.[40] The latter statement misleads the reader to conceive al-Ghazālī's "conversion" as a symptom of a disease rather than a genuine religious experience.

Al-Ghazālī's declared motives for his departure from Baghdad in *al-Munqidh* have been challenged by several scholars. Duncan Black Macdonald argued that Al-Ghazālī left Baghdad because he felt that he was *persona non grata* with the Sultan Barkyāruq.[41] According to Macdonald, this was because al-Ghazālī sided with Tutush (d. 488 A.H. / 1095 C.E.), uncle and rival of Barkyāruq. In

---

[38] Al-Ghazālī, *al-Munqidh*, p. 131.

[39] This statement was accepted by Dimashqiyyah, who is an avid critic of al-Ghazālī, without any qualifications. 'Abd al-Raḥmān Sa'īd Dimashqiyyah, *Abū Ḥāmid al-Ghazālī wa 'l-Taṣawwuf* (Riyad: Dār Ṭībah, 1409 A.H), 45.

[40] Farrūkh, 494-496.

[41] W. Montgomery Watt, *Muslim Intellectual: A Study of Al-Ghazālī* (Edinburgh: The Edinburgh University Press, 1963), p. 140.

fact, this opinion goes back in history to the time of al-Ghazālī who mentioned it in *al-Munqidh.* It contradicts, however, al-Ghazālī's own account of his relationship with those in authority at the time. It is quite clear, rather, that he was courted by them. He was convinced that the Caliph would not understand his reasons for leaving Baghdad and thus would prevent him from doing so.[42] Besides, if his only goal was to disappear from Baghdad in order to escape political difficulties, he could have done so without the trouble of becoming a Sufi, the hardships associated with the distribution of his wealth and leaving his family behind in Baghdad.

Another challenge to al-Ghazālī's account was set forth by Farid Jabre who claimed that al-Ghazālī fled Baghdad for fear of assassination by the Bāṭinites.[43] The above-mentioned criticism of Macdonald's opinion also applies here. In addition, one could argue that if it were true that al-Ghazālī feared for his life, he would have looked for places located far away from the influence of the Bāṭinites. However, he went to Damascus and Jerusalem which were under the direct influence of the Fāṭimids. Furthermore, at the end of his journey, he returned to Nishapur, which was very close to the strongholds of the Bāṭinites, during the peak of political assassinations.[44] Among the many dignitaries who were systematically assassinated by the Bāṭinites was Fakhr al-Mulk, son of Niẓām al-Mulk and vizier for Sanjar in Nishapur, who met the same fate as his father in 500 A.H. / 1106,[45] the same year al-Ghazālī resumed public teaching at the Niẓāmiyyah of Nishapur. The description of his return reflects his awareness of the great danger awaiting him in Nishapur, for he wondered in *al-*

---

[42] Al-Ghazālī, *al-Munqidh*, p. 137.

[43] Watt, p. 140.

[44] Watt, pp. 140-143.

[45] Ibn Kathīr, *al-Bidāyah wa 'l-Nihāyah* (Beirut: Maktabah al-Ma'ārif, n.d.), 12: p. 167.

Munqidh whether he would be able to fulfill his duty of spreading knowledge or be cut off by death. He faced the latter possibility with a faith as certain as direct vision that there was no protection nor refuge save in Allah, the Sublime, the Mighty.[46] He believed that Allah facilitated his movement to Nishapur and, indeed, that it was He who was moving him.[47]

Another fact that can be cited against Jabre's claim is that the teachings and the activities of the Bāṭinites prompted al-Ghazālī to devote at least seven books and treatises to what appears to be a systematic confrontation of their positions, which ironically commenced in Baghdad by writing *Faḍā'iḥ al-Bāṭiniyyah wa Faḍā'il al-Mustaẓhiriyyah* and continued throughout the rest of his life.[48] Obviously, such a commitment and determination to undermine the Bāṭinites' position could only be an expression of a deeply motivated, knowledgeable and courageous scholar.

The basic problem of Jabre's claim is his interpretation of a statement reported by 'Abd al-Ghāfir al-Fārisī in which al-Ghazālī professed that, before leaving Baghdad, "a door of fear was opened

---

[46] McCarthy, p. 107.

[47] Al-Ghazālī, *al-Munqidh*, p. 146.

[48] These books are: 1. *al-Mustaẓhirī fī'l-Rad 'alā al-Bāṭiniyyah*, also known as *Faḍā'iḥ al-Bāṭiniyyah wa Faḍā'il al-Mustaẓhiriyyah*; Al-Ghazālī wrote it at the request of the 'Abbasid Caliph al-Mustaẓhir (d. 512 A.H. / 1118 C.E.) against the Bāṭiniyyah; 2. *Ḥujjat al-Ḥaqq*, was written in Baghdad but has been lost. Also, both *Qawāsim al- Bāṭiniyyah* and *al-Darj al-Marqūm bi'l-Jadāwil*, which was written in Ṭūs, are lost; 3. *Qawāsim al-Bāṭiniyyah.* 4. *Jawāb al-Masā'il al-Arba' allatī Sa'lahā al-Bāṭiniyyah bi Hamadān* [published in Al-Manar 11 (1908), pp. 601-608]; 5. *al-Darj al-Marqūm bi al-Jadāwil*; 6. *Faiṣal al-Tafriqah bain al-Islām wa'l-Zandaqah*; 7. *al-Qisṭās al-Mustaqīm*, and the section on Ahl al-Ta'līm in *al-Munqidh min al-Ḍalāl* which is a critique of their methodology; Al-Ghazālī, *al-Munqidh*, pp. 117-129. The above mentioned books are listed in chronological order as they appear in 'Abd al-Raḥmān Badawī's *Mu'llafāt al-Ghazālī* (Kuwait: Wikalah al-Matbu'at, 1977).

upon him" [*futiḥa 'alayhi bābun min al-khawf*] and that it preoccupied him, so much so, that he could not pay attention to anything else.[49] According to Jabre, this statement reflected al-Ghazālī's fear of being assassinated at the hands of the Bāṭinites, and not his fear of Hellfire as he claimed in *al-Munqidh*. After citing Jabre's argument, Nakamura criticized it by stating that he simply did not "understand why this 'fear' cannot be that of Hellfire as Ghazālī himself confesses."[50] The context in which al-Ghazālī mentioned his fear of Hellfire in *al-Munqidh*, reflects Sufi themes and terminology. Indeed, it is mentioned in the introduction to the section on "the Ways of the Sufis", after he declares his preference for their path which, by definition, requires him to be detached from worldly affairs, and his intention to follow it. It took al-Ghazālī six months, beginning in Rajab 488 A.H., to reach the point in his profound spiritual experience where he severed his ties with worldliness. One can only ask: why would he wait for a total of six months in Baghdad, before embarking on his journey if there was an imminent danger and if he was preoccupied with his personal safety? He expected the scholars of Iraq neither to accept nor to understand the religious reasons behind his action; he blamed their position on their level of understanding.[51] Thus, it is untenable that al-Ghazālī's fear of assassination could have played any role in his departure from Baghdad. His own account, on the other hand, is perfectly comprehensible.

Among those who appear to have reconciled the positions of Macdonald and Jabre is al-'Uthmān who thought that it is not strange to interpret al-Ghazālī's "excessive fear" in terms of the "choking political crises" that prevailed during that time.[52] He was

---

[49] Al-Subkī, 4: p. 209.

[50] Nakamura, p. 50.

[51] Al-Ghazālī, *al-Munqidh*, pp. 131-135.

[52] 'Abd al-Karīm al-'Uthmān, *Sīrat al-Ghazālī wa Aqwāl al-Mutaqaddimīn*

only to be followed by al-A'sam who cited both Macdonald and al-'Uthmān in concluding that "al-Ghazālī saw himself, beyond doubt, threatened by the danger that encircled him." He added that al-Ghazālī's increasing anxiety, due to his fear, was accompanied by his "consciousness of the threatening political danger."[53] It should be noted that there are two possibilities for interpreting "beyond doubt" in the above statement as it is read in Arabic.[54] The first is that al-Ghazālī did not have any doubt in seeing himself encircled by danger, and the second is that al-A'sam did not have any doubt that Al-Ghazālī saw himself encircled by danger; there remains nothing, understandably, in al-A'sam's account to substantiate any of the two possibilities. In addition, al-A'sam cited Watt regarding the same notion, yet he failed to mention that, on the same page he cited, Watt considered that Macdonald's position that al-Ghazālī was persona non grata with Barkyāruq "was probably not intended to do more than call attention to a secondary factor, since he accepted al-Ghazālī's 'conversion' to the mystic life as genuine."[55] It is obvious that such a citation would have undermined al-A'sam's straightforward following of the position handed down by Macdonald.

One last odd addition to what seems to be the unreasonable skepticism of some scholars about al-Ghazālī's "conversion" and abandonment of Al-Niẓamiyyah, came from Victor Sa'īd Bāsil, who said, in his *Manhaj al-Baḥth 'an al-Ma'rifah 'ind al-Ghazālī*—(a work for which Farid Jabre wrote an introduction)—that among other reasons "al-Ghazālī was also bored with teaching"![56]

---

fih (Damascus: Dār al-Fikr, n.d.), p. 20.

[53] 'Abd al-Amīr al-A'sam, *al-Faylasūf al-Ghazālī: I'ādah Taqwīm li Munḥanā Taṭawwurihi al-Fikrī* (Beirut: Dar al-Andalus, 1981), 39-40.

[54] *Ba'da 'idhin ra'ā al-Ghazālī nafsah, bimā lā yaqbal al-shakk, qad aṣbaḥ muhaddad bi 'l-khaṭṭar al-muḥdiq bih min kulli jānib. Loc. cit.*

[55] Watt, *Muslim Intellectual*, p. 140.

[56] Victor Sa'īd Bāsil, *Minhaj al-Baḥth 'an al-Ma'rifah 'ind al-Ghazālī* (Beirut:

Al-Ghazālī's abandonment of almost everything he possessed and his choice of the spiritual path of taṣawwuf should not come as a surprise. He read the books of Sufis such as Abu Ṭālib al-Makkī's *Qūt al-Qulūb* (Food of Hearts), the books of al-Ḥarith al-Muḥāsibī, and the writings of al-Junayd, al-Shiblī, and Abū Yazīd al-Bisṭāmī.[57] Al-Ghazālī's position was consistent with those of the above-mentioned Sufi masters. He chose their methodology as the one that could best fulfill his quest for knowledge. Al-Muḥāsibī (d. 243 A.H. / 857 C.E.), for example, withdrew from public life and died in want.[58] Likewise, al-Junayd (d. 298 A.H. / 910 C.E.), a student of al-Muḥāsibī, had doubts whether he was worthy of giving lectures.[59] Al-Shiblī (d. 334 A.H. / 946 C.E.), a student of al-Junayd, was the governor of Dunbawind, canton of Rayy, and also renounced the world and asked of the inhabitants forgiveness for his past conduct. He then submitted his resignation.[60] Al-Bisṭāmī (d. 261 A.H. / 874 C.E.) stated that he gained knowledge of the world by means of a hungry belly.[61] Following suit, al-Makkī (d. 386 A.H. / 996 C.E.) advocated self-mortification: he lived for a considerable time on nothing but wild herbs.[62] Their influence on al-Ghazālī is obvious and demonstrable.

Al-Ghazālī's internal struggle might have been triggered by the visit of Abu al-Ḥusayn Ardashīr Ibn Manṣūr al-'Abbadī to the Niẓāmiyyah of Baghdad in 486 A.H. / 1093 C.E. His preaching; which al-Ghazālī attended, was so moving that "more than thirty

---

Darr al-Kitab al-Lubnani, n.d.), p. 18.

[57] Al-Ghazālī, *al-Munqidh*, p. 131.

[58] Ibn Khallikān, *Wafayāt al-A'yān wa Anbā' Abnā' al-Zamān*, trans. B. Mac Guckin De Slane (Paris: Printed for the Oriental Translation Fund of Great Britain and Ireland, 1843) 1: p. 365.

[59] Ibn Khallikān, 1: p. 338.

[60] Ibn Khallikān, 1: p. 511.

[61] Ibn Khallikān, 1: p. 662.

[62] Al-Ghazālī, *al-Munqidh*, p. 131.

thousand men and women were present at his circles, many people left their livelihood, many people repented and returned to mosques, alcoholic drinks were spilled and instruments of play [i.e. music] were broken."[63]

Furthermore, al-Ghazālī's departure from Baghdad was consistent with the activities of a typical Sufi. It was a part of the path of the Sufi to travel from one place to another and to visit tombs of good people. Visiting cemeteries was intended to help the Sufi purify his soul, since the sight of the graves teaches one about the temporal and limited nature of life on earth, and that one should treat it as a passage to the hereafter. A different perspective concerning al-Ghazālī's journey came from Zwemer, who said: "When al-Ghazālī determined to abandon the world and set out as a pilgrim he was only following the custom of the time." To "prove" his point, Zwemer narrated the travels of al-Tabrīzī and the Persian poet Sa'ādī; both narrations, although full of adventures, are devoid of any religious connotations.[64]

Thus, describing al-Ghazālī's journey as a "custom" unfairly and arbitrarily reduces it to a simple this-worldly affair!

It is theoretically possible that a certain text can be proven forged, or it may not reflect historical facts; however, this does not apply to *al-Munqidh*, whose authenticity has already been demonstrated on sound grounds. In addition, my acceptance of al-Ghazālī's account contained therein, on its own merit, as an authentic source, does not entail accepting every idea mentioned in it. Thus, proving the authenticity of *al-Munqidh* renders the interpretation and criticism of al-Ghazālī's description as mere

---

[63] Ibn Kathīr, al-*Bidāyah wa'l-Nihāyah* (Beiruti Maktabah al-Ma'ārif, n.d.) 12: 144.

[64] Samuel M. Zwemer, *A Moslem Seeker after God: Showing Islam at its Best in the Life and Teaching of Al-Ghazālī Mystic and Theologian of the Eleventh Century* (New York: Fleming H. Revel Co., 1920), p. 105.

conjectures, or at best as an intellectual exercise. Al-Ghazālī accounted for the people of his days who, once they learned of his departure from Baghdad and rejected his declared religious reasons, became confused and entangled in devising explanations for his conduct.[65] It is interesting to note that this is still the case, nine centuries later!

[65] McCarthy, p. 93.

ESSAY FIVE

Logic in Al-Ghazālī's Theory of Certitude

Mohd Zaidi bin Ismail

Although certitude might be considered by many to be very personal, and because, of that, too subjective, one needs more than just gallantry to make an outright denial of its importance in life. Perhaps it is precisely because of its being objectively subjective that one cannot do without it. Indeed, nobody can be a total sceptic, at least when dealing with some urgent practical problems in this temporal existence. Hence, to live a normal life, one cannot help being a realist in the sense of having certitude concerning the truth of some matters—however small they might be. Nevertheless, man is a complex personality, possessing a number of abilities and faculties which, at times, are at odds with each other. One of these inherent faculties is reason-intellect (*al-'aql*). In fact, not many have dared dispute the intimate presence of this distinctively human faculty. Having accepted these two facts, namely, the importance of certitude and the presence of reason, one can go even further to inquire whether a person can be sure of something which his reason considers entirely impossible. Or, to put it differently, is it conceivable that we have certitude concerning a matter which is totally rejected by our reason? This question, for us, is by no means artificial. Rather, it provides the necessary framework for our present discussion.

It is not hard to see why al-Ghazālī, as a scholar who was very much interested in the problem of knowledge and faith, was so involved in the problem of certitude. Since logic is the property of reason, concerns the correct laws of thought, and is highly regarded by al-Ghazālī, he could not but give as well an account of its status in his overall solution to that problem. In the present paper, we will concern ourselves with surveying what al-Ghazālī's answer is and how he provides such a solution. But before that, and since certitude, truth and knowledge are only different aspects of a single item, it is very relevant to see how he perceives truth-reality (*al-ḥaqq*)[1]

Certitude in Relation to Truth and Knowledge

Truth is one of the Divine Names. This, in turn, is very closely related to al-Ghazālī's understanding of Existence. In this regard, he claims,

> ... everything of which one is aware may be absolutely false (*baṭil muṭlaqan*), absolutely real (*ḥaqq muṭlaqan*), or real in, one respect and false in another (*ḥaqq min wajh baṭil min wajh*). Whatever is impossible in itself (a*l-mumtan' bi dhātih*) is absolutely false, while that which is necessary in itself (*al-wājib bi dhātih*) is absolutely real, and whatever is possible in itself and necessary by another (*al-mumkin bi*

[1] When referring to the word *al-ḥaqq*, we have to combine these two English words, 'truth' and 'reality', for in Arabic such a word connotes both meanings. For further; analysis of this terra, and how it is related to *taṣdīq*, see Syed Muhammad Naquib al-Attas, *Islām and the Philosophy of Science* (Kuala Lumpur: ISTAC, 1989), pp. 17-25; and his *A Commentary on the Ḥujjat al-Ṣiddīq of Nūr al-Din al-Rānīrī* (Kuala Lumpur: Ministry of Culture, 1986), pp. 128-129, 149-153, 183, 187, and 234.

> *dhātih al-wājib bi ghayrih*) is real in one respect and false in another. For this last has no existence in itself and so is false, yet acquires existence from the side of what is other than it, so it is, in that respect, real ...[2]

For al-Ghazālī, truth-reality (*al-ḥaqq*) can be applied to external existence (*al-wujūd fi al-a'yān*); to mental existence (*al-wujūd fi al-adhhān*), that is, the intelligible (*al-ma'qūl*) or knowledge (*al-ma'rifah*); and to verbal existence (*al-wujūd alladhī fī al-lisān*), namely, speech (*al-aqwāl or al-nuṭq*).[3] The intelligible, in his view, is that by which the intellect comes in contact with the

---

[2] Al-Ghazālī, *Al-Maqṣad al-Asnā fi Sharḥ, Ma'ānī Asmā' Allāh al-Ḥusnā* (Limassol: al-Jaffan and al-Jabi, 1987), hereafter cited as *Maqṣad*, pp. 126-127. Full English annotated trans, by David B. Burell and Nazih Daher, The *Ninety-Nine Beautiful Names of God* (Cambridge: The Islamic Texts Society 1992), henceforth abbreviated as NN, p. 124.

[3] For al-Ghazālī's explanation of various modes of existence, see *Fayṣal al-Tafriqah bayna 'l-Islām wa 'l-Zandaqah*, ed. Riyad Mustafa (Damascus: Dar al-Ḥikmah, 1986), hereafter abbreviated as *FT*, p. 50. English trans. R.J. McCarthy, "Appendix I," chap, in *Freedom and Fulfillment: An Annotated Translation of al-Ghazālī's al-Munqidh min al-Ḍalāl and other Relevant Works of al-Ghazālī* (Boston: Twayne Publishers, 1980), pp. 151-52; *Maqṣad*, p. 25 (NN, 6-7, 19); *Iḥyā' 'Ulūm al-Dīn* with Zayn al-Din 'Irāqīs *al-Mughnī 'an Ḥaml al-Asfār fi al-Asfār fi Takhrīj mā fi al-Iḥyā' min al-Akhbār* (Beirut: Dar al-Kutub al-'Ilmiyyah, 1986) hereinafter cited as *Iḥyā'*, 3: pp. 22-23; *Kitāb al-Imlā' fi Ishkālāt al-Iḥyā'*, in *Iḥyā'*, 5: p. 21; *al-Mustaṣfā min 'Ilm al-Uṣūl* (Cairo: Mu'assasat al-Ḥalabi, n.d.), henceforth abbreviated as *MSTF*, 1: pp. 21-22; *Mi'yār al-'Ilm fi Fann al-Manṭiq* (Beirut: Dar al-Andalus, 1964), hereinafter identified as *MFFM*, pp. 50-52 and pp. 138-140; *al-Iqtiṣād fi'l-I'tiqād*, partial English trans. 'Abd Raḥmān Abū Zayd, *Al-Ghazālī on Divine Predicate* (Lahore: Sh. Muhammad Ashraf, 1974), pp. 47-64; and *Iljām al-'Awāmm 'an 'Ilm al-Kalām*, ed. Riyad Mustafa (Damascus: Dar al-Ḥikmah, 1986), hereafter cited as *Iljām*, pp. 125-128. See also our "The Sources of Knowledge in al-Ghazālī: A Psychological Framework of Epistemology" (master's thesis, ISTAC, August 1995), hereafter cited as *Sources*, pp. 83-84.

existent (*al-mawjūd*). Truth occurs when the intelligible corresponds to the existent. Therefore, when the thing is considered in itself (*min ḥayth dhātih*), it is named existent. However, considered in relation to the intellect which perceives it as it is, it is qualified as "true". The one which most deserves to be called real-true should be that whose existence is established by virtue of its own essence, eternally and everlastingly. Likewise is the knowledge about Him, and such professed, verbal witness (*al-shahādah*) to Him as "there is no god but Allāh". In this manner, only the essence of the truly existing One (*dhāt al-mawjūd al-ḥaqīqī*), i.e. God, is qualified to be attributed as such.[4]

Knowledge (*al-'ilm*) of anything other than Him, on the contrary, holds good insomuch as that thing exists. Should it become nothing, the belief (*al-i'tiqād*) in it will be false (*baṭil*). That belief as well is not true by virtue of the essence of the thing believed (*dhāt al-mu'taqad*), since that very thing exists not by itself, but by virtue of another Being, that is, God.[5] Hence, we may claim at this stage that one of those factors characteristic of truth is "permanence" in contrast to "relativity" or "change". Permanence in a simple sense can be said to consist in the duration of "the thing as it is". This becomes even more significant when connected with the notion of "clarity" which is inherent in al-Ghazālī's conception of knowledge and certainty.[6]

Al-Ghazālī once mentioned that knowledge can be regarded as "the recognition of the thing as it is (*ma'rifat al-shay' 'alā mā huwa bih*).[7] In fact, the main objective of his search is the

---

[4] *Maqṣad*, p. 127 (NN, 124-125).

[5] Ibid.; and *MIFM*, p. 184 and pp. 191-193.

[6] See *Sources*, pp. 3-10.

[7] Al-Ghazālī, "Kitāb al-'Ilm," chap, in *Iḥyā'*, 1: 41. English trans. Nabih Amin Faris, *The Book of Knowledge* (reprint, Lahore: Sh. Muhammad Ashraf, 1991), henceforth cited as KI, p. 73.

knowledge about the realities of things (*al-'ilm bi ḥaqā'iq al-umūr*), especially as perceived in the soul's primordial existence (*fiṭrah*). Therefore, it is necessary that the reality of knowledge (*ḥaqīqat al-'ilm*) be understood first. For him, it is none other than certain knowledge (*'ilm al-yaqīn*). Real certitude in his scheme is commensurate with complete unveiling, and to be sure, consists in the utmost degree of clarity of the thing known so much so that no negation of that degree is possible, actually or potentially.[8] Since we are here attending to the ultimate degree of certitude, are there, by implication, levels below such a climax? If so, what exactly is the hierarchy and what does it look like? This is the issue which will occupy us next.

Levels of Certitude

In our estimation, were al-Ghazālī asked to give the equivalent of certitude in a single word, he would most probably have chosen the term "clarity". Indeed, it was with the criterion of clarity that he evaluated his "stock" of knowledge, namely, whatever conviction he had by way of mere following (*taqlīd*), sense-perceptions and reason. Each of these three elements, when scrutinized independently from other higher sources, did not pass his vigorous test of certainty. So was the case with the existing methodologies aiming at certainty such as theology, philosophy and *Ta'līmite-Bāṭinite* doctrine, with the exception of the mystical method.[9]

---

[8] Al-Ghazālī, *Qaḍiyyat al-Taṣawwuf: al-Munqidh min al-Ḍalāl*, edited together with other articles by 'Abdul Ḥalīm Maḥmūd (Cairo: Dar al-Ma'ārif, 1988), henceforth abbreviated as *Munqidh*, p. 330. English trans. R. J. McCarthy, *Freedom and Fulfillment*, op. cit., hereafter cited as *MMD*, p. 63. Cf *MIFM*, p. 184.

[9] Al-Ghazālī considered those approaches as exhaustive. See *Munqidh*, pp. 335-380 (*MMD*, 65-91).

Accordingly, al-Ghazālī identified three levels of certitude and their order of priority.[10] The first and highest in intensity is that of the gnostics (*al-'ārifūn*), consisting of two groups, namely, *al-muqarrabūn* and *al-ṣiddīqūn*; and involving the very state of unveiling (*al-mukāshafah or al-kashf*), direct witnessing (*al-mushāhadah*), and spiritual tasting (*dhawq*). This realm constitutes the level of the transcendental prophetic spirit (*al-rūḥ al-quds al-nabawī*). Nevertheless, even at this state, the intensity of experience of each individual is not the same.[11] The second in nobility and strength is that of the theologians, consisting in the ascertainment, by reasoning (*istidlāl*) and syllogism (*qiyās*), of the possibility of such mystical states. This level leads only to the knowledge (*'ilm*) about such spiritual states. It is important to note that once the existence of such states is rendered possible, their contents-whether communicated to others or not-are also possible. For were it not because of the experiential contents, there would be no such urgency to prove the possibility of those transcendental states. The lowest stage of certitude characteristic of the common people is faith (*imān*), and is to be understood in this particular context as a favourable acceptance of those supra-ordinary states, based on mere following, hearsay and experience of others.[12]

---

[10] Ibid., p. 379 (*MMD*), 95-96); KI, p. 141; *NN*, 30-31, al-Ghazālī's *Kitāb Dhikr al-Mawt wa mā ba'dahu*, English trans. T. J. Winter, *The Remembrance of Death and the Afterlife* (Cambridge: The Islamic Texts Society, 1989), hereafter abbreviated as *Death*, p. 139 and 143; and *Iḥyā'*, 3: pp. 17-18.

[11] Al-Ghazālī's *Mishkāt al-Anwār*, ed. Abū al-'Alā 'Afifi (Cairo: al-Dār al-Qawmiyyah, 1964), hereafter cited as *Mishkāt*, 57, 63-64, and 77-78. English trans. W. H. T. Gairdner, *The Niche of Lights* (Lahore: Sh. Muhammad Ashraf, 1952), henceforth cited as MA, pp. 146-147, and 153; and *Sharḥ Kitāb 'Ajā'ib al-Qalb* of *Iḥyā'*, Malay trans. Nurhickmah, *Keajaiban Hati* (Singapore: Pustaka Nasional, 1991), hereafter cited as KH, pp. 54-56.

[12] In MMD only the supremacy of the first is clearly indicated but the order

For us, it is the issue of upgrading the intensity of certitude that resulted in the two types of internal conflict in al-Ghazālī's life. The initial tension relates to the improvement of level 3 in order to reach level 2, and this type of personal conflict is considered to be his epistemologico-methodical crisis. The later crisis refers to the upgrading of level 2 to level 1, a process-period that is regarded as his spiritual crisis. In this latter crisis, the matter at stake is the actual experience of what has been so far rendered rationally possible at the level of theory. In al-Ghazālī's system, as it appears to us, there is no urge for "doubt" as a necessary tool at least once in a person's life.[13] His concern, particularly during his mystical period, is more with the intensity

---

of priority of the other two states is not explicitly laid down. However, this arrangement of the order of intensity is based on his *Mishkāt*, pp. 77-78 (MA, 148-149); NN, p. 31; KI, p. 141 and 209; *al-Arba'īn fi Uṣūl al-Dīn*. (Beirut: Dar al-Jīl, 1988), henceforth abbreviated as ARB, pp. 45-46, and 111; and KH, pp. 35-37, in all of which the order is obviously stated. See also al-Ghazālī's *Ma'ārij al-Quds*, English trans. Yusuf Easa Shammas, "*Al-Ghazālī's the Ascent to the Divine Through the path of self-Knowledge*" (Ph.D. diss., Hartford Seminary Foundation, 1958, obtained through Michigan: U-M-I, 1987), p. 129; "The Book of Reflection (al-*fikr*)", *Iḥyā'*, 4: pp. 451-452; and al-Ghazālī's *Masā'il fī Ma'rifat Allāh*, ed. Nabih Amin Faris, al-*Abḥāth* XIV, 1 (March 1961), 220.

[13] This becomes even more obvious when his expositions in one of his last writings, namely, *Iljām al-'Awāmm 'an 'Ilm al-Kalām* are taken into account. There, he argues for the adequacy of mere faith in something true, no matter how one gains it. Consistent with his previous views, as found especially in his *Iḥyā'* and *al-Munqidh*, he reasserts that doubt is a serious sickness in regard to which only *kalām* is very useful as a remedy. Cf Osman Bakar, "The Place of Doubt in Islamic Epistemology: Al-Ghazzali's Philosophical Experience," in *Tawhid and Science* (Penang: Secretariat for Islamic Philosophy and Science, and Nurin Enterprise, 1991), pp. 39-60; and Eric L. Ormsby, "The Taste of Truth: The Structure of Experience in al-Ghazālī's *al-Munqidh min al-Ḍalāl*," in *Islamic Studies Presented to Charles J. Adams*, ed. Wael B. Hallaq and D. Little (Leiden: E.J. Brill, 1991).

of certitude rather than with the negative aspect of it, which will be elaborated later.

Since the ultimate concern of a Muslim should be the realization of *tawhīd* in its truest sense, it is by no accident that al-Ghazālī treats the problem of certitude along with his exposition of this central, fundamental theme. Accordingly, he enumerates four grades of *tawhīd*: the first being that of the hypocrites (*al-munāfiqūn*) namely, the affirmation of the Divine Unity, not by heart, but merely by tongue. The second is the *tawhīd* of the common masses (*al-'awāmm*) which includes the affirmation at both levels, verbal as well as by heart. Nevertheless, this second grade can be considered as a genus with two species: one is the *tawhīd* of the ordinary man and the other, that of the theologians (*al-mutakallimūn*). Its differentia then is constituted by the criterion "knowing how to defend one's faith", based on which the former is not qualified.[14] The third grade is that of the people who are brought near to God (*al-muqarrabūn*), and it is also known as "The Belief in One Actor" (*tawḥīd fl'lī*). The fourth grade involves the *tawhīd* of the veracious (*al-siddīqūn*). This grade is called "Annihilation in Unity" (*fana' fī al-tawhīd*), and can also be summarized, albeit inadequately, as the belief in "nothing in existence except the One Real Being".[15] Only those who are in

---

[14] For more on theology, see KI, pp. 53 55, 84, 104, 135 and 141; *Iḥyā"*, 1: pp. 113-119, English trans. Nabih Amin Faris, *The Foundations of the Articles of Faith* (reprint, Lahore: Sh. Muhammad Ashraf, 1974), henceforth cited as FAF, pp. 13-34; ARB, pp. 20-21, and 181; *MSTF*, 44; al-Ghazālī's *Jawāhir al-Qur'ān* (Beirut: Mashhūrāt Dār al-Āfāq al-Jadīdah, 1983), pp. 21-23, 33, and 36-37; MMD, pp. 68-69; and *al-Iqtiṣād fī'l-I'tiqād* (Beirut: Dār al-Kutub al-'Ilmiyyah, 1983), hereinafter cited as *II*, pp. 6-18. Theological certainty achieved through the employment of valid logical tools only leads one to the highest negative certainty.

[15] See also *Iljām*, pp. 94-95; and *NN*, p. 126, and 128-129. As we have seen, people of the third and fourth grades can also be grouped under a single genus, the gnostics (*al-'ārifūn*).

either the second, third or fourth Stage are considered as "believers", and accordingly, have certainty although with different intensity.[16]

To the best of our knowledge, the most detailed elaboration of certitude can be found in al-Ghazālī's *Kitāb al-'Ilm of Iḥyā*. There, he approaches certainty from two angles, resulting in two views of certitude: the negative and the positive aspects, so to speak. What is here to be understood as constituting the negative aspect of certainty is all those answers to the fundamental question, "what is not certainty?" It is the method of understanding certainty by virtue of knowing its negations. On the contrary, its positive aspect is to be comprehended as the explanation of those very elements that constitute certainty. These two aspects of certainty, taken together, form al-Ghazālī's holistic understanding of it.

The first aspect has to do with the concern of the logicians-philosophers (*nuẓẓār*) and the scholastic theologians (*mutakallimūn*). It is identified with the lack of doubt, in the sense of the soul's inclination towards affirming the object (*'adam al-shakk idh mayl al-nafs ilā'l-taṣdīq bi 'l-Shay'*).[17] Insofar as this aspect of certitude is concerned, there are altogether four psychic states, namely, the state of doubt (*shakk*), defined as the state in which the degree of the affirmative inclination (or belief) equals that of the negative inclination (or disbelief); the state of conjecture-probability (*ẓann*) understood as the condition in which the degree of belief exceeds that of disbelief, but not to the extent of rejecting totally the possibility of the latter; the state of belief approaching certainty (*i'tiqād muqārib li al-yaqīn*) which is

---

[16] For details, see *Iḥyā'*, 4: pp. 259-275; Abdul Haq Ansari, "*The Doctrine of Divine Command: A Study in the Development of Ghazālī's View of Reality*," *Islamic Studies* XXI, 3 (1982); and M. Smith, *Al-Ghazālī the Mystic* (London: Luzac and Co., 1944), pp. 166-169.

[17] *Iḥyā*, 1: p. 88 (KI, 193).

the psychologico-emotional affirmation, not on the basis of definite knowledge and thorough examination, but by mere hearsay, confidence and following (*taqlīd*); and lastly, certitude (*yaqīn*), identified by al-Ghazālī with true knowledge (*ma'rifah ḥaqīqiyyah*), and characterized accordingly by the impossibility of its negation, that is, doubt.[18]

For al-Ghazālī, in the case of certainty wherein the soul assents (*al-taṣdīq*) willingly to a proposition and becomes tranquil with it, three conditions are fulfilled. First, the soul becomes definitely convinced of the truth of such a proposition, and introspectively, definite as well of the validity of its conclusiveness, which by no means is due to negligence, absent-mindedness, error and confusion. Second, the soul affirms conclusively the proposition and by no means feels the possibility of its opposite. Even if the soul were to entertain such a possibility, it would be very hard for the soul to accept such a case. Third, the soul becomes at rest with a thing as well as confirms it, whether or not the soul feels its opposite.[19]

In the case where the soul yields to a belief, and subsequently, an opposite case is narrated by the most learned of men, like a prophet or a trustworthy man; if that contradicting view leaves the soul with such an impact as the suspension of judgment, then this psychic state is named firm belief (*i'tiqād juzm*). This seems to us to be only another equivalent description of what was previously termed *i'tiqād muqārib li 'l-yaqīn.*

Most of the convictions of the Muslim masses, similarly also of the Jews and the Christians, are of this nature. In fact, the belief of most of the theologians, in serving and defending their schools by means of argumentation (*bi ṭarīq al-adillah*), is of the same kind. More often than not, they accept the doctrines and proofs of

---

[18] Ibid., pp. 88-89 (KI, pp. 193-194). Cf. *FT*, pp. 73-74.

[19] *MSTF*, pp. 43-44.

their school in toto, based merely upon good faith which has been nurtured since adolescence and upon which their upbringing was based.[20] There is no single comprehensive way to produce such a firm belief. Indeed, as clearly exposed in *Iljām*, the manner varies according to the psychology of a person involved.[21] In cases where the soul feels the opposite of its belief and cannot, by nature, flee from the possibility of accepting it, such a state is called conjecture *(ẓann)*. This state, however, has innumerable receptive degrees of improvement or decline. It can therefore be gradually improved such that it ends up in becoming knowledge (*'ilm*) and certitude (*yaqīn*). This is so in regard to the *tawātur* case.[22]

In al-Ghazālī's view, real affirmation, looked at from its negative aspect, is achieved through demonstration (*burhān*), consisting generally of six channels, to wit, discursive reasoning (*naẓar*), sense-perception (*ḥiss*), mental instinct (*gharīzat al-'aql*), innumerable indisputable narration (*tawātur*), empirical experience (*tajribah*), and some combinations of the preceding channels (*dalīl*).[23] In short, this state of certitude is logical, arrived at through valid inferences (*al-istidlāl*) from certain premisses.[24] It constitutes the basis and the lowest degree of the positive aspect of

---

[20] Ibid.

[21] *Iljām*, pp. 132-136. See our last section here, *Analysis*.

[22] *MSTF*, p. 44.

[23] *Iḥyā'*, 1: p. 89 (KI, pp. 194-195); in Faris' translation, sense-perception (*ḥiss*) could not be found.

[24] See also al-Ghazālī's *Mi'rāj al-Sālikīn*, in *al-Quṣūr al-'Awā'il min Rasā'il al-Imām al-Ghazālī*, compiled by Abū Muḥammad Muṣṭafā Abū al-'Alā (Cairo: Maktabah al- Jundi, 1972), pp. 170-177. The detailed verification of this logical aspect-degree of certainty can be found in al-Ghazālī's logical writings among which are his *Maqāṣid al-Falāsifah*, ed. Sulaymān Dunyā (Cairo: Dar al-Ma'ārif, 1961), henceforth abbreviated as *MF; MIFM*; *Qisṭās al-Mustaqīm*, ed. Riyad Mustafa (Damascus: Dar al-Ḥikmah, 1986), hereafter cited as *Qisṭās*; and *Miḥakk al-Naẓar*. Refer especially to those chapters on the "Matters of the Syllogism" (*Māddat al-Qiyās*).

certitude.

This latter aspect of certitude, which is really the concern and aim of the ṣūfīs and most of the religious scholars, consists of (our developmental levels; first, logical certitude; second, the prevalence of one's affirmation of something in one's heart; third, its dominance over and its taking hold of the heart; and lastly, its ruling over the soul, leading either to action or avoidance (*famahmā mālat al-nafs ilā'l-taṣdīq bi shay' wa ghalaba dhālik 'alā'l-qalb wa istawlā ḥattā ṣāra huwa al-mutaḥakkim wa 'l-mutaṣarrif fi'l-nafs bi 'l-tajwīz wa 'l-man' summiya dhālik yaqīnan*).[25] Indeed, as we have explained elsewhere, this stage is precisely the fourth meaning of "intellect" in al-Ghazālī's scheme.[26]

In al-Ghazālī's comprehension, the negative aspect of certainty is found among all believers, but this positive aspect is only possessed by those people brought near to God (*al-muqarrabūn*). Furthermore, only the description of certitude as vague (*al-khafā'*) or clear (*al-jalā'*) is attributable to both aspects, whereas the qualification of certainty as either weak (*al-ḍa'īf*) and little (*al-qillah*), or strong (*al-quwwah*) and great (*al-kathrah*), is solely confined to the latter aspect. Therefore, whatever comes below logical certitude is regarded as vague, while whatever is above is considered clear. Nevertheless, the degree of clarity differs-it might be strong and great, or weak and small. This degree is determined, among others, by the mystical experiential certitude one possesses. Implied, thus, from such an explanation is al-Ghazālī's regarding disbelief as pure darkness.[27] Such an

---

[25] *Iḥyā'*, 1: p. 89 (KI, 195).

[26] *Sources*, p. 9 and 30-32.

[27] *Iḥyā'*, 1: pp. 89-90. However, the consideration that disbelief or unbelief is pure darkness is clearly asserted by al-Ghazālī in his Mishkāt especially in its second section on the veils (*al-ḥijāb*).

understanding suits exactly his explanation regarding man's knowledge-during his worldly life-of God and of other realities, in relation to man's vision of God and the unveiling of other realities to him in the Hereafter. For al-Ghazālī, knowledge and the vision that is attained through unveiling do not differ in kind, but only in degree of clarity.[28]

In brief, the negative aspect of certainty can be viewed as its objective demarcating part, while the positive aspect, its subjective intensive part.[29] Taking into account such a conception of certainty, al-Ghazālī's classification of certitude and the paths leading to it into three grades, as presented previously, can be better grasped. For him, although the psychologico-emotional affirmation, generally named "the common belief and being the consequence of *taqlīd*, is still valid when applied to the common masses, it is still within the mixture of belief and disbelief, or pure light and absolute darkness. Such is the case because, through thorough examination, this kind of belief can be stirred up and transformed subsequently into either logical certitude, or the opposite lower case".[30]

Therefore, the lowest level to which the term "certitude" is validly applied is logical certitude, achieved mainly through *al-istidlāl*. This minor degree of certitude can be continuously upgraded until it reaches, through unveiling (*kashf*) and inspiration (*ilhām*), the highest level of experiential certitude. Ultimately, this level is constituted by one's immediate experience

---

[28] ARB, pp. 196-197, and 205-207; *Ma'ārij al-Quds fī Madārij Ma'rifat al-Nafs* (reprint, Beirut: Dār al-Āfāq al-Jadīdah, 1978), pp. 157-163; and *Iḥyā'*, 4, p. 269, 329-332.

[29] Cf. Azmi T. al-Sayyed Ahmad, "*Al-Ghazālī's Views on Logic*" (Ph.D. diss., Faculty of Arts, University of Edinburgh, February 1981), pp. 61-124.

[30] This is really the case with regard to al-Ghazālī's stock of knowledge and conviction achieved mainly through *taqlīd*, after having been subjected to his critical analysis, as explained in his *MMD*.

of the Real Existence or the Real Unity so much so that this certitude overrules one's soul, leading either to action towards or avoidance of something, in conformity with such an intuitive knowledge. It is here that the intellectual will (*irādah*)—as opposed to the sensitive—animal will-comes into the picture; a will that integrates the subsequent practices with the antecedent knowledge, leading gradually to a transformation of being.[31] Although al-Ghazālī ascribes this level of certainty to *al-muqarrabūn*, which is the lowest species of the gnostics (*al-'ārifūn*), this does not necessarily imply that the *al-ṣiddīqūn* as the highest species of the gnostics are excluded. On the contrary, it unavoidably includes the latter, for he himself describes that there is no limit for such an experiential certitude.[32]

Certitude in Relation to the Premisses of Syllogism

It has been made clear in the last section that the highest level of negative certitude is achieved by means of logical proofs. On this particular issue, al-Ghazālī has left us numerous elucidations, the basic framework of which has not gone through any significant change. Nevertheless, his explanation can be better understood when one has a good grasp of the subject-matter of logic as understood traditionally. Most of the discussion of this negative certitude falls in the section on the matters (or premisses) of a valid syllogism. Since al-Ghazālī does approve of the science of logic as developed by the Muslim philosophers-especially Ibn Sīnā, taking the summary account of it as expounded in *Maqāṣid*

[31] Muhd. Yasir Nasution, *Manusia Menurut al-Ghazālī* (Jakarta: Rajawali Pers, 1988), p. 82; and AW, pp. 31-32. It should be emphasized here that, in al-Ghazālī's whole scheme, practices are not only necessary as the result of such intuitions but are also indispensable for the realization of those intuitions. We can therefore claim that both are in a continuous reciprocal relationship.

[32] See *Kl*, p. 135; *NN*, pp. 45-46; and *Iljām*, 94.

al-Falāsifah as our starting point can serve our purpose well. Any addition or minor changes undertaken by al-Ghazālī in his subsequent writings will be incorporated as we proceed.

There are altogether thirteen types of premisses which could in turn be used in a valid syllogism. The degrees of certainty under which each of those premisses falls are not the same and are not as many as the types of premisses. Thus, more than one premiss will share the same degree of certainty, and following that, the same kind of syllogism. Yet, each premiss is useful for an argument as well as instrumental in effecting certainty only in regard to those who accept it in its alleged status. In this manner, the extent of application of each premise is not the same. Generally, the highest certainty is effected out of the demonstrative (*burhān*) syllogism. Lower than that is the dialectical (*al-jadālī*), followed then by the rhetorical (*al-khiṭābī*), also known as the jurisprudential-legal (*fiqhī*) Syllogism. The rest of the syllogisms, which have no place in a scholarly discussion aiming at certainty, are the poetical, and the fallacious-sophistical.[33]

Those premisses, which share the degree of certainty effective of demonstrative syllogism, are intellectual a priori (*al-awwaliyyāt*), sensory (*al-maḥsūsāt*), empirical (*al-tajribiyyāt*), the impeccable transmission (*al-mutawātirāt*) and the propositions whose syllogisms are naturally together with them (*al-qaḍāyā allati qiyāsātuhā fi al-tab' ma'hā*).[34] They are all regarded as certain (*yaqīniyyatan*) and true (*ṣādiqatan*), without any doubt (*shakk*) or ambiguity (*shubhah*), thus are necessarily accepted (*wājibat al-qabūl*)[35] In other words, the outcome of demonstration is to make the truth manifest (*ẓuhūr al-ḥaqq*) and

[33] *MF*, p. 101, and pp. 110-112; and II, pp. 17-18.

[34] *MF*, p. 110. Cf. *FT*, p. 74.

[35] *MF*, p. 101; *MIFM*, p. 142.

attain certainty (*ḥuṣūl al-yaqīn*).[36] What follows is the nature of each premiss as conceived by al-Ghazālī.

A priori propositions (*al-awwaliyyāt*)[37] are like "two is bigger than one", "three plus three equals six", "one thing cannot be simultaneously eternal and contingent", and "negation and affirmation cannot be predicated simultaneously to a single item." These propositions are purely intellectual (*al-'aqliyyāt al-maḥḍah*), in the sense that, given the natural disposition of the intellect alone, they are necessarily and instinctively consented.[38] In all these, one needs only the mind wherein are imprinted the isolatory concepts, and the cogitative-imaginative faculty which relates some of them to the other. Such a judgment, which is universally fixed in the mind, is not done by the senses, for the latter do not perceive save limited items and events.[39]

Sense-perceptions (*al-maḥsūsāt or al-ḥissiyyāt*) are divided into two groups. The first kind is the internal perceptions (*al-mushāhadāt al-bāṭinah*), involving all internal states (*al-aḥwāl al-bāṭinah*) like hunger, thirst, anger, fear, etc. The second group, on the other hand, includes the external sense-perceptions (*al-maḥsūsāt al-ẓāhirah*) such as "the snow is white", "the moon is

---

[36] *MF*, p. 110. For the relation between these premisses and a person's psychology, see *Sources*.

[37] At least in *MIFM*, al-Ghazālī considers that there are two types of a priori propositions, possibly in the sense of immediate, that is, the purely intellectual (*al-awwaliyyāt al-'aqliyyāt al-maḥḍah*) and the sensory (*awwaliyyāt ḥissiyya*h). See pp. 142-146. In Qisṭās, he says that the a priori necessary cognitions (*al-'ulūm al-awwaliyyah al-ḍarūriyyah*) are effected either from senses (*al-ḥiss*), from experience (*al-tajribah*), or from intellectual instinct (*gharīzah al-'aql*). See p. 45.

[38] *MF*, p. 102; *MSTF*, p. 44; II, p. 16; and *MIFM*, pp. 142-146.

[39] *MF*, p. 102; *MSTF*, pp. 44-45; and *MIFM*, pp. 142-146. As to how these isolatory abstract concepts come to be inscribed in one's intellect, see our Sources, chapters one and two.

round" and "the sun is shining". The intellect alone, without associating with the senses, cannot pass such judgments as these. Such propositions are evident but error penetrates these observations because of several impediments like extreme distance or intimacy of the perceived object, the density of the mediums, and the weakness of the eye. Nevertheless, one should not doubt the trustworthiness of sense-perceptions when freed from such impediments.[40]

The empirical propositions (*al-tajribiyyāt* or *al-mujarrabāt*) such as "fire burns" and "wine intoxicates" are sometimes known as the regular sequence of Divine habit (*iṭṭirād al-'ādāt*). These propositions are the result of the combined operation of the intellect and the senses. The judgement rendered in this sort of propositions is general (*qaḍiyyah 'āmmah*) and is applicable to the whole (*al-ḥukm fī'l-kull*).[41] A person requires numerous, indeed uncountable, recurrences of similar events in various conditions—as in the case of the innumerable number of narrators of the impeccable reports (*al-tawātur*)—so as to effect firm belief (*'aqd qawī*), certitude and knowledge in the soul.[42] These propositions occur by means of a hidden syllogism (*qiyās khafī*) of the intellect, following the memorized, recurring sensory perceptions.[43]

---

[40] *MF*, p. 102; *MSTF*, p. 45; *II*, pp. 15-16; and *MIFM*, pp. 142-146.

[41] *MSTF*, p. 45.

[42] Indeed, al-Ghazālī regards every occurrence in the case of *al-mujarrabāt* as similar to a narrating observer in the case of *tawātur* reports. Therefore, both kinds of premisses are of the same 'genus', the difference between them is only of the nature of 'species'. In this respect, the former is more general for it includes the perceptions of various senses, while the latter is limited only to the sense of hearing. See *MIFM*, pp. 142-146.

[43] The hidden syllogism necessarily has as one of its premisses what is known as the principle of coincidence. The principle is once formulated by al-Ghazālī to be "if the event were coincidental or accidental and not necessary, it would never continue to be as such in most cases without variation (*law kāna hādhā al-amr ittifāqiyyan aw 'araḍiyyan lamā istamarra*

Perhaps such experiences necessitate conclusive judgment, and yet, at times, they necessitate only probability. Empirical knowledge is certain for those who experience it. However, men differ in this knowledge due to differences in their experience.[44]

Of the same kind with *al-mujarrabāt* are the intuitive propositions (*al-ḥadsiyyāt*) as the result of one's intuitive insight (*al-ḥads*). Their presence is due to a person's purity of mind, its strength and its attentive observation of matters, leading to the soul's definite affirmation of such matters. However, if that person is contested by either a believing or a non-believing disputer, it is not possible for the latter to recognize this so long as his sagacity is not strong, and so far as he does not go through the same experience and does not hold the belief which is held by the former. Whoever pursues the sciences seriously, numerous propositions will appear to him by way of intuitive insight and discursive inference (*'alā ṭarīq al-ḥads wa 'l-i'tibār*). It is in accordance with this state that it is said: "Whoever does not taste [or experience] will not know, and whoever does not attain will not understand (*man lam yadhuq lam ya'rif wa man lam yaṣil lam yudrik*)".[45]

The impeccable narrations (*al-mutawātirāt*) are those propositions which are known through a group's narration

---

fi'l-akthar min ghayr ikhtilāf)." As a matter of fact, al-Ghazālī never doubted the very connection (*nafs al-iqtirān*) existing between two events. Rather, the matter concerning which he was really at odds with the Muslim philosophers is the mode of such a connection (*wajh al-iqtirān*), regarding which he proposed a philosophical stand that came to be known as "occasionalism." See *MIFM*, pp. 143-145. For his elabourate discussion of occasionalism, and his refutation of Peripatetic causality, see his *Tahāfut al-Falāsifah*, ed. Sulaymān Dunyā (Cairo: Dar al-Ma'ārif, 1957), pp. 239-251.

[44] *MF*, p. 103; *FF*, p. 74; and *MSTF*, pp. 45-46.

[45] *MIFM*, pp. 142-146. For another brief description of this kind of propositions, see also *MIFM*, pp. 185-186.

(*ikhbār jamā'ah*) that is impossible to be doubted, like our knowledge of Mecca.[46] This is a matter beyond mere sense-perception since the senses are capable only of hearing the voice of the narrator regarding the existence of Mecca. The judgement as to the truthfulness of such reports, hence, is left to the intellect. Obviously, its instrument is the sense of hearing, but not a single hearing; rather the innumerable repetition of hearing necessarily effective of knowledge (*takarrur al-samā' wa lā yanḥaṣir al-'adad al-mūjib li 'l-'ilm fī 'adad*). This means that every condition of tawātur must equally be satisfied in each period, leading finally, without any interruption, to the original source.[47]

Propositions whose syllogisms are naturally together with them (*al-qaḍāyā allatī qiyāsātuhā fi'l-ṭab' ma'ahā*) consist of propositions which are not present in the mind save through middle terms (*bi ḥudūdihā al-wusṭā*). Nevertheless, these middle terms escape the mind such that one is led to regard those propositions as being *a priori* and immediately known, though in reality they are known by means of a mediation, like our saying, "two is one third of six". Such a matter as "two is one third of six" is in no need of serious contemplation (*ta'ammul*). Whenever the particular sought is present, then is present too the assent of it because of the presence of the middle term together with it.[48] This proposition thus acts like a priori propositions and is valid to be among the matters (or the premisses) of syllogisms. In fact, propositions that come to be as the results of syllogisms, composed out of the premisses of the preceding three kinds (namely, *al-awwaliyyāt, al-maḥsūsāt* and *al-mujarrabāt* (which

---

[46] *MF*, p. 103; and II, p. 16.

[47] *FT*, p. 74, and 87-88, 91-94; and *MSTF*, pp. 46-48. For a detailed exposition of *tawātur*, see pp. 132-145. Cf. Bernard Weiss, "*Knowledge of the Past: The Theory of Tawātur According to Ghazālī*," in Studia Islamica LXI (MCMLXXXV).

[48] *MF*, p. 104; and *MIFM*, pp. 142-146.

includes necessarily *al-tawātur* as a species)), are qualified to be premisses of syllogisms.[49] All the above-mentioned propositions are real, certain, and usable as premisses of the demonstrative syllogism.

The second type of syllogism is dialectical. It occupies a lower degree of certainty, and is formed out of premises of the well-known (*al-mashhūrāt*) or the approved (*al-musallamāt*) type. Nonetheless, *a priori* propositions, which are stronger than the above two kinds of premisses, can also be used in dialectic (*al-jadal*) but only on account of its popularity. For such an art of argument does not require of its premisses more than just fame. These two premisses as well as the conclusions reached through such an inference approximate certainty (*muqāribatan li'l-yaqīn*), and are acceptable to all people at their face value. It is hard for the mind to entertain the possibility of error in them and to instantly conceive their contraries as being possible, though there is still room for such a possibility if meticulous observation and serious reflection are carried out. The syllogism is called dialectical (*jadaliyyan*) because of its usefulness in arguing against an opponent.[50] Some of the Qur'anic proofs occupy this status since the claims cited, though neither necessarily true nor perforce constitutive of Qur'anic teachings, are still instrumental to dumbfound the opponents who believe and recognize them.[51] Below are the descriptions of propositions of the dialectical nature.

The well-known propositions (*al-mashhūrāt*), such as "lying is bad", are those praiseworthy opinions (*ārā' maḥmūdah*) the affirmation of which is made compulsory on the basis of mere popularity, and by virtue of the testimony (*shahādāt*) of the

[49] *II*, p.16; *Qista*. pp. 101-102; and *MWM*, pp. 142-146.

[50] *MIFM*, p. 140; *MF*, p. 101, and 110-111; and *Qisṭās*, p. 102.

[51] Ibid.; pp. 66-67, 102, and 121-122.

whole, the majority, or the multitude of learned men. These judgements are neither absolutely true nor totally false. Neither are they *a priori*, nor estimative. Their truth requires further scrutiny and is so only when certain subtle conditions, which escape most people's minds, obtain. One way to differentiate this kind of propositions from *a priori* ones is to suppose an imaginary case wherein one is born of a sudden as a person; fully mature, intelligent and rational, being shown these two kinds of propositions—the *a priori* as well as the well-known. In such a case, one will then be able to doubt the well-known premisses or, at least, hesitate in assenting to them, and thus, will finally come to understand that those propositions are neither self-evident nor *a priori*.

The acceptance of such well-known premisses is founded merely on varieties of accidental causes and factors, nurtured since early childhood. It is these elements, which are mostly psychologico-circumstantial, that confirm and fix such propositions in the soul. Those causes are, at least, five in number. First, tenderness of heart, by virtue of innate disposition. Second, the inborn disposition of a man to be violently proud and disdainful. Third, the love of peace-making, conciliation and cooperation in the quest of livelihoods. Fourth, the disciplinary, repeated inculcations of the religious law, from parents and teachers, for setting people's lives aright since early childhood. Fifth, the inductive inference of a general law from only a number of particulars. All these are hence the underlying reasons that induce the soul to make such judgments. Because of all these "background" factors, nurtured especially since adolescence, propositions of this type are subject to varying degrees of strength and weakness. Most of the premisses used by the theologians as well as the jurists are of this type, accepted on the basis of mere popularity.[52] The approved propositions (*al-musallamāt*), on the other hand, involve those premisses which either are accepted by the opposite party or are famous only among two opposing parties. They are put ahead by one party against its opponent, without the same case being applied to the former.[53]

Sometimes, the matters of syllogism are belief in the sense of being preponderantly probable (*ẓannun ghālibun*), thus, are not categorically affirmed. The soul is content with the belief and, in most cases, is unaware of its opposite. However, when considered seriously, the soul may entertain the possibility of error, thus, may accept its opposite. The syllogism formed out of this third kind is called rhetorical (*khiṭābiyan*) or jurisprudential. Such a syllogism is effective in inducing the soul towards truth and hindering it from falsehood. It is acceptable for the purpose of teaching (*al-ta'līmāt*) and preaching (*al-mukhāṭabāt*), and is usable in every matter in which certainty in its complete sense is not sought. It is composed of the accepted (*al-maqbūlat*), the apparently famous (*al-mashhūrāt fī al-ẓāhir*) and the conjectural-probable (*al-maẓnūnāt*) propositions.[54]

The accepted propositions (*al-maqbūlat*) are those propositions of which we have become convinced, by believing whosoever relates them to us when such an authority consists either of a group of individuals whose number falls short of the size required to give conclusive corroborative reporting (*tawātur*), or of a single individual distinguished by manifest justice or abundant learning. All these statements are suitable for legal

---

[52] *MSTF*, pp. 48-49; M. E. Marmura, "*Ghazālī on Ethical Premises*" and "*Premises that are Not Certain and Usable in Demonstrations*," The Philosophical Forum 1, 3 (1969), 395, and 399-402; *FT*, pp. 73-74; and *MF*, pp. 106-107.

[53] Ibid., p. 107; and II, p. 17.

[54] *MWM*, p. 140; *MF*, p. 101, and 111-112; and Marmura, *op. cit.*, p. 399.

analogical arguments, but not for rational demonstrations. Their power of evoking varying degrees of belief is obvious. Therefore, their degrees of credibility in all these are innumerable.[55]

The apparently famous propositions (*al-mashhūrāt fi'l-ẓāhir*), such as the saying "Help your brother, whether he is unjust or being unjustly treated", consist of every claim the whole of which is accepted right away by the one who hears it. Nevertheless, if he reflects and investigates it, he will find out that—taken at face value—it is unacceptable and invalid.[56] The conjectural-probable propositions (*al-maẓnunāt*) involve whatever case that is effective of preponderant probability, though it is still accompanied by the feeling of the possibility of the contrary case. One thus inclines to believe rather than to disbelieve it—not in an unshakeable way—lending it that kind of inclination whereon one's strategy for action is based. That person, however, continues to be conscious of the possibility of its opposite. When both the well-known and the accepted propositions are considered as propositions the opposite of which, in one way or another, one is conscious, they can be; classified as "conjectural-probable".[57]

In some other cases, the matters of syllogism resemble either the certain or the well-known; which apparently, thus not really, approximates the former. These propositions are pure ignorance (*al-jahl al maḥḍ*), depicted in the guise of certainty, being neither probable nor certain. The syllogism resulting from them is termed fallacious-sophistrical (*mughāliṭiyyan wa sūfasṭā'iyyan*) because it is not intended but for deception and sophistry. It violates the

---

[55] *MF*, p. 107; and Marmura, *op. cit.*, pp. 402-403. Another type of proposition, that is, *al-sam'iyyāt*, appearing only in his al-*Iqtiṣād fi'l-I'tiqād*, can fall into either *al-mashhūrāt* or *al-maqbūlat*, depending upon the number of the narrators. See *II*, p. 17.

[56] *MF*, pp. 107-108.

[57] Ibid., p. 109; and Marmura, *op. cit.*, p. 403.

realities (*ibṭāl al-ḥaqā'iq*). The propositions that constitute such a syllogism are the estimative (*al-wahmiyyāt*) and the ambiguous (*al-mutashabihāt*).[58] The ambiguous propositions (*al-mutashabihāt*) are those propositions which are deceitful in their resembling the a priori, the empirical and the popular ones, though, in reality, they are not so. They approximate the rest of the latter only apparently.[59]

The estimative propositions (*al-wahmiyyāt*) are the outcome of the judgment of the estimative faculty in regard to non-sensible matters. This faculty does not accept anything except in conformity with the sense-data. Its very nature then is to contradict and reject anything which does not conform with its compositions and assessment of the sense-perceptions. Its judgments, i.e., the *al-wahmiyyāt,* become very firmly implanted in the soul such that one's ability to doubt them is hindered. Such judgements are only true, certain, and reliable, so long as they relate to the realm of sense perceptions. However, they are regarded as spurious premisses (*muqaddimāt bāṭilah*) when applied to non-sensible matters.[60]

As for the fifth kind, known as poetical syllogism (*qiyāsan shi'riyyan*), it is not effective of knowledge (*'ilm*) or probability (*ẓann*). It is made up of imaginary propositions (*al-mukhayyalāt*) which we know to be false, but towards which the soul inclines by

---

[58] *MF,* p. 101 and 111; *FT,* p. 74; and *MWM,* p. 140.

[59] *MF,* p. 107. In his *Mi'yār,* however, he considers *al-mushābbihat* in its most general sense, that is, as a 'genus', in which we find three 'species' of propositions, to wit, that which resembles the primary intellectual ones, namely, *al-wahmiyyāt,* that which resembles the probable ones, namely, *al-mukhayyalāt,* used in poetical syllogism; and that which results from errors and confusions (*al-aghālīṭ*), either in the expression (*lafẓ*) or in the meaning (*ma'nā*). See *MIFM,* pp. 150-154.

[60] *MSTF,* pp. 46-48; *MF,* pp. 104-111; *MIFM,* pp. 33-43, 63-66, and 151-152; and Sources, pp. 17-28 and 70-76.

way of incitement, repulsion, granting, withholding, intimidation or encouragement. Their impact on the soul is through the repetitions of all those conditions, mainly contraction and expansion, such that they are affirmed though one is aware of their falsity.[61]

Analysis

So far, it is widely accepted that *Iljām* is one of al-Ghazālī's latest writings, if not the very last. In many instances, the chronological posteriority of this book has led some scholars to regard it as decisive wherever there are apparent inconsistencies between its contents and those of his earlier writings. Be that as it may, if one can be sure at all of al-Ghazālī's stand in his *Iljām*, it is, in our view, his consistency in holding the importance of logic within his overall scheme of knowledge and certitude. It is in strict accordance with such a hierarchical framework of certitude that al-Ghazālī accounts for the problem of faith, achieved through various channels. Faith (*al-imān*) is an expression of a conclusive affirmation (*taṣdīq jāzim la taraddud fīhi*) which the person involved does not think of as capable of error (*wa la yash'ur ṣāḥibuhu bi imkān wuqū' al-khaṭa' fīhi*). Such a categorical consent is effected at six different levels.[62]

The first level, which is the highest and constitutes the ultimate aim (*al-ghāyah al-quswā*), is attained through demonstration (*al-burhān*). Perhaps, in each period these qualities gather only in one or two persons who attain such a level. Yet a period may totally lack such a qualified person. Al-Ghazālī also maintains that there are many Qur'anic proofs which, when scrutinized carefully, are of this nature, though because of the

[61] *MIFM*, p. 140; and *MF*, p. 101, 109, and 112.

[62] Cf Binyamin Abrahamov, "Al-Ghazālī's Supreme Way to Know God," *Studia Islamica* LXXVII (1991), pp. 143-144.

conciseness of the Qur'an, they are not enumerated in the complete forms of various types of valid-cum-certain syllogism.[63] If salvation were to be limited only to the like of this level knowledge (*al-ma'rifah*), then salvation will be small in number and those successful, quantitatively insignificant.[64]

The second level is attained through theological (or in this context, dialectical) estimative proofs (*al-adillah al-wahmiyyah al-kalāmiyyah*), composed of those matters which are acceptable and affirmed on the basis of their popularity among great scholars, the repulsiveness of disobeying them, and the reluctance of the soul to initiate dispute in these matters. In some matters and concerning some people, this is effective as well of conclusive affirmation in such a manner that a person does not in principle feel the possibility of the opposite case.[65] We have stated before that some of the claims cited in the Qur'an, when arguing against its opponents, are of this dialectical type.

The third level is the result of rhetorical proof (*al-adillah* al-*khiṭābiyyah*), that is, the aptitude that is customarily used in ordinary dialogues and public addresses. In the case of most people, this produces right-away affirmation prior to any real comprehension insofar as one's heart is not laden with fanaticism and deep-rooted belief in the opposite of the requirements of the proof.[66] In al-Ghazālī's view, many of the Qur'anic proofs are of this third kind so as to be understood by and be appealing to the masses.[67]

The fourth level consists of the affirmation that is based solely on hearing (*mujarrad al-samā'*) from someone in whom one has

---

[63] *Qisṭās*. pp. 19-91.

[64] *Iljām*, p. 132.

[65] Ibid.

[66] Ibid.

[67] Ibid., p. 133.

good faith on the basis of people's numerous praises of him, such as one's father, teacher or public figures of one's time.[68] The fifth level involves that kind of affirmation to which one's heart spontaneously turns, upon hearing something, despite the fact that the circumstantial evidences (*qarā'in al-aḥwāl*) are not conclusive in the eye of a true investigator though they are effective of definite belief as regards the masses.[69] The sixth level, on the other hand, is that affirmation which takes place upon hearing a report or saying that suits one's temperament and character. The prompt affirmation is solely because of its conformity with his temperament, and is neither due to good faith in the reporter nor to the proof presented.[70]

The belief maintained by the masses is, for al-Ghazālī, acceptable—indeed, sufficient—on account of the above-mentioned levels, the highest of which, in their case, are the proofs of the Qur'an.[71] All but the first level in fact boil down to those affirmations determined mainly by psychologico-circumstantial factors that surround a person since his childhood. More often than not, they are of the kind of mere following, unquestionable acceptance (*taqlīd*) and good faith (*ḥusn al-ẓann*).[72] Nevertheless, such affirmative beliefs are equally applicable to both truth and falsehood, thus, are inadequate in the eye of a real seeker of truth and knowledge. This is why al-Ghazālī reasserts his position: "... the [real] conclusive affirmation is established upon argument and precise formulation of proofs (*al-baḥth wa taḥrīr al-adillah*).[73]

It is not just the acceptance of the truth of the content of prophecy by various ways of *taqlīd* that matters but also the

[68] Ibid., pp. 133-134.

[69] Ibid., p. 134.

[70] Ibid., pp. 134-135.

[71] Ibid., p. 135.

[72] Ibid., pp. 135-136.

[73] Ibid., p. 136.

realization and verification (*taḥqiq*) of such truth. The latter, as has been repeated several times already, is possible only through the method of the Sufis.[74] "By various ways of *taqlīd*." we mean, based on al-Ghazālī's framework, any means save necessary *a priori* intellectual knowledge and direct perceptions—whether ordinary or supra-ordinary. Thus, in this sense, those ways include the *tawātur* type of acceptance as well as any other method that results in concomitant sorts of propositions, used as premisses in a valid syllogism. This is especially true with regard to those matters of belief, concerning unseen realities and hidden realm that come to us through authentic lines of transmission. It is within this context, we again think, that al-Ghazālī regards the theologians as a special kind of *muqallid*, being differentiated from the rest by their mastery of the art of argument in defense of their belief. Nevertheless, this theological method is of two types: one is by means of demonstration, and the other, by those non-demonstrative syllogisms—especially the dialectical one—as well as other such formal sorts of reasoning as induction (*al-istiqrā'*) and analogy (*al-tamthīl*).[75] It is the former method of the theologians that is taken by al-Ghazālī to constitute certitude, looked at negatively.

In al-Ghazālī's view, *taqlīd*, regardless of its various modes and in as long as it leads one to a belief corresponding to truth, is acceptable. Belief indeed is the image formed in one's soul. It is the correspondence of this image to the actual object that counts rather than the means of arriving at such a correspondence. In this sense, therefore, the basic criterion is the question, "Does the reflected image in one's soul correspond to the reality or true object?" Only then can one question the degree of clarity of

---

[74] *Death*, pp. 143-144. See the section *Levels of Certitude* of this article; and our *Sources*, chapters three and four.

[75] For details on induction and analogy, see *MIFM*, pp. 121-122, 142-146 and 191-193; and *Qisṭās*, pp. 131-139.

the image; whether weak and low, or strong and high. In general, however, it is the former question that matters. In line with such an understanding, al-Ghazālī emphasizes psychologico-circumstantial factors that are inculcated especially through acculturation, and which play a vital role in shaping the belief of a child.[76] All these elements, when properly upgraded and with guidance from God, will result in one's gaining knowledge. In fact, knowledge is a sort of belief, albeit, a true, certain one.

Besides the necessary intellectual knowledge, the significant role of the sensible particulars of this physical world is very obvious in al-Ghazālī's framework. These particulars are very instrumental in providing the intellect with raw data from which—through the illumination of the Divine Intellect—it abstracts basic universal concepts which in turn act as units of propositions. We thus find in those matters of demonstration, three types of propositions—*al-maḥsūsāt, al-mujarrabāt* and *al-tawātur*—that have their roots in one's observation of the particular physical objects or events.[77] Sense-perception, as a basic constitutive unit of the other two kinds of propositions, is rendered reliable as long as one is conscious of various impediments possible in it, is aware of the role of the intellect in scrutinizing it, and does not reduce everything merely to sensible reality.

Previously, we have stated that logical certitude, which is the result of demonstrative syllogism, constitutes the lowest level of positive certainty. This becomes even clearer when al-Ghazālī himself includes intuitive propositions (*ḥadsiyyāt*) among the

---

[76] *Iljām*, pp. 137-140; *II*, p. 12; *FT*, pp. 96-101; and *FAF*, pp.13-16. Cf. Our account of *taqlīd* in al-Ghazālī's classification of knowledge, viewed from its sources and modes of arrival, in *Sources*, pp. 64-69; and R. M. Frank, "*Al-Ghazālī on Taqlīd: Scholars, Theologians, and Philosophers*," Zeitschrift fur Geschichte der Arabisch-Islamischen Wissenschaften Band 7 (1991 / 92).
[77] See our *Sources*, pp. 41-46.

certain matters of a valid syllogism. As discussed elsewhere, *ḥads* (the intuitive insight) is a kind of intuition, albeit the lowest one.[78] The acceptance of higher sorts of intuition is therefore rendered possible once the lowest one is acquiesced.

In this respect, although various sorts of intuition are levels of perception beyond ordinary reason, they by no means contradict reason.[79] Therefore, they possess rational contents which appear in the form of "matters" of sound reasoning or, to be more specific, valid syllogistic inference. This fact is better appreciated when viewed from the traditional understanding of logic. Logic, as rules of correct reasoning and valid inference, has two constitutive parts; one is formal, another, material. Reason in a sense pertains to the former, and thus, when considered in isolation from the second part, is devoid of content. Matters of reasoning, in fact, are very epistemological in nature, and involve those propositions formulated as a result of true, certain intuitions.

We can at least say that in al-Ghazālī's framework, knowledge, certitude and truth are synonymous with each other. They are a single item, viewed differently. Two elements play a fundamental role in shaping this item: the factor of "permanence", which refers more to the object of knowledge; and the principle of "clarity", which concerns more the perceiving subject. Knowledge or certainty relates more to the degree of clarity, while truth-reality is connected more with the extent of permanence. Permanence in a way already subsumes another basic factor, namely, "universality". In this way, the more universal a thing is, the more permanent is its "unitary" relation with all the particular units. However, God in His essence is above all such categories. He thus transcends all these conceptual ultimatums.

Finally, after being sure of all this, it becomes rather easier to

---

[78] Ibid., pp. 54-69 and 78-79.

[79] Ibid., pp. 49-51.

formulate those which are pseudo-knowledge, which—starting from the highest to the lowest—are belief approximating certainty, conjecture-probability, doubt, and unbelief. In each category, one finds various sorts of alleged propositions which, when arranged as arguments, produce a distinct type of syllogism. Thus, dialectical form, as an argument, occupies the status of "beliefs that approximate certainty". Rhetorical argument in turn is of the nature of "conjecture-probability". After these come poetical and sophistic inferences which might fall within the areas of doubt and unbelief. Nevertheless, in contrast to al-Ghazālī's demarcation in regard to other higher levels of negative and positive certitude, his elucidation of the premisses of the nature of doubt and total unbelief is not as lucid as his treatment of the rest mentioned above.

Major Terms in Al-Ghazālī's Child-Educational Theory: An Example of Islamization of Contemporary Knowledge

Asmaa' Mohd. Arshad**

The process of Islamization of contemporary knowledge, which Syed Muhammad Naquib al-Attas originally conceptualized and developed, involved two inter-related aspects, namely, the isolation of key concepts and elements that constitute the substance, the spirit, character and personality of alien culture and civilization,[1] and the formulation and integration that refers to the

** This article is a revised version of a chapter from my M.A. thesis: *Ethical Dimension of Child Education of Abū Ḥāmid al-Ghazālī*: An Early Example of Islamization of Contemporary Knowledge. I would like to express my gratitude to Prof Dr. Wan Mohd. Nor for his supervision of the thesis and revision ofthis article.

[1] See al-Attas, *Islam and Secularism*, reprint 1978 (Kuala Lumpur: ISTAC, 1993), 137 cited hereafter as *IS*; Wan Mohd. Nor Wan Daud, *The Educational Philosophy and Practice of Syed Muhammad Naquib al-Attas* (Kuala Lumpur: ISTAC, 1998), 313 cited hereafter as *EPS*. The isolation of

infusion of Islamic elements and key concepts in every branch of relevant contemporary knowledge. It includes the infusion of some fundamental key concepts of Islam such as the [Islamic] concept of religion (*dīn*), of man (*insān*), of knowledge (*'ilm* and *ma'rifah*), of justice (*'adl*), of right action (*'amal as adab*), etc.[2]

Wan Daud further explains that the process of Islamization of contemporary knowledge itself initially occurred with the very first revelation when God revealed the first five verses of *Sūrat al-'Alaq* to the Holy Prophet ﷺ.[3] This process, or the "epistemological revolution",[4] as al-Attas calls it, reached its culmination in the writings of al-Ghazālī (d. 1111), the reviver (*mujaddid*) of the fifth century, who systematically studied, reported and refuted the philosophers,[5] and integrated some of their ideas into the teachings of Islam, especially as understood

---

foreign elements refers mainly to the human science besides the natural and applied sciences particularly where they deal with the interpretation of facts and formulation of theories. It is used by al-Attas with reference to the:

i) reliance upon human reason alone to guide man through life.
ii) adherence to belief in the validity of the dualistic vision ofreality and truth.
iii) affirmation of the evanescent aspect of existence projecting a secular worldview.
iv) espousal of the doctrine of humanism.
v) emulation of the allegedly universal reality of drama and tragedy in the spiritual, or transcendental, or inner life of man, making drama and tragedy real and dominant elements in human nature and existence.

[2] See *IS*, 163-164. For deliberate and Systematic discussion on these concepts, see Wan Mohd. Nor Wan Daud, *EPS*, 35-67, 225-227.

[3] A brief historical account on the process of Islamization of knowledge is elucidated by Wan Daud in *EPS*, 316-330.

[4] Ibid., 371 citing "The Corruption of Knowledge," unpublished lecture in Istanbul, 1985. The term "epistemological revolution" was introduced by al-Attas in his lecture in Istanbul, 1985.

[5] Ibid., 323.

by the Sufis. This intellectual tradition was continued by his successors such as Fakhr al-Dīn al-Razī, 'Adūd al-Dīn 'Abd Al-Raḥman al-Ījī, Ibn Khaldūn, etc. It declined during the subsequent centuries due to many reasons, and worsened with the arrival of the modern secular Western worldview and concepts until it was later revived and conceptually articulated in this century by al-Attas who clearly understood and explained the challenge of secularism at the philosophical level. It might be of interest to note here that there are indeed methodological similarities between al-Ghazālī and al-Attas since the latter is very much influenced and inspired by the former. One of the most distinctive aspects commonly shared by the two scholars is their concern about the proper usage of key terms in their writings. Al-Ghazālī for instance, criticized the limitation of the usage of terms like *fiqh, dhikr, ḥikmah*, etc. In addition he did not uncritically use any philosophical terms[6] (which were mostly neo-Platonic, but to a certain extent Aristotelian)[7] in his works, which he considered incongruent with the Islamic worldview, though it is well-known that he was more conversant with the said philosophical doctrines and their technical terms than was any other Muslim thinker before him.[8] In her findings, Rava Lazarus-Yafeh said:

> Yet here is a most astonishing linguistic fact that in a large number of his books including his major works, there is

---

[6] To my mind it is more accurate to state that al-Ghazālī: did not use any 'metaphysical terms' like *al-fā'il, al-'aql al-awwal* as highlighted by Rava Lazarus-Yafeh herself, except for the purpose of refuting the philosophers. As far as the philosophical terms are concerned, he did use some of the terms in relation to ethics, such as *ḥikmah, shajā'ah, 'iffah, 'adālah*, etc, since these words conform to the Islamic worldview.

[7] Rava Lazarus-Yafeh, *Studies in Ghazzali* (Jerusalem: The Magnes Press & The Hebrew, University, 1975), p. 249, cited hereafter as *SIG*.

[8] See for instance, Mustafa Abū-Sway, *Al-Ghazzāliyy A Study in Islamic Epistemology* (Kuala Lumpur: Dewan Bahasa dan Pustaka, 1996), p. 88, cited hereafter as *GE*.

> nowhere any use of a single philosophical [metaphysical] term; even when al-Ghazālī deals with typical metaphysical subjects and not in the usual orthodox way.[9]

However, in ethics, al-Ghazālī does use Some terms that were used by Muslim philosophers, especially Miskawayh. He Islamized some of the fundamental concepts, as observed by some scholars. Gil'adi, for instance suggested that:

> ... changing key terms, adding references to the Islamic religious sources and making some modifications in content, Ghazālī conferred on the Greek philosophical ideas a new meaning, integrating them into an Islamic moral-educational system.[10]

Thus, it is the purpose of this article to examine some of the key ethical terms used by al-Ghazālī to reinterpret and reformulate the subject matter that is originally adapted from the philosophers but later transformed into his Sufi spirit and framework. In fact the transformation of key terms and concepts that determine and project the conceptual structure of Islamic worldview according to al-Attas,[11] signifies a very important process of Islamization. It involves firstly, the islamization of language that brings about the islamization of thought and reason. Language, thought and reason are closely interconnected and interdependent in projecting to man his worldview or vision of reality.[12] One of the most substantial aspects that distinguishes al-Ghazālī from Miskawayh is his extensive usage of Sufi concepts

---

[9] Ibid, citing *SIG*, 249. The findings of Lazarus-Yafeh's study are based on al- Ghazālī's works that are commonly accepted to be authentic.

[10] See Avner Giladi, *Children of Islam: Concepts of Childhood in Medieval Muslim Society* (Oxford: Macmillan, 1992), 4 cited hereafter as COL.

[11] See Al-Attas, *The Concept of Education in Islam: A Framework for an Islamic Philosophy of Education*, reprint 1980 (Kuala Lumpur: ISTAC, 1991), 10 cited hereafter as *CEII*.

[12] Ibid., pp. 2-11.

and terminology. Our analysis in this article is based on the explication of child rearing and education of the former in his third volume of his *magnum opus*, *Iḥyā' 'Ulūm al-Dīn*. There are remarkable similarities between this section and Miskawayh's chapter of *Ta'dīb al-Aḥdāth wa 'l-Sibyān* in his *Tahdhīb al-Akhlāq* which is mainly adopted from Bryson's *Oikonomikos.*[13] In comparison to Miskawayh's philosophical approach, al-Ghazālī opts for a Sufi interpretation of the subject. In this article we shall further analyze five major terms used by al-Ghazālī that project the inherent Sūfī conceptual structure pertaining to his educational method. The most important key terms in this field are *ta'dīb* (education), *riyāḍah* (training), *ta'līm* (instruction), *tarbiyah* (upbringing) and *tahdhīb* (refinement).[14]

1. *Ta'dīb* (Education)

In al-Ghazālī's framework, *adab*[15] is to bring out (*istikhrāj*) the inner faculty and latent character trait (*mā fi'l-quwwah wa 'l-khuluq*) into action (*ilā al-fl'l*) by actualizing the good natural

[13] See Abū Ḥāmid al-Ghazālī, *Iḥyā' 'Ulūm al-Dīn*, 4 vols. (Beirut: Dār Iḥyā' Turāth al-'Arabī, n.d), 3:72-74 cited hereafter as *Iḥyā'*; see M. Abul Quasem, "Ghazālī's Rejection of Philosophic Ethics," *Islamic Studies* 13, no. 2 (June 1974), 124 cited hereafter as *GR*, n. 29; see al-Ghazālī, *Kitāb Riyāḍat al-Nafs & Kitāb Kasr al-Shahwatayn,* trans. By T. J. Winter, *al-Ghazālī on Disciplining the Soul and Breaking the Two Desires: Books XXII and XXIII of the Revival of the Religious Sciences* (Cambridge: The Islamic Texts Society, 1995), Ixiv cited hereafter as *RN.*

[14] For an exposition of these terms in Islamic educational discourse, see Ahmad Bazli Shafie, *The Educational Philosophy of Muhammad Abduh* (M.A. thesis. International Institute of lslamic Thought and Civilization (ISTAC), 1998), pp. 22-34.

[15] In the philosophical terminology of Miskawayh, *adab* is identified as *Khuluq* see Ahmad bin Muhammad ibn Miskawayh, *Tahdhīb al-Akhlāq wa Taṭhīr al-A'rāq* (Beirut: Mashhūrāt Diir Maktabat al-Ḥayāt, 1977), p. 53 cited hereafter as *Tahdhīb.*

disposition (*al-sajiyyah* al-*sāliḥah*)[16] which is solely a Divine gift. This process encompasses two aspects of *ādāb*-the divinely gifted origin of the innate natural disposition (*sajiyyah*)[17] and the acquisition of human action (*kasb al-ādamī*) through righteous practice and self-discipline (*ḥusn al-mumārasah wa 'l-riyāḍah*). Apparently, the above conception implies human freedom of will (*ikhtiyār*) which forms the basis of al-Ghazālī's ethical system.[18] Al-Ghazālī, citing a ḥadīth of the Holy Prophet ﷺ, maintains that every child is born in equilibrium and sound natural disposition (*mu'tadilan ṣaḥīḥ al-.fiṭrah*).[19] This conception of *fiṭrah* is primarily based on the ḥadīth:

> Every child is born with the sound natural disposition (*al-fiṭrah*), it is only his parents who make of him a Jew, a Christian or a Zoroastrian.[20]

Al-fiṭrah[21] in this sense is the natural inclination in man to assent to the existence of God (*al-taṣdīq bi'l-rubūbiyyah*).[22] It is

---

[16] See Abū Ḥāmid al-Ghazālī, *Rauḍāt al-Ṭālibīn fi Majmū'āt al-Rasā'il al-Imām al-Ghazālī* (Beirut: Dār al-Fikr, 1998), p. 100, cited hereafter as *RT*.

[17] See *Tahdhīb*, p. 51.

[18] See Abdul Khaliq, "Ethics [al-Ghazālī]," *A History of Muslim Philosophy*, 2 vols., ed. M.M. Sharif, reprint of 1961, 2nd ed. (New Delhi: Low price publications, 1995), 1: 626, cited hereafter as Ethics. 1961, 2nd. ed. (New Delhi: Low Price).

[19] *Iḥyā'*, 3: p.60. the ḥadīth is not mentioned in Miskawayh's *Tahdhīb al-Akhlāq*.

[20] Ibid., 3: 74 citing al-Bukhārī, 'Kitāb al-Janā'iz', *al-Jāmi' al-Ṣaḥīḥ* no. 92. The parental religious accountability in child education is not emphasized by Miskawayh.

[21] Miskawayh uses the term *ṭab'* or *ṭabī'ah* pl. *ṭabā'ī* instead of *fiṭrah*. The above-mentioned Qur'anic verse and ḥadīth pertaining to the concept of *fiṭrah* is not mentioned in his *Tahdhīb al-Akhlāq*. According to al-Attas, *ṭabī'ah* is not exactly the same as nature which does not imply any creation. *ṭabī'ah* on the other hand, implies *Ṭābi'*, the Printer which refers to God.

[22] Abū Ḥāmid al-Ghazālī, *Kimiyā' al-Sa'ādah fi Majmū'āt Rasā'il al-Imām*

mentioned in the Qur'an:

> *So set thou thy face truly to the religion being upright, the nature in which Allah has made mankind."*[23]

However, the nature of man is created to be receptive to both good and evil.[24] In some instances, children are born gifted with perfect innate disposition (*kamāl fiṭrī*), possessing sound intellect and good character. They are inherently inclined to be generous, truthful and courageous in nature, particularly in the case of the prophets, saints and sages. While in some other cases, they are born with the opposite characteristics. Nonetheless, good character according to al-Ghazālī, can be acquired through habituation, association with those who possess noble traits, and education.[25] Thus, parents are the main social factor responsible for moulding a child's character to be either good or bad. They are also the first who exercise and implement the second aspect of adab which requires human action through the process of *ta'dīb* that involves the inculcation of knowledge through instruction (*al-ta'līm*) and habituation (*al-i'tiyād*).[26]

Hence adab is disciplining[27] the physical and spiritual self

---

al-Ghazālī (Beirut: Dar al-Fikr, 1998), p. 426, cited hereafter as *KS*.

[23] Surah al-Rum: 30 cited in *KS*, p. 426.

[24] *Iḥyā'*, 3:74. In this regard, Miskawayh holds the same position as al-Ghazālī. According to him, every character is subject to change. However the admonitions and the education (*al-mawā'iẓ wa 'l-ta'dīb*) produce different results for different people; some are responsive to discipline and acquire virtue rapidly; while others are also responsive but slowly accustom themselves to it. See *Tahdhīb*, 53; Miskawayh, *Tahdhīb al-Akhlāq wa Taṭhīr al-A'rāq*, trans. Constantine K. Zurayk, *The Refinement of Character* (Beirut: Centennial Publication, 1968), 31, cited hereafter as *RC*.

[25] *Iḥyā'* 3:5; *RN*, 31.

[26] See Abū Ḥāmid al-Ghazālī, *Mīzān al-'Amal*, ed. by Ahmad Shams al-Din (Beirut: Dar al-Kutub al-'Ilmiyyah, 1989), 70, cited hereafter as *MA*.

[27] My rendition of *adab* as 'disciplining' is inspired by al-Attas' conception

(*al-adab ta'dīb al-ẓāhir wa 'l-bāṭin*), encompassing the four realms of an individual life: words, deeds, belief and intention.[28] The physical self refers to the outward forms of bodily constitution whereas the spiritual self is the inner heart (*al-qalb*) which he uses interchangeably with the term rational soul (*al-nafs al-nāṭiqah*)[29] and Spirit (*al-rūḥ*).[30] Although the soul and the body are two distinct entities, they interactively affect each other and mutually determine their courses. According to al-Ghazālī, every bodily act produces an effect which forms a direct bearing on the quality of the soul. When the act is repeated and performed deliberately, its effect on the soul becomes established. As bodily action influences the soul, similarly the soul influences the physical performance. Consequently, when the quality of the soul is established, relevant bodily action necessarily proceeds from it. Nevertheless, the level of willingness in the execution of an act depends on the strength or weakness of the soul.[31] The established state or quality of the soul is called character (*al-khuluq*) which refers to the inward form (*al-ṣūrah al-bāṭinah*), whereas the physical creation (*al-khalq*) is referred to as the outward form (*al-ṣūrah al-ẓāhirah)* of

---

of *adab* and *ta'dib*. In one of his works, he states that "*Adab* is the discipline of body, mind and soul". A fuller treatment of this concept is articulated in his monograph: *The Concept of Education in Islam*. See *CEII*, 22-27.

[28] See *RT*, 99.

[29] See Abū Ḥāmid al-Ghazālī, *Al-Risālah al-Ladunniyyah fi Majmū'āt Rasā'il al-Imām al-Ghazālī* (Beirut: Dar al-Fikr, 1998), 225, cited hereafter as *RL*. Al-Ghazālī maintains that the Qur'anic terms *'al-nafs al-muṭma'innah'* of which the Sufis name *'al-qalb'* and the philosophers call *'al-nafs al-nāṭiqah'* refers to the same spiritual substance which lives, acts and comprehends. In this regard he does not refrain from using the philosophers' term: *al-nafs al-nāṭiqah* (the rational soul) due to its conformity with the Qur'an. See *RL*, 225-226.

[30] See *KS*, p. 420.

[31] See *EG*. pp. 47-48.

the human being.[32] In his interpretation, al-Ghazālī reiterates that character (*al-khuluq*) is a firmly established condition of the soul (*hay 'ah fī'l-nafs rāsikhah*), from which actions proceed easily without any need for deliberation or forethought (*fikr wa rawiyyah*).[33] If the condition of the soul is disposed towards the production of praise-worthy deeds acknowledged by the Intellect and the Religious Law (*'aqlan wa Shar'an*), it is named a 'good character trait' (*ḥusn al-khuluq*); and if blameworthy deeds proceed from it, the condition is called a 'bad character trait' (*sū' al-khuluq*).[34] Due to his interactive theory of the soul and body, al-Ghazālī believes in the susceptibility of the character (*al-khuluq*) to change through discipline.[35] He said:

Were the traits of character not susceptible to change there

---

[32] *Iḥyā'* 3:53; *RN*, 16; see M. Abul Quasem, *Ethics of Ghazālī* (New York: Caravan Books, 1978), 80 cited hereafter as *EG*.

[33] See *Iḥyā'*, 3:53. This definition is originally derived from Galen's ethical treatise through the medium of Miskawayh's *Tahdhīb al-Akhlāq*. Miskawayh defines *Akhlāq* (character) as a state of the soul which causes it to perform its actions without thought or deliberation. According to him, *adab* is similar to *khuluq*. The same definition is also cited by Ibn 'Adī, al-Rāghib al-Iṣfahānī, Fakhr al-Din al-Rāzī, Naṣīr al-Din al-Ṭūsī, Ibn 'Ajība and 'Abdullah al-Ḥaddād. For further analysis, see *RN*, 17. See Miskawayh's definition of *Akhlāq* in *Tahdhīb*, 51; *RC*, 29.

[34] *Iḥyā'* 3:53; *RN*, 17.

[35] Similarly, Miskawayh maintains the same position in the susceptibility of character to change through education and admonition (*bi'l-ta'dīb wa 'l-mawā'iẓ*) even though the result varies from one person to another. However, the discussion pertaining to this issue mainly refers to the ancient philosophers (*al-qudamā'*) particularly the Stoics, Galen and Aristotle. Miskawayh opts for Aristotle's position in his *Kitāb al-Akhlāq* and *Kitāb al-Maqūlāt*: He further demonstrated his view in the Aristotelian principles of syllogism: "Every character is subject to change. Nothing which is subject to change is natural (*bi 'l-ṭab'*). Therefore, no single character is natural." It differs from al-Ghazālī whose argument is based on the Qur'anic sources. See *Tahdhīb*, 51-53; *RC*, 29-31; *Iḥyā'*, 3:55-56.

would be no value in counsels, sermons and discipline (*al-ta'dībāt*), and the Prophet ﷺ would not have said, "Improve your characters".[36]

Hence *ta'dīb* in the ethical framework of al-Ghazālī is a process of disciplining the physical and spiritual aspects of man which involves the acquisition of knowledge and transformation of his personality in order to possess good character traits (*ḥusn al-khuluq*). This process entails spiritual struggle (*al-mujāhadah*) and discipline (*al-riyāḍah*),[37] leading towards purification of the soul (*tazkiyat al-nafs*) and refinement of the character (*tahdhīb al-akhlāq*). Indeed, *akhlāq* is the content (*mawḍū'*)[38] and the ultimate result of *ta'dib*, whereby the highest form of ethics (*akhlāq*) according to al-Ghazālī, is the adab in religion (*al-adab fī'l-dīn*) as confirmed in the Qur'an, manifested by the *Sunnah* of His Prophet ﷺ, the *Ṣaḥābah, Tābi'ūn* and the men of *adab*.[39] Indeed, the perfect outcome of this Divine educational curriculum is the Holy Prophet ﷺ himself as the exemplary model, as acknowledged in one of his ḥadīth: "My Lord has educated me (*addabanī*) and so made my education (*ta'dībī*) most excellent.[40] Al-Ghazālī further said:

---

[36] *Iḥyā'*, 3:55, *RN*, 25.

[37] *Iḥyā'*, 3:56.

[38] *EPS*, 136 citing Mahmud Qambar, *Dirāsah Turāthiyyah fī'l-Tarbiyah al-lslāmiyyah*, 2 vols. (Qatar: Dar al-Thaqāfah, 1985), 1:406, cited hereafter as *DT*.

[39] Al-Ghazālī, *Al-Adab fī'l-Dīn fi Majmū'āt Rasā'il al-Imām al-Ghazālī* (Beirut: Dar al-Fikr, 1998), 403, cited hereafter as *AFD*. Al-Attas uses the term *insān adabī* to indicate the meaning of *ahl al-adab* (man of *adab*) as mentioned by al-Ghazālī. See *EPS*, 133 citing *Risālah*, para. 15, p. 54.

[40] *RT*, 99; *EPS*, 135. Wan Daud highlights that S. M. N. al-Attas is the first to interpret and translate *'addabanī'* as 'educated me'. It is notably important to highlight that our rendition of *'ta'dīb'* as education is, in fact inspired by his definition of education (*ta'dīb*) in his interpretation of the word. See in *CEII* 26-27.

> Indeed the most perfect and highest conduct, the best and the most beautiful deeds are *adab* in religion through which the believer follows the deed of the Lord of the Universe and the conduct of Prophets and Messengers. God has educated us (*addabanā*) with what He has shown and explained in the Qur'an. He also has educated us (*addabanā*) through his Prophet Muhammad ﷺ, by the means of his *Sunnah* which is incumbent upon us, and blessing is upon us, and blessing is for him. Similarly, we have to follow the Companions (*al-ṣaḥābah*) and the Followers (*al-Tābi'īn*), as well as the people of adab (*ahl al-adab*) among the believers.[41]

The above quotation does, in fact, support Lapidus, Gabrieli and al-Attas' thesis suggesting that from the first century of *hijrah*, adab has acquired a broad meaning which includes the intellectual, social and ethical aspects of life.[42] In this classical era of Islam, *adab* was used to imply learning and knowledge acquired for the sake of right living. It was a concept of what a person should know, be, and do to perfect the art of living.[43] The term has an epistemological bearing upon the Qur'an and *Sunnah*[44] as the ultimate sources of *adab*. In fact Prophet

---

[41] *AFD*, 403. The Qur'anic and prophetic exemplary model of good character is rarely mentioned in *Tahdhīb al-Akhlāq*. Nevertheless, he acknowledges the role of Sharī'ah in the acquisition of virtues, and the attainment of wisdom and happiness. See *Tahdhīb*, 54; *RC*, 32.

[42] See *CEII*, 25-26, 35-36; *The Encyclopedia of Islam*. New edition (Leiden: E. J. Brill, 1986) s.v. "*ADAB*," 1: 175, cited hereafter as *EI*. Ira M. Lapidus, "Knowledge, Virtue and Action: The Classical Muslim Conception of *Adab* and the Nature of Fulfillment in Islam," in Barbara Daly Metcalf, ed. *Moral Conduct and Authority: The Place of Adab in South Asian Islam* (Berkeley: University of California Press, 1984), 38-39, cited hereafter as *KVA*.

[43] *KVA*, p. 39.

[44] *Sunnah* is apprehended in its larger context, including *Sunnah* of the Companions (*ṣaḥābah*) and the followers (*Tābi'īn*) who are the custodians

Muhammad ﷺ was the first beneficiary and recipient of the Qur'anic educational content (*al-ta'dibāt fi'l-Qur'ān*). In the history of Islam, he was the first being educated by the Lord Himself through His Divine Speech until his character and personality became equivalent to the Qur'an.[45] His perfect manifestation of the Qur'anic ethical model thus illuminates the whole creation of God which he acknowledged in one of the ḥadīths: "*I am raised up to accomplish noble character.*"[46]

Adab contains within its conceptual structure, according to al-Attas, the meaning of knowledge and action (*'ilm wa 'l-'amal*),[47] the activities of the body and soul (*al-jasad wa 'l-rūḥ*), of the physical and spiritual (*al-ẓāhir wa 'l-bāṭin*), as well as the vertical and horizontal relationship of mankind (with God and fellow human beings).[48] Nevertheless, this comprehensive meaning of adab has been gradually narrowed down into the specific sphere of 'Arabic belles-lettres'.[49]

2. *Riyāḍah* (Self-discipline)

Riyāḍah, from the linguistic point of view, is a substitution of the blameworthy state with the praiseworthy (*istibdāl al-ḥāl al-madhmūmah bi 'l-ḥāl al-maḥmūdah*).[50] Philosophers define

of the prophetic *Sunnah*.

[45] *Iḥyā'*, 2:358. In this regard al-Ghazālī used the term *ta'dīb* in his subtitle on the explication of the way Allah educated the Prophet Muhammad ﷺ (*bayān ta'dīb Allāh Ta'ālā ḥabībahu wa ṣafiyyahu Muḥammad* ﷺ *bi'l-Qur'ān*).

[46] Ibid, citing the Prophetic ḥadīth: '*bu'ithtu li utammim makārim al-akhlāq*.'

[47] *CEII*, p.26.

[48] Ibid., pp. 21-22; *EPS*, p. 167.

[49] *EL* 1: 176; *CEII*, p. 36.

[50] See Muhammad 'Ali al-Tahānawī, *Kashshāf Isṭilāḥāt al-Funūn*, 4 vols. (Beirut: Dar al-Kutub al-'Ilmiyyah, 1998), 2:226, cited hereafter as *Kashshāf*.

riyāḍah as abstinence from the accidental states of desire (*al-i'rāḍ 'an al-a'rāḍ al-shahwāniyyah*). *Riyāḍah* also includes the customary prayer and fasting (*mulāzamat al-ṣalāh wa 'l-sawm*) as well as constant vigilance from sin and censure (*'an mūjibāt al-ithm wa 'l-lawm*), restraint from the gate of sleeping (*wa sadd bāb al-nawm*) and avoidance from the acquaintance with people (*ṣuḥbat al-qawm*).[51] In al-Ghazālī's ethical framework, *riyāḍah* is defined as training of the soul for the good, and developing it from a trivial to an intense struggle through a gentle and gradual effort, until difficult states and practices become plain and simple.[52] *Riyāḍah* is one of the means for the acquisition of good character traits (*ḥusn al-khuluq*).[53] While it is possible to possess good character through Divine gift, al-Ghazālī suggests the common means of achieving it, i.e., through self-mortification (*mujāhadah*) and self-discipline (*riyāḍah*),[54] which he refers to as the painstaking effort (*ḥaml al-nafs*) in performing those actions that necessarily proceed from the good traits until they become habitual and pleasant. Indeed, it implies the meaning of

[51] Ibid.

[52] See *RT*, p. 149.

[53] In a like manner, Miskawayh uses the term *riyāḍah* in the sense of disciplining the beastly and irascible soul *(al-nafs al-bahīmiyyah wa 'l-nafs al-ghaḍabiyyah*). However, the term is rarely mentioned in his literature. He indicates that animals cannot be a subject of *riyāḍah*. It is mentioned in *Tahdhīb al-akhlāq*: "As it is impossible to discipline the wild beasts (*riyāḍat al-sibā' al-bahā'im al-waḥshiyyah*) which do not respond to education (*al-ta'dīb*), as such it is impossible to discipline the person who grows up in this way (*riyāḍat man nasha'a 'alā hādhihī al-ṭar'īqah*) ... See *Tahdhīb*, p. 75; *RC*, p. 57.

[54] Likewise, Miskawayh believes in the mutability of character. However, instead of using the terms *mujāhadah* and *riyāḍah*, he uses the terms *bi al-'ādah wa al-tadrīb* as the disciplinary method for character formation. See *Tahdhīb*, p. 51; *RC*, p. 29.

gradualness (*al-tadarruj*).[55] For instance, a man who wishes to acquire the quality of generosity must oblige himself to perform generous acts, continuously struggling with his soul in giving away some particular possession until his nature conforms to it. Thus, the action becomes one of his traits and part of his nature, at which time it will become easy and habitual.[56]

Al-Ghazālī further divides *riyāḍah* into two: the first refers to the inculcation of adab (*riyaḍāt al-adab*) meaning withdrawal from the innate nature of the soul (*al-khurūj 'an ṭab' al-nafs*); and the second is pursuing the right objective (*riyaḍāt al-ṭalab*), which refers to intentional well-being (*siḥḥat al-murād*).[57] Self-discipline thus, includes both physical devotion and spiritual endeavor since man is composed of both. The real purpose of *riyāḍah* (self-discipline) is to attain self-purification from spiritual impurities[58] by subjecting the faculty of anger and desire (*quwwat al-ghaḍab wa'l-shahwah*)[59] under the authority of reason and Revelation (*al-'aql wa 'l-Shar'*)[60] which ultimately leads to the refinement of character[61] reflected in outward actions and deeds. Following his predecessors,[62] al-Ghazālī maintains that good character depends

---

[55] See *Iḥyā'*, 3:89.

[56] Ibid., 3:58; see *RN*, p. 32; *EG*, p. 89.

[57] Dr George M. Abdul-Massih, rev. ed. *A Dictionary of Sufism Terminology: Arabic—Arabic* (Beirut: Librairie Du Liban Publishers, 1993), p. 93 citing al-Ghazālī, *al-Imlā' 'an Ishkālāt al-Iḥyā'*, p. 63.

[58] See *Itḥāf*, 14 vols. (Beirut: Dar al-Kutub al-'Ilmiyyah, 1989), 8:587-8.

[59] *MA*, 62.

[60] See *Iḥyā'*, 3:54. Similar to Miskawayh, al-Ghazālī draws up the analogy of the beast (*al-sab'*) or dog (*al-kalb*) to illustrate the irascible quality of the soul, and the pig (*al-khinzīr*) for its appetitive faculty. Besides the irascible (*al-sab'iyyah*) and the appetitive (*al-bahīmiyyah*), al-Ghazālī adds the term *al-shayṭāniyyah* for the evil and *al-rabbāniyyah* for its divine quality. See *Iḥyā'*, 3:10-11; *Tahdhīb*, p. 65-66.

[61] See *MA*, p. 63. *Tahdhīb*. pp. 67-68; *RC*, p. 49.

[62] In this regard, al-Ghazālī agrees with al-Iṣfahānī, Miskawayh and Ibn Sina

upon the harmonious relationship of the three faculties of the soul, namely: the faculty of reason (*quwwat al-tafakkur*), the faculty of anger (*al-ghaḍab*) and the faculty of desire (*al-shahwah*). The harmonious relationship among these three faculties would lead to justice (*al-'adālah*),[63] the power which maintains the equilibrium (*al-i'tidāl*)[64] of the three faculties. A sound faculty of reason or knowledge distinguishes between true and false statements, between right and wrong beliefs and between good and evil actions by which it generates the virtue of wisdom (*al-ḥikmah*) in the soul. The sound faculty of anger and desire yields and obeys the authority of reason and Revelation (*al-'aql wa 'l-Shar'*). Then, the virtues of courage (*shajā'ah*) and temperance (*'iffah*) spring and emanate from the soul.[65] The faculty of justice is thus, a power (*qudrah*) that controls the two faculties to be

---

whose ideas on some points run parallel to the Platonic theory of the tripartite nature of the soul and Aristotelian theory of the mean (*al-wasaṭ*). See *ET*, p. 196. See M. Abul Quasem, "Al-Ghazālī's Theory of Good Character," *Islamic Culture* 51, no. 4 (October 1977): p. 231, hereafter cited as *TGC*; M. E. Marmura, "Ghazālī's Attitude to the Secular Sciences and Logic" in *Essays on Islamic Philosophy and Science*, ed. by George F. Hourani, (New York: Albany, 1975), p. 102.

[63] *Tahdhib*, pp. 37-38; *MA*, p. 62-63.

[64] Aristotelian theory of the mean (*al-i'tidāl or al-wasaṭ*) is incorporated by Miskawayh and later modified by al-Ghazālī into a religious framework. See *Tahdhīb*, p.38, pp. 45-46; *RC*, p. 17 and 22; *Iḥyā'*, 3:58; *MA*, p. 12. Further analysis of this concept is found in *ET*, p. 113; *RN*, lix; see also D. M. Donaldson, *Studies in Muslim Ethics* (London: S. P. C. K, 1953), p. 126 and 128, cited hereafter as *SME*.

[65] Parallel with the philosophers, particularly Miskawayh, al-Ghazālī too affirms the four cardinal virtues (*ummahāt al-akhlāq*): wisdom, temperance (moderation), courage and justice. However, these philosophic virtues in al-Ghazālī's literature are incorporated into the ṣūfī framework. See *Tahdhīb*, pp. 38-44; *MA*, pp. 74-91; F. Rosenthal, *The Classical Heritage in Islam*, trans, from German by Emile & Jenny Marmorstein (London: Routledge and Kegan Paul, 1975), p. 96.

submissive to the pronouncements of reason and *Sharī'ah*.[66] In this case, it is notice worthy that al-Ghazālī opts for the authority of transmitted knowledge (i.e. Revelation and Tradition) that is supplemented by reason, a position which is upheld by the Sunni Muslims.[67]

Self-discipline (*riyāḍah*) is a pre-requisite for the harmonious balance and equilibrium of the character (*al-i'tidāl fi'l-akhlāq*) which is defined by al-Ghazālī as spiritual health (*siḥḥat al-nafs*).[68] Thus, the aim of self-discipline (*riyāḍah*) and mortification (*mujāhadah*)[69] is to bring the soul back to its primordial state of equilibrium (*i'tidāl*), for it constitutes the health of the soul, while deviation from it constitutes its sickness.[70] The mean or equilibrium is a state in which all the faculties of the soul remain in order so that good character may be achieved. The observance of the mean results in four fundamental traits of character (*ummahāt al-akhlāq*):[71] the virtues of wisdom, courage,

---

[66] *TGC*, p. 231. The purpose of Shari'ah, according to Miskawayh, is to prepare and accustom the young to perform good deeds, and prepare the soul for the attainment of wisdom and the acquisition of virtues, besides the actualization of human happiness through sound thinking and correct reasoning. See *Tahdhīb*, p. 54; *RC*, p. 32.

[67] G. F. Hourani, *Reason and Tradition in Islamic Ethics* (Cambridge: Cambridge University Press, 1985), 272, 275. The majority opinion of the Sunnites (*ahl al-Sunnah*) upholds the authority of Revelation that is supplemented by dependent reason to be the prime source of legal judgment. This view was elaborated thoroughly in the work of Imam al-Shafi'i who extended the range of coverage of the Qur'an and the *Sunnah* by supporting the method of analogy, which is a method of dependent reason in the service of Revelation. This point differentiates al-Ghazālī from Miskawayh who, following the philosophers' line, founded his arguments primarily on reason. See the above reference, 270-276.

[68] *Iḥyā'*, 3:60.

[69] Ibid., 3: 58.

[70] *TGC*, p. 237.

[71] There is a slight difference between al-Ghazālī's usage of this term, before

temperance and justice.[72] Wisdom (*al-ḥikmah*), according to al-Ghazālī, is a state of the soul which enables man to distinguish between right and wrong beliefs (*al-i'tiqādāt*); between true and false statements (*al-aqwāl*) and between good and evil actions (*al-af'āl*).[73] Courage (*al-shajā'ah*) is a state of the soul in which the faculty of anger is always obedient to wisdom (*al-ḥikmah*),[74] and temperance (*al-'iffah*) is a state of the soul in which the faculty of desire is disciplined under the commands of reason and *Sharī'ah.* As for justice (*al-'adl*), it is the state and power of the soul in which the faculties of anger and desire are controlled under the dictates of wisdom that is guided by reason and *Sharī'ah.*[75] As Abul Quasem pointed out, al-Ghazālī was more consistent than Miskawayh in his affirmation of *Sharī'ah* as the standard principle besides reason in determining the right mean (*al-wasaṭ al-ḥaqīqī*),[76] by which he maintains that Prophet Muhammad ﷺ is the perfect model who possesses the right equilibrium of character.[77] In relation to child education, *riyāḍah*[78] (self-discipline) is the most important term to denote the significance of character formation in the early phase of childhood particularly

---

and after he became a ṣūfī. In *Mīzān al-'Amal,* he extensively uses the philosophical term: '*ummahāt al-faḍā'il*'; whereas in *Iḥyā'* he uses '*ummahāt al-akhlāq*' since it is more consistent with the Qur'anic terminology. The term '*akhlāq*' is in fact the Qur'anic expression for 'character'. See *Iḥyā',* 3: 54; *MA,* 74; *Tahdhīb,* 40; *Sūrah al-Qalam*: 4; *Sūrah al-Shu'arā'*: 137.

[72] *TGC,* pp. 237-238.

[73] Ibid, p. 237; *RT,* p. 146; *Iḥyā'.*

[74] *RT,* p. 146.

[75] *Iḥyā',* 3: 54; *TGC,* 237; *RN,* 20-21.

[76] See *TGC,* 234-235. In many cases, Miskawayh frequently mentions reason alone though he does mention *Sharī'ah* in some places. See *Tahdhīb,* 54.

[77] *Iḥyā',* 3: 55.

[78] The usage of *riyāḍah* further reveals al-Ghazālī's awareness of the ṣūfī tradition, in comparison with Miskawayh's philosophical approach pertaining to child education.

during the age of discernment (*tamyīz*),[79] before they can discern good from evil. Character formation is, in fact, of the utmost importance during this period due to the immaturity of their reasoning faculty,[80] at a time when they are highly receptive to either positive or negative influences.

3. *Ta'līm* (Instruction)

The word *Ta'līm* is derived from its root *'allama* which means to make someone *'alim* and *'alīm* (the infinite form) or to make him possess knowledge (*al-'ilm*) so that it becomes firmly rooted in his mind.[81] It is the infinite noun signifying the meaning he taught him knowledge or sciences (*'allamahū al-'ilm or a'lamahū*).[82] Al-Rāghib al-Ifahānī proposes that *Ta'līm* is particularly applied to that which is repeated to such an extent that it produces an impression or effect (*athar*) upon the soul of the learner (*nafs al-muta'allim*). It is also said that *al-ta'līm* refers to exciting the attention of the soul to the conception of meanings (*tanbīh al-nafs li taṣawwur al-ma'ānī*).[83] According to al-Ghazālī, *al-ta'līm* is the means for the acquisition of knowledge,[84] through which men are elevated from the level of beasts (*ḥadd al-bahīmiyyah*) to that of

---

[79] See *Tahdhīb*, pp. 68-69; *Iḥyā'*, 3:72.

[80] Al-Ghazālī maintains that the faculty of discernment will attain its maturity (*kamāl al-'aql*) during puberty (*bulūgh*). See *Iḥyā'*, 3:72.

[81] See *AEL*, 5:2139.

[82] Ibid.

[83] Ibid.; Al-Zabīdī, *Tāj al-'Arūs*, 10 vols. (Beirut: Dar al-Sādir, n.d), 8: 405-6.

[84] *RL*, 230. Miskawayh believes in the twofold perfection (*kamāl*) of the human being: one is the cognitive (*al-'ālimah*) and the other is the practical (*al-'āmilah*). The first is the one through which he desires knowledge and sciences; and the second is the one that leads towards the organization and arrangement of things into their proper order. Neither one can be completed without the other, for knowledge is the beginning (*mabda'*) and action is the end (*tamām*). See *Tahdhīb*, 57-58; *RC*, 36-37.

human beings (*ḥadd al-insāniyyah*).[85] He further divides the means of acquiring human knowledge (*al-'ilm al-insānī*) into two: through human teaching (*al-ta'līm al-insānī*) and Divine teaching (*al-ta'līm al-rabbānī*).[86] The first, is a familiar method and a path which is easily perceived; as for Divine teaching, it is of two aspects: from without which is attained through learning (*al-taḥṣīl bi 'l-ta'allum*); and from within which refers to the preoccupation with reflection (*al-ishtighāl bi 'l-tafakkur*).[87]

Knowledge is potentially ingrained in the souls at the beginning of their creation, like the seed in the earth and the gem in the depths of the sea, or in the heart of a mine.[88] Similar to Iṣfahānī's argument, al-Ghazālī quotes a number of Qur'anic verses in support of this point. The most important argument is

---

[85] See *Iḥyā'*, 1:11; *BOK*, 23. There are technological and ontological similarities between al-Ghazālī and Miskawayh pertaining to this point. According to Miskawayh, man is distinguished from all other existents (*sā'ir al-mawjūdāt*) by his discerning and reflective faculty (*quwwatihī al-mumayyizah al-marwiyyah*) that is not shared by any other creature. Through this reflective faculty, man is able to transcend the purely human level to acquire angelic qualities. Thus, he whose discernment is truer, whose reflection is more sound, and whose choice is better has achieved greater perfection in his humanity ... But when his reflection is imperfect and his actions fall short of the purpose for which he was created, he deserves to be degraded from the human rank (*martabat al-insāniyyah*) to the beastly (*ilā martabat al-bahīmiyyah*). See *Tahdhīb*, 35-36; *RC*, 12-13.

[86] *RL*, 230. Al-Ghazālī's classification of the means of acquiring knowledge is almost the same as al-Farābī's distinction between human and Divine teaching in the pursuit of knowledge. For further analysis on al-Farābī's theory of instruction see Fuad Said Haddad, "An Early Arab Theory of Instruction," *International Journal of Middle Eastern Studies* 5, (1974): pp. 240-259.

[87] *RL*, 230. See al-Ghazālī, *al-Risālatu 'l-Ladunniyyah*, trans, by Margaret Smith in *Journal of the Royal Asiatic Society*, part 2 (April 1938): pp. 360-361, cited hereafter as *RL*(t).

[88] See *RL*(t), pp. 360-361.

substantially based on verse 172 of *sūrat al-a'rāf* referring to the Covenant testified by the sons of Adam ﷺ:

> When thy Lord drew forth from the children of Adam—from their loins—their descendants, and made them testify concerning themselves, (saying): "Am I not your Lord?" They said: "Yea! We do testify!" (*alastu bi rabbikum qālū balā shahidnā*).[89]

Hence, learning (*al-ta'allum*) is the quest to bring forth (*ṭalab khurūj*) the thing from potentiality to actuality (*min al-quwwah ilā al-fi'l*) (in oneself); while teaching or instruction (*al-ta'līm*) is the action of bringing forth the thing (*ikrājuhū*) from potentiality to actuality (in someone else).[90] In his analogy, al-Ghazālī illustrates the learned (*al-'ālim*) as a sower, and the learner (*al-muta'allim*) as the earth in deriving its profit; and knowledge, with its potentiality is like the seed, and its actuality is like the plant. Then when the soul of a learner is perfected, it is like a tree which bears fruit, or like the pearl brought forth from the depths of the sea.[91] Hence, the process of *ta'līm* (instruction) consists of the three main components: the learned (*al-'ālim*), the learner (*muta'allim*) and knowledge (*'ilm*). Knowledge as the gist of this process is defined by al-Ghazālī as knowing the thing as it is (*ma'rifat al-shay' 'alā ma huwa bihī*).[92] It is the presentation to the learner by the rational and tranquil soul (*taṣawwur al-nafs al-nāṭiqah al-muṭma'innah*) of the realities of things and their forms (*ḥaqā'iq al-ashyā' wa ṣuwarihā*), divested of the matter in themselves and of their modes, quantities, substances and essences, if they are simple (*mufradah*).[93] Thus the process of

---

[89] Surat al-A'rāf:172 quoted and further interpreted in al-Ghazālī's *Mīzān al-'Amal*. See *MA*, 124-125; IS, 56.

[90] *RL*(t), pp. 360-361.

[91] Ibid.

[92] *Iḥyā·*, 1:29.

[93] See *RL*, 224; *RL*(t), 191.

ta'līm necessarily involves the cultivation of knowledge[94] (as its content) in the rational soul as its recipient, since the first manifestation of its light is in the brain (*al-dimāgh*)[95] or intellect (*al-'aql*) that is the source, foundation and fountain pad of knowledge.[96] Knowledge springs from the intellect as the fruit springs from the tree, the light from the sun and the vision from the eyes.[97] Hence, *ta'līm*, as emphasized by al-Attas, is distinct from *ta'dīb* since the former generally refers to the instructional

---

[94] Al-Ghazālī differs from Miskawayh with regard to which type of knowledge needs to be first acquired. Al-Ghazālī emphasizes the obligatory knowledge (*farḍ 'ayn*) that is binding upon every Muslim i.e., the five pillars of Islam beginning with the confession of faith (*al-shahādah*) besides the prior importance of instrumental knowledge like language, etc.; while Miskawayh emphasizes the study of logic that is the tool (*al-ālat*) of correct understanding and instinctive reasoning (*al-fahm wa 'l-'aql gharīzī*) to be the prerequisite for the Divine knowledge. See *Iḥyā'*, 1:14; *BOK*, 30-31; *Tahdhīb*, 19; *RC*, 62.

[95] *RL*, 226. *RL*(t), 199. Miskawayh differs from the ṣūfis on the question of how the faculties of the soul work. He maintains that the rational faculty (*al-quwwah al-nāṭiqah*) which deals with reflection, discernment and thought, operates through the brain (*al-dimāgh*). The irascible faculty (*al-quwwah al-ghaḍabiyyah*) through which the soul exercises anger, vigor, etc. operates through the heart (*al-qalb*); while the faculty of desire (*al-quwwah al-shahwiyyah*) that deals with passion and desire works through the liver (*al-kabid*). On the contrary, in the ṣūfis, inducing al-Ghazālī's terminology, 'intellect' (*al-'aql*) is used interchangeably with 'heart' (*al-qalb*). Heart is the subtle divinely spiritual substance (*laṭīfah rabbāniyyah rūḥāniyyah*) perceived as the king that controls the passionate and subordinate faculties of the soul. See *Tahdhīb*, 38; *RC*, 15; *Iḥyā'*, 3:3; see also Mohammed Nasir Omar, "Miskawayh's Theory of Self-Purification and the Relationship Between Philosophy and Sufism," *Journal of Islamic Studies* 5, no.1 (January 1994): pp. 48-49. For a better exposition of the ṣūfi meanings of *'aql, qalb, rūḥ and nafs* in modern discussion, see al-Attas, *The Nature of Man and The Psychology of Human Soul* (Kuala Lumpur: ISTAC, 1990), 2, 5, 40.

[96] *Iḥyā'*, 1:83.

[97] Ibid.

and cognitive aspects of education, whereas the latter includes both aspects as well as the physical, emotional and spiritual.[98]

4. *Tarbiyah* (Good Breeding)

The term *tarbiyah*, derived from its roots *rabba* and *rabā*, literally means to feed, to nourish, to nurture, to bear, to foster, to cause increase in, to rear, to bring forth mature product, to domesticate.[99] This activity is usually exercised by the possessor of the objects. *Tarbiyah* bears the meaning of 'bringing of a thing to a state of completion by degrees'[100] which is applicable even to stones as pearls.[101] The semantic field of *tarbiyah* is not restricted to man alone, but is extended to other species: animals, plants and minerals.[102] The primary signification of *al-rabb* is *al-tarbiyah* which basically implies the meaning of possession, ownership and authority[103] by which the true possession belongs to God (*al-Rabb*) alone who is the Creator, Nourisher, Sustainer, Provider, Cherisher and Possessor of all creation.[104] Ḥassān ibn Thābit in one of his poems said: "… than a white clear pearl, of those which the sea has brought to maturity", meaning a pearl which the shell has reared, or brought to maturity, at the bottom of the water.[105] The most common application of the term tarbiyah is for child-

[98] *EPS*, p. 140.

[99] *CEII* 29 citing lbn Manzur, *Lisān al-'Arab*, 14: 307, col. l; E. W. Lane, *An Arabic-English Lexicon*, 8 vols. (Beirut: Librairie du Liban, 1980), 3: 1002, cited hereafter as *AEL*.

[100] *CEII* 29; *AEL*, 1002.

[101] *AEL*, 1002.

[102] *CEII*, 29-30. The term *tarbiyah* is not only applied to children but extends to pearls, prosperity or grace (*ni'mah*), plants, herbage, horses, etc. See the examples given in *AEL*, 3:1003.

[103] *AEL*, 3:1002.

[104] *CEII*, pp. 29-30.

[105] *AEL*, 3:1002.

rearing and upbringing: *rabbāhu* taking good care of him, acting as a guardian until he attains puberty, or to the utmost term of youth (either his own child or other's).[106] In a like manner, it is also used in relation to the offspring of an animal other than man.[107] Hence stock breeding, chicken farming and plant cultivation are forms of tarbiyah respectively.[108] Thus, it is interpreted by al-Attas that tarbiyah simply means cherishing, without necessarily including the inculcation of knowledge in the process.[109]

Similarly *tarbiyah* in al-Ghazālī's literature, is a general term used to indicate progress towards a state of perfection or completion[110] by degrees (*'alā al-tadrīj*).[111] In a like manner, the application of the term *'tarbiyah'* extends to species other than human. For instance, he says:

> ... for a seed is not an apple tree or a date-palm: it has merely been created in such a way as to permit it to become one when it is properly nurtured (*idhā anḍaf al-tarbiyah ilaihā*), and even when nurtured (*wa lā bi'l-tarbiyah*) a date-stone can never become an apple tree.[112]

His conception of *tarbiyah* is further illustrated by a comparison of a *shaykh* with a farmer in his chores. As a farmer weeds out the invasive plants to ensure the full growth of his plantation, the *shaykh* uproots the bad character of his disciple and transforms him into a virtuous person. This process will be accomplished through discipline and guidance to the path of

---

[106] Ibid.; lbn Manzur, *Lisān al-'Arab*, 15 vols. (Beirut: Dar al-Sādir, 1994), 1:401.

[107] *AEL*, 3:1002.

[108] *CEII*, p. 29.

[109] Ibid., p. 32.

[110] See *Iḥyā'*, 3: 61; *MA*, p. 70.

[111] See *Itḥāf*, 7: 343.

[112] *RN*, 25; *Iḥyā'*, 3:56.

Allah.[113] Hence, with reference to the soul, al-Ghazālī uses the term *tarbiyah* to convey the meaning of *tazkiyah* (purification) as a part of the overall educational development of a human being.[114] He explains:

> ... just as the body is not initially created complete (*kāmil*), but rather moves towards completion and strength through its growth (provided by nourishment) and upbringing (*tarbiyah*), so too the soul is created deficient, with its completion and perfection (*qābilah li 'l-kamāl*) being present in a latent form, and will only become perfected through training (*tarbiyah*)[115] or purification (*tazkiyah*)[116], refinement of character (*tahdhīb al-akhlāq*) and

[113] See al-Ghazālī, *Ayyuhā al-Walad*, ed. Riyāḍ Muṣṭafā al-'Abdullah (Beirut: Dar al-ḥikmah, 1986), pp. 74-75 cited hereafter as *AW*.

[114] In relation to the usage of the term *'tarbiyah'*, al-Attas argues that all the inherent concepts couched in the term *'tarbiyah'* pertain to physical and material growth and maturity only. In most cases, al-Ghazālī's usage of this term are generally consistent with al-Attas' except in one or two instances. In the above example, al-Ghazālī did apply the term to the spiritual growth of a man. Nonetheless, it is important to note that the term is used in quite a loose and rare manner in his *Iḥyā' 'Ulūm al-Dīn* and *Ayyuhā al-Walad* since the two books are meant for everyone including beginners on the ṣufi path. Al-Ghazālī even admits to his reluctance in revealing the illuminative knowledge (*'ilm al-mukāshafah*) in *Iḥyā' 'Ulūm al-Dīn*. In this sense, *Mīzān al-'Amal* is more philosophical, though it was written earlier before he became a ṣūfi. See *Iḥyā'*., 1:3-4; *BOK*, 6; see also George F. Hourani, "The Chronology of Ghazālī's Writings," *Journal of the American Oriental Society* 79, part 2 (1959): pp. 225-233, cited hereafter as *CGW*, and, al-Attas semantic analysis of the term *'tarbiyah'* in his *CEII* 28-33.

[115] *Iḥyā'*, p. 61. The term *'tarbiyah'* in this context means *'tazkiyah'* (purification). The former is the one that is used in *Iḥyā'* while the later (*tazkiyah*) is the one that is used in the same phrase written in his earlier work *Mīzān al-'Amal.*

[116] *MA*, p. 70.

nourishment with knowledge (*al-taghdhiyah bi 'l-'ilm*).[117]

Thus *tarbiyah* in the literature of al-Ghazālī is associated with the nourishment of body and soul; and in its particular relation to the soul, *tarbiyah* is used interchangeably with *tazkiyah*[118] (purification), indicating a certain degree of flexibility in that context. Nevertheless, this term is hardly used in his more specialized writings like *Mīzān al-'Amal*, *Al-Risālah al-Qudsiyyah*, *Kimiyā' al-Sa'ādah*, etc.[119] In fact, the above examples of the usage of tarbiyah are only mentioned in *Iḥyā' 'Ulūm al-Din* and *Ayyuhā al-Walad* which are meant for everyone including the masses (*al-'awām*) and beginners on the spiritual path (*murīd*).[120]

5. *Tahdhīb* (Refinement)

Another key term that al-Ghazālī frequently uses in his ethical theory is *'tahdhīb'* (refinement). The term *tahdhīb* literally means refining, cleansing, purifying, clearing away of any dirt and filth.[121] The term has the original meaning of the clearing and trimming of trees, by cutting off the extremities of the branches in order that they may increase in growth and beauty. It is then generally accepted and used to signify the cleansing or purifying; and putting a thing into its right and proper state; trimming or adjusting it; and clearing it from any filthy thing.[122] Thus, in relation to Islamic ethical terminology, *tahdhīb al-akhlāq* precisely means the refinement of character, inclusive of cleansing and purifying it. In reference to al-Ghazālī's ṣūfistic definition,

---

[117] Ibid.; *Iḥyā'*, *3*: 61; *RN*, p. 39.

[118] See *AM*, 70; *Iḥyā'*, 3:61.

[119] Similarly, it is rarely mentioned in Miskawayh's: *Tahdhīb al-akhlāq*. He primarily uses the term *'ta'dīb'* and *'tahdhīb'* in relation to the ethical aspect of child education. See *Tahdhīb*, pp. 68-70; *RC*, pp. 50-51.

[120] See *AW* (Beirut: Mu'assasah al-Risālah, 1987), pp. 3-4.

[121] *AEL*, 1: 2887.

[122] Ibid.

tahdhīb refers to self-examination (*imtiḥāin al-nafs*) and to choosing appropriate options for the progress of the states[123] (*ikhtiyār aḥwālihā*) of the soul according to its stations (*maqāmāt*). For instance, the sign of which a person is at the station of patience (*ṣabr*) is when his good deeds are performed easily without any hesitation,[124] or when a generous man constantly takes pleasure in giving his money with no reluctance.[125] Thus, in the ethics of al-Ghazālī, a person who insincerely gives away his money is not a generous person.

The concept of the refinement of character (*tahdhīb al-akhlāq*) reveals the meaning of proper governance over the faculties of anger (*al-ghaḍab*) and desire (*al-shahwah*).[126] It is in fact, the result of self-mortification (*mujāhadah*) and self-discipline (*riyaḍāt al-nafs*),[127] which ultimately lead towards the equilibrium of the rational faculty and the perfection of wisdom

---

[123] State (*ḥāl*—pl. *aḥwāl*) in the ṣūfis' terminology is the conditions that come to the heart gratuitously, without any effort or inducement to which the *'abd* is transferred by purifying his *nafs*; conditions that overshadow one's being spontaneously-in the form of sorrow, fear, expansiveness, contraction, desire or pleasure. If it endures and becomes permanent, it is called Stage (*Maqām*). See Al-Qāshānī, *Iṣṭilāḥāt al-Ṣūfiyyah*, ed. Muḥammad Kamāl Ibrahīm Ja'far (Cairo: Markaz Taḥqīq al-Turāth, 1981), 57; Al-Qāshānī, *Iṣṭilāḥāt al-Ṣūfiyyah*, trans, by Nabil Safwat, rev. & ed. by David Pendlebury (London: The Octagon Press Ltd., n.d. 1991), p. 114.

[124] *RT*, p. 149.

[125] *RN*, p. 32.

[126] See *Itḥāf*, 7:334. In relation to its proper governance, Miskawayh incorporates the Platonic analogy of a man who mounted a vigorous beast and lead a dog or a hunting panther. Life would be harmonious if the man manages to tame his beast and lead a dog (*dābbatahu wa kalbahū*), but should the beast have the upper hand, the three would be in bad conditions. See *Tahdhīb*, 66-67; *RC*, A6-Al; *SME*, 129.

[127] *Itḥāf*, 7:337. Miskawayh maintains that character would undergo changes under the influence of education (*al-ta'dīb*), age (*al-sunan*) and experience (*al-tajārib*). See *Tahdhīb*, 70; *RC*, 52.

(*i'tidāl quwwat al-'aql wa kamāl al-ḥikmah*); as well as the equilibrium of the faculty of anger and desire (*i'tidāl quwwat al-ghaḍab wa 'l-shahwah*) through their submission under the authority of reason and *Sharī'ah* (*wa kaunuhā li'l-'aql muṭī'atan wa 'l-Shar'*).[128] The sound faculty of justice is able to control the faculties of anger and desire according to the pronouncement of reason and *Sharī'ah.*[129] It reduces the greed of desire by arousing anger against it, and lessens the rage of anger by arousing a strong desire against it in order for both desire and anger to become submissive to reason and *Sharī'ah.*[130] This harmonious condition will ultimately lead towards a spiritual transformation from the base attributes to the virtuous. While the heart is purely refined from the stains of illness,[131] the character (*al-akhlāq*) will be purified from all its impurities. Simultaneously, the gate that conceals him from the Truth will be opened and unveiled for a servant to receive gnosis (*ma'rifah*) and the secrets of religious commandments by which he acknowledges his Lord.[132] Hence the purpose of *tahdhīb* (refinement)[133] is to purify oneself from the stains of illness that veil him from acknowledging the Truth from his Lord. According to al-Ghazālī, if a child is purely brought up through the process of refinement (*tahdhīb*), he will genuinely understand the reason and wisdom underlying this disciplinary

---

[128] *Iḥyā'*, 3:58; *RT*, 146.

[129] Ibid., 3:53.

[130] *TGC*, p. 231.

[131] Al-Muṭaffifin: 14. See the Qur'anic translation of A. Yusuf Ali where he renders *rāna* as stain of the illness that stands in the way of his perceiving Truths which are obvious to others. It becomes the obstacle that turns him to mock at Truth and embrace Falsehood.

[132] *Itḥāf*, 7:587-588.

[133] According to Miskawayh, the purpose of *tahdhīb* is to accomplish obedience to Allah in which lies salvation and everlasting bliss. See *Tahdhīb*, 67; *RC*, 48.

process (*riyāḍah*) when he approaches puberty[134] which represents his mature age of reasoning (*kamāl al-'aql*).[135] At this stage, he will understand at the rational level, the concept of life and death, as well as the accountability underlying every act in the hereafter. The worldly life is merely a transitional period through which man should gather up provisions for his ultimate destiny in the hereafter.[136] Hence, it is my conviction that the preparation for *taklīf* (accountability) before the age of puberty is the most substantial foundation for child education in Islam.

Based on the above analysis, the term *ta'dīb*, as al-Attas has been arguing, is the most inclusive and accurate term to convey the meaning of education in Islam. In agreement with al-Ghazālī, al-Attas reiterates that the term *ta'dīb* includes within its conceptual structure the elements of knowledge (*'ilm*), instruction (*ta'līm*) and good breeding (*tarbiyah*).[137] It conclusively reveals the person-centered[138] aim of Islamic education, that is the development of a well-balanced personality (*al-i'tidāl fi'l-akhlāq*),[139] through the actualization of inner

---

[134] *Iḥyā'*, 3:74.

[135] Ibid., 3:72.

[136] Ibid., 3:74.

[137] *CEH*, 34. In a like manner, al-Ghazālī and Miskawayh use the term *'ta'dīb'* instead of *'tarbiyah'* to denote the meaning of education in its comprehensive manner. Nonetheless, al-Ghazālī emphasizes a full expression of the term *'riyāḍah'* in its particular relation to child education.

[138] Wan Daud illustrates two main positions with regard to the aim and purpose of education. There are basically two positions concerning this matter; the first is the utilitarian and pragmatic view which is more dominant in this modern world. It refers to the society-centered position whereby education is perceived as a vehicle to produce good citizens. Secondly is the person-centered position that stresses individual development espoused by most of the dominant religions in the world. See *EPS*, 121-132.

[139] In this regard, Miskawayh uses the term *al-wasaṭ min al-faḍīlah* or

potential faculties and quality of the soul (*al-quwwāt wa 'l-khuluq*).[140] It is the actualization of the inherent natural disposition (*al-fiṭrah*)[141] of man from its potentiality (to recognize the essence of things and to recognize God)[142] into actuality, that is to acknowledge God through religious fulfillment. It is accomplished through the educational process (*ta'dīb*) which includes the transmission of knowledge (*ta'līm*), good breeding (*tarbiyah*) and self-discipline (*riyāḍah*) which results in the refinement of character (*tahdhīb al-akhlāq*). Good character in this sense is the equilibrium (*i'tidāl*) of the three faculties of the soul. Wisdom is the highest ethical virtue when the faculties of desire and anger are governed by the faculty of reason and by Revelation.[143] Hence, al-Ghazālī strongly emphasizes the formation of this good character since it is one of the essential pre-requisites of happiness (*al-sa'ādah*)[144] in this world and in the hereafter.

---

wasaṭiyyat al- faḍā'il (moderation of virtues). See *Tahdhīb*, 45-46.

[140] See *RT*, p. 100.

[141] Miskawayh in this sense, opts for the term al-*tab'* or *al-ṭabī'ah* (nature). See *Tahdhīb*, pp. 51-53.

[142] See. *KVA*, p. 46.

[143] *TGC*, pp. 237-238.

[144] The primary means of happiness are the virtues of the soul that lie in the faith (*īmān*) or knowledge, and good character (*ḥusn al-khuluq*). The virtues of the soul (*al-faḍā'il al-nafsiyyah*) can only be acquired with the help of bodily virtues (*al-faḍā'il al-jismiyyah*), external virtues (*al-faḍā'il al-khārijiyyah*) and the virtues of divine grace (*al-faḍā'il al-tawfīqiyyah*). For further explanation on al-Ghazālī's conception of happiness, see *EG*, pp. 58-63.

Additional Considerations

The above conceptual and terminological transformation reflect some of al-Ghazālī's principles and methods of Islamization. He argues in *al-Munqidh min al-Ḍalāl* concerning knowledge from external sources:

> … assuming that these are found only in the philosopher's writings, if they are reasonable in themselves and supported by proofs; and do not contradict the Qur'an and *Sunnah*, then why should it be shunned and rejected? If we were to open this door and adopt the attitude of rejecting every truth that has been apprehended by a forger (*mubṭil*), we would have to abstain from a great deal of truth (*al-ḥaq*).[145]

In this regard, al-Ghazālī's approach to Islamization[146] is primarily epistemological. He holds that the subject of ethics promulgated by the philosophers has been an amalgam of truth and falsehood[147], where truth originates from prophetic and Sufi teachings, and falsehood comes from their own disquisitions.[148] In this respect, he quoted the sayings of Sayyidinā 'Ali:

> "Do not know the truth by the men (who speak it), but know the truth (by itself), and then you will know its adherents"[149] (*la ta'rif al-ḥaqq bi 'l-rijāl, bal a'rif al-ḥaqq ta*

---

[145] See *al-Munqidh min al-Ḍalāl fī Majmū'āt al-Rasā'il al-Imām al-Ghazālī* (Beirut: Dār al-Fikr, 1998), p. 547, cited hereafter as *MDI.*

[146] In this regard, our analysis is based on his position towards philosophical sciences particularly ethics, as documented in his own autobiography: *al-Munqidh min al-Ḍalāl.*

[147] *MDI*, pp. 546-547.

[148] Ibid.; see Montgomery Watt, *The Faith and Practice of al-Ghazālī,* reprint of 1953, 3rd ed. (Oxford: Oneworld Publications, 1998), 39 cited hereafter as *FPG.*

[149] See *FPG*, pp. 40-41.

'rif ahlahū).[150]

Hence, the truth should be extricated from the statements or the positions of the people of error (*intizā' al-ḥaqq min aqāwīl ahl al-ḍalāl*)[151], since truth is sometimes mixed with falsehood, similar to gold which is found mixed with gravel and dross.[152] This extrication, however, can only be done by the learned (*al-'āqil*), not the ignorant;[153] for knowing the truth itself is a prerequisite for this process.[154] Al-Ghazālī further illustrates his position with reference to the analogy of a money-changer who suffers no harm if he puts his hand into the counterfeiter's purse. By virtue of his professional acumen, he will extract the authentic coins from among the spurious and counterfeit ones. Similarly, the peasant who does not possess such skills must be restrained from dealing in such an activity.[155] Likewise a clumsy and stupid person must be kept away from the seashore, but not the proficient swimmer and a child must be prevented from handling a snake, but not a

---

[150] *MDI*, 546.

[151] Ibid. Al-Attas' conception of lslamization of present-day knowledge: "the deliverance of knowledge from its interpretation based on secular ideology; and from the meaning and expression of secular ideology," is parallel to al-Ghazālī's principle of "extricating the truth from the false." It indicates a methodological similarity between al-Ghazālī's approach in his revivification of the Islamic sciences and al-Attas' Islamization of present-day knowledge as a process of isolating the Western elements and key concepts and infusing it with the Islamic elements and key concepts, which imbue knowledge with the quality of its natural function and purpose, and thus make it true knowledge. See *CEII*, 24; IS, 162-163. For further details, see *EPS*. 291-369.

[152] See *FPG*, pp. 41-42.

[153] Ibid.

[154] See *MDI* p. 546.

[155] See *FPG*, 40; *MDI*, 546; see Richard J. McCarthy, *Freedom and Fulfillment: An Annotated Translation of al-Ghazālī's al-Munqidh min al-Ḍalāl and Other Relevant Works of al-Ghazālī* (Boston: Twayne Publishers, 1980), p. 79 cited hereafter as *FF*.

skilled snake charmer.

In this respect, he compromises with neither those who have blindly accepted nor those who have totally rejected the philosophers' ethical thought. Total rejection means denying part of the truth, since some aspects of their teachings are reasonable and not in conflict with the Qur'an and the *Sunnah.*[156] Al-Ghazālī further highlights the example of lkhwān al-Ṣafā who mixed and even tried to support their falsehoods with some Qur'anic verses, prophetic traditions as well as the sayings of sages and Sūfīs.[157] In this case, total rejection of their works means abstaining from adopting part of the truth which originated from the said authentic sources of knowledge. On the other hand, he was convinced that total acceptance of the philosophers' ideas would inevitably mean a gradual slipping into falsehood (*istidrāj ilā 'l-baṭil*),[158] since one would then almost certainly accept at least some of their errors that are mixed with the truth.[159] In this regard, he illustrates by way of an analogy of the learned man who can appreciate and feel no aversion to honey, even if he finds it in a cupping glass, for it does not alter the essence of honey itself (*dhāt al-'asal*).[160] whereas the ignorant man assumes that the honey is impure because it is in a cupping glass, his attitude being based on an unexamined foresurption that the cupping glass is made only for impure blood. Thus, the man in question does not realize that the impurity of the cupping glass is essentially due to the attribute of the blood itself (*li ṣfatin fi dhātih*).[161] Yet it is rampant among the majority to falsely ascribe man as the criterion of truth (*ya'rifūna 'l-ḥaqq bi 'l-rijāl*); instead of truth as

[156] See *MDI* 547; *FF*, 79.

[157] *MDI* 547.

[158] Ibid.

[159] See *FF*, 80; *FPG*, 42.

[160] See *MDI* 547; *FF*, 80; *FPG*, 41.

[161] *MDI* 547.

the criterion of man (*wa la ya'rifūna 'l-rijāl bi 'l-ḥaqq*).[162] Hence, the public, according to al-Ghazālī, should be restrained from reading the philosophers' works due to their possible tendency to be impressed and ultimately blindly accept those false theories.[163]

The process of extricating or uprooting (*intizā'*) the truth from falsehood by a profound scholar (*al-'ālim al-rāsikh*) is symbolically illustrated by the analogy of a skillful snake-charmer who discerns between the antidote and the poison from a snake. He extracts the antidote while destroying the poison, and will not withhold the antidote from anyone in need.[164] It is also similar to an experienced money-changer, after picking up and extracting the authentic gold coins from the counterfeiter's purse, he will throw away the counterfeits but not withhold the authentic coins from the needy.[165] The apparent similarity between the authentic coins and the counterfeits does not make the authentic coins counterfeits; just as it does not render the counterfeits authentic.[166] Similarly, the apparent similarity between truth and falsehood does not make the true false, or vice versa.[167] Hence, one should be able to access the true aspects of the philosophers' teachings after identifying and further extricating the truth from falsehood.

Al-Ghazālī's view on ethics articulated in *Kitāb Riyaḍāt al-Nafs wa Tahdhīb al-akhlāq* of *Iḥyā'*, is a clear manifestation of his Islamization approach which is further deliberated on in *al-Munqidh min al-Ḍalal.* It clearly shows his 'epistemological

---

[162] Se al-Ghazālī, *Al-Munqidh min al-Ḍalāl wa ma 'ahu Kimiyā al-Sa'ādah wa 'l-Qawā'id 'id al-'Asharah wa 'l-Adab fi'l-Dīn* (Beirut: Mu'assasah al-Kutub al-Thaqāfiyyah, 1987), p. 50, cited hereafter as *MP2*; *FPG*, 42.

[163] See *MDI*, 547; *FF*, 79.

[164] Ibid., 547-548; *FPG*, 43.

[165] See *MDI*, 547-548; *FPG*, 43.

[166] See *MDI*, 548; FPG, 43; *FF*, 81.

[167] See *MDI*, 548; *FF*, 81.

revolution' against Hellenistic sources of knowledge promulgated by the philosophers. He neither opts for a total acceptance nor a total rejection of these foreign elements by virtue of the fact that truth is sometimes mixed with falsehood, as gold is sometimes mixed with gravel and dross. Hence, the process of Islamization carried out by him, involves at least two major steps: **1.** discernment between truth and falsehood; and **2.** extrication of truth from falsehood. These methods can only be exercised by profound scholars (*al-rāsikhūn fi'l-'ilm*), since knowledge of the truth itself is a prerequisite to discern between what is true and false. In this context, he further outlines two primary criteria for knowledge to be qualified as 'truth':

1. its cohesion with the principles of reason that is supported by proof (*burhān*);[168]
2. its conformity with the ultimate sources of knowledge derived from Divine Revelation, particularly the Qur'an and *Sunnah* of the Prophet ﷺ.[169]

In spite of his moderate attitude towards philosophical sciences, al-Ghazālī was nonetheless critical in dealing with the philosophers' theological or metaphysical doctrines which originated from the Hellenistic sources. His attitude is apparently discernible, even in dealing with the practical disciplines, including the moral education of children. In this context, he does not only eliminate certain foreign conceptual elements from its framework, but also infuses certain key Islamic fundamental concepts in relation to the methodological aspect of Child Education, such as *ta'dīb* (education), *riyāḍah* (self-discipline), *ta'līm* (instruction), *tarbiyah* (good breeding) and *tahdhīb* (refinement). The most important philosophical key term eliminated by al-Ghazālī, is the theory of natural order (*al-niẓām*

[168] See *MDI* p. 547.
[169] *MDI* p. 547.

al-tabīʿī), which was initially deliberated on by Miskawayh in his *Tahdhīb al-Akhlāq*. Al-Ghazālī replaced the said theory with the Qur'anic concept of *fiṭrah* in his chapter on child education. The concept of *fiṭrah*, as discussed by the higher Sūfis, refers to the essence of human nature that naturally inclines to recognize and acknowledge the Lordship of God, provided it is liberated from external distractive influences and guided by truth.[170] The concept of *fiṭrah* and moral education is further supported by the concept of prophecy (*nubuwwah*)[171] as the perfect exemplary model to guide and lead all of humanity towards the Straight Path (*al-ṣirāṭ al-mustaqīm*).[172] Al-Ghazālī further assimilates the Islamic concept of the 'Straight Path' with the philosophers' conception of the right mean (*al-wasaṭ al-ḥaqīqī*).[173] The above concepts are ingrained in the concept of parental religious accountability (*amānah or taklīf*) which distinguishes him from Miskawayh's conception of child education. It is thus, a major responsibility of the parents to prepare the child for the process of recollection (*al-tadhakkur*) of his true nature (*fiṭrah*) to assent to the existence and Lordship of God (*al-taṣdīq bi'l-rubūbiyyah*).[174] Apart from the above conceptual assimilation, al-Ghazālī concurrently accepts and incorporates the disciplinary methods of child upbringing of Muslim philosophers such as Miskawayh. These methods including habituation (*i'tiyād*), socialization (*mukhālaṭah*) and learning (*ta'allum*) are further reiterated and even simplified by al-Ghazālī in his *Iḥyā'*. However, the latter substantially differs from the former in several fundamental aspects, particularly in relation to the curriculum of learning. While his predecessor

---

[170] See Ali Issa Othman, *The Concept of Man in Islam* (Cairo: Dar al-Ma'ārif, 1960), p. 7, cited hereafter as *CMI*.

[171] See *MDI*, p. 556.

[172] See *Iḥyā'*, 3:64.

[173] Ibid., 3: 63.

[174] See *KS*, p. 426.

suggests Logic (*al-Manṭiq*) as the primary subject to be acquired by elementary students, al-Ghazālī proposes that al-Qur'an should be the utmost priority to be taught. It is further in line with the religious and cultural norms of his period, as al-Qur'an was indeed the main subject being taught in the *Kuttāb*.[175] Furthermore, it was a religious symbol for children to primarily learn the Qur'an,[176] known to be a common practice in Muslim countries at that time.

---

175 See HME, p. 19.

176 Ibid., p. 23 citing Ibn Khaldūn, al-*Muqaddimah*, pp. 397-399.

Preliminary Remarks on Al-Ghazālī's Spiritual Approach to Theology

Ssekamanya Siraje Abdullah**

In his discussion of the development of Islamic Theology, the great Muslim historian and philosopher of history Ibn Khaldūn refers to what he calls "the school of the recent scholars", a new phase in the development of the Ash'arite school of theology. According to Ibn Khaldūn, this phase is characterized by the use of logical arguments and the refutation of the opinions of philosophers. He adds that "the first scholar to write in accordance with the (new) theological approach was al-Ghazālī"[1]

Ibn Khaldūn's description of al-Ghazālī's approach to

** I wish to express my profound thanks to my supervisor Professor Alparslan Acikgenc for his guidance. Professor Syed Muhammad Naquib al-Attas was very generous with his insightful comments. Professors Wan Mohd Nor Wan Daud, Omar Jah, Ferid Muhic, Muddathir Abdel Rahim, Karim Crow, Bilal Kuspinar all read and commented on the manuscript.

[1] Ibn Khaldūn, al-*Muqaddimah*, (Beirut: Dār al-Qalam,1984), pp. 465-466 {Trans. Franz Rosenthal, *The Muqaddimah of Ibn Khaldūn*, 3 vols. (New York: Pantheon, 1958), 3:51-52}.

theology is rather incomplete in that it leaves out *taṣawwuf*, a key element in al-Ghazālī's thought and practice. In this paper an attempt is made at demonstrating that *taṣawwuf* served as the integrating element in al-Ghazālī's theological thought. It cannot be denied that in addition to his introduction of logical demonstration into theology, al-Ghazālī's spiritual orientation colored most of his theological discussions as well as his evaluation of the approach of previous generations of theologians. Thus al-Ghazālī should be given credit not only for initiating the logical approach to speculative theology (*kalām*), but also for articulating the metaphysical approach of Ṣūfism based on a direct intuition of existence. In the following pages al-Ghazālī's relationship with and evaluation of the characteristic dialectical approach of early *kalām* will be examined, followed by his introduction and defense of logic, and, finally, his elaboration of the ṣūfī spiritual approach to *kalām*.

Al-Ghazālī and Dialectical *Kalām*

Considering the fact that al-Ghazālī's early training was as a Shāfi'ite jurist and an Ash'arite *mutakallim*, it is by no means surprising that his early theological works were in accordance with the characteristic method of early Ash'arite *kalām*. As a result of the polemical nature of this science, its characteristic method was basically dialectical. It always involved advancing arguments against real or imaginary opponents. In accordance with this method, the *mutakallimūn* used to hold public debates or disputations for the exposition of their arguments as well as the refutation of their opponents' contrary arguments.[2]

---

[2] On the dialectical nature of *kalām*, see J. Van Ess, "The Logical Structure of Islamic Theology." In *Logic in Classical Islamic Culture* ed. G. E. von Grunebaum (Wiesbaden: Otto Harassowitz, 1970), 21-50, henceforth cited as "*Logical Structure*." See also Ahmet Adanali, "Dialectical Method and its

A survey of al-Ghazālī's philosophical and theological works show that he was an expert in the method of dialectics and often applied it to good advantage. In the introduction to his main *kalām* tract, *al-Iqtiṣād fī'l-i'tiqād*, al-Ghazālī acknowledges having relied on the various dialectical techniques.[3] He considered such techniques very useful for silencing heretics who do not comprehend demonstrative arguments but accept reputable premises (*al-mashhūrāt*) as true. On the other hand, dialectics is useful for convincing people who are not satisfied with rhetorical arguments and are unable to understand demonstrative arguments. It is also useful for investigating the opposite arguments on an issue.[4]

It is apparently because of the above considerations that the dialectical method features prominently in many of his major *kalām* works, regardless of the period during which they were composed. Among al-Ghazālī's works wherein the dialectical method is predominant are *Tahāfut al-Falāsifah*, *Fayṣal al-Tafriqah bayna 'l-Islām wa 'l-Zandaqah*,[5] *al-Qisṭās al-Mustaqīm*,[6]

Critique: Ghaziili as a Case Study" (Ph.D. Dissertation, University of Chicago, 1995), henceforth cited as "*Dialectical Method*." George Makdisi has observed that unlike Christian theology, which is concerned with "understanding faith, the dialectical method of kaliim makes it concerned primarily with defending formulations of the faith against doubters and negators." He contrasts this polemical *kalām* with the traditionalists' science of *'uṣūl al-dīn*, which serves an 'illuminative' rather than an 'apologetic' purpose. See his "Hanbalite Islam," 262.

[3] Al-Ghazālī, *Kitāb al-Iqtiṣād fī'l-I'tiqād* (Beirut: Dār al-Kutub al-'Ilmiyyah, 1983),pp. 12-14.

[4] Adanali, "Dialectical Method," p. 103; al-Ghazālī, *Maqāṣid al-Falāsifah* (Cairo: al-Maṭba'ah al-Maḥmūdiyyah. 1936), 1: 53.

[5] al-Ghazālī, *Fayṣal al-Tafriqah bayna 'l-Islām wa 'l-Zandaqah, In Majmū'āt Rasā'il al- Imām al-Ghazālī*, vol. 3 (Beirut: Dar al-Kutub al-'Ilmiyyah, 1994). Henceforth cited as *Fayṣal.*

[6] Idem, al-*Qisṭās al-Mustaqīm*, In *Majmū'āt Rasā'il al-Imām al-Ghazālī*, vol.

and *Faḍā'iḥ al-Bāṭiniyyah.*[7] In most of these works, he debates with an imaginary opponent, citing both arguments for and against his adversaries' positions.

There is sufficient evidence to prove that as al-Ghazālī used the dialectical method in his works, he was clearly aware of its shortcomings. He noted, for instance, that dialectics, in its pure form, involves the refutation of arguments simply because they are advanced by the opponents, a procedure which may inadvertently lead to the rejection of the truth.[8] The best approach should be to examine the validity of each argument before accepting or refuting it. This explains why in his refutation of philosophers, he set very stringent conditions for the refutation of any discipline, including the necessity of mastering its methods, understanding its principles, and emulating its authorities by raising new questions.[9] Thus before embarking on the refutation of the doctrines of the philosophers, he made it a point to understand and present them as objectively as possible.[10] In that manner, he reformed the method of dialectics, consequently presenting a wonderful refutation of the doctrines of philosophers. His method in the *Tahāfut* was so excellent that it has been considered by Carre de Vaux, a 19th century Orientalist, as "the first masterpiece" in the art of dialectics.[11]

In his *Faḍā'iḥ al-Bāṭiniyyah*, al-Ghazālī observed that although he used the dialectical method of argument presented in

---

3. (Beirut: Dar al-Kutub al-'Ilmiyyah, 1994). Henceforth cited as *Fayṣal.*

[7] Idem, *Faḍā'iḥ al-Bāṭiniyyah*, ed. 'Abd al-Raḥmān Badawī. (Cairo: al-Dar al-Qawmiyyah, 1964). Henceforth cited as *Faḍā'iḥ.*

[8] Idem, *al-Munqidh min al-Ḍalāl*, Trans. R. J. McCarthy in *Freedom and Fulfillment* (Boston: G. K. Hall, 19Bp), 27 and 83.

[9] Ibid, p. 18.

[10] Ibid, p. 108; *Maqāṣid*, 1: 2.

[11] Bernard Carre de Vaux, *Ghazzālī* (Paris: F. Akan, 1902), 61. Quoted by Adanali, "Dialectical Methodology", p. 56.

the form of dialogue in order to facilitate its understanding by common people, he was fully aware that this method was not satisfactory for the scholars.[12] He therefore combined it with the analytical techniques in which he stressed the importance of paying attention to the meaning of words as well as their underlying intentions and connotations. Besides showing al-Ghazālī's inclination to the logical methods of the philosophers, the above examples also demonstrate his mastery and conscious utilization of the dialectical method of argumentation in his *kalām* works.

In addition to his exposure to other forms of argumentation—particularly the demonstrative syllogism (*al-burhān*) al-Ghazālī's mastery of dialectics apparently contributed to his awareness of the existence of basic flaws in the dialectical arguments of the *mutakallimūn*. The various references in his works in which he appears to question the legitimacy of the science of *kalām* have to be understood to be directed against the numerous flaws in its method. For instance, in the context of describing his experience in search of true and certain knowledge, he maintains that he found the dialectical methods used by the *mutakallimūn* to be nothing more than empty talk which did not prove anything. Whatever is valid and beneficial in dialectical *kalām* had already been clearly explained in the Qur'an.[13]

In other words, the methods used by the *mutakallimūn* could not lead him to the sure and certain knowledge he was seek.[14]

---

[12] *Faḍā'iḥ*, pp. 7-8.

[13] *Munqidh*, p. 22.

[14] *Munqidh*, McCarthy's translation, p. 63; Idem, *Iḥyā' 'Ulūm al-Dīn*, 4 vols. (Beirut: Dār al-Ma'rifah, 1982), 1:133. Henceforth cited as *Iḥyā'*. Cf. al-Juwaynī, who argued that dialectics cannot lead to knowledge of the reality of the divine Essence (*dhāt*). For more discussion about this, see: Ahmad Mahmud Ṣubhī, *Fi 'Ilm al-Kalām*, 3 Vols. (Beirut: Dār al-Nahḍah, 1985), 2:164.

Al-Ghazālī argues that the science of *kalām*, based on the dialectical method, was mostly aimed at showing the inconsistency of the adversaries. However, this is only useful for someone who has premises to defend. It is useless for the skeptic who admits nothing at all except the primary and self-evident truths.[15] In one of his epistles with a Ṣūfī orientation al-Ghazālī considers the *mutakallimūn* among the *maghrūrūn* (vainglorious) individuals. This is because "they spent their time in *kalām* and dialectics and refuting their opponents and following their inconsistencies ... who spent their time also in teaching methods of debating with [their opponents] and defeating them."[16] The *mutakallimūn*, however, did not master the application of the proofs. Therefore, they mixed up things, considering a *shubhah* (doubt) to be a proof and vice-versa. Moreover, they considered dialectics the most important religious duty and even went to the extent of excluding from the faith those who do not base their belief on *al-naẓar* (rational contemplation).[17]

---

[15] *Munqidh*, McCarthy's translation, p. 69.

[16] Idem, *al-Kashf wa 'l-Tabyīn fī Ghurūr al-Khalq Ajma'īn*, In *Majmū'āt Rasā'il al-Imām al-Ghazālī*, vol. 5 (Beirut: Dār al-Kutub al-'Ilmiyyah, 1994), p. 168. Henceforth cited as *Ghurūr*. Fazlur Rahman rightly observed that al-Ghazālī's hostile remarks against *kalām* were "not because of the metaphysical beliefs it sought to inculcate but with the purely dialectical method it employed." *Prophecy in Islam: Philosophy and Orthodoxy*, (Chicago and London: University of Chicago Press, 1958. Repr. N.p.: Midway Reprint, 1979), 95, henceforth cited as *Prophecy*. Although this author's comments about al-Ghazālī's attitude to dialectics are valid, his view that al-Ghazālī adopted the metaphysics of philosophers is open for discussion.

[17] Al-Ghazālī, *al-Kashf wa'l-Tabyīn fi Ghurūr al-Khalq Ajma'īn*, p. 168. For the arguments of the Mu'tazilah on the necessity of rational contemplation, see 'Abd al-Jabbār ibn Aḥmad, *Sharḥ Al-'Uṣūl al-Khamsat*, e.d. 'Abd al-Karīm 'Uthmān, (Cairo: Maktabah Wahbah, 1965), p. 39, pp. 60-63, and p. 88. See also idem, *al-Mughnī fi Abwāb al-Tawhīd wa 'l-'Adl*, 12: 237-259,

Those remarks were apparently aimed at all *mutakallimūn* regardless of whether they were Mu'tazilites or Ash'arites. In al-Ghazālī's view, most of them missed the point by using the dialectical method which, according to him, does not prove anything. Al-Ghazālī's disapproval of the dialectical method took him to the extent of rejecting and refuting one of the most important arguments advanced by the earlier *mutakallimūn* in defense of the legitimacy of *kalām*, that is the necessity of *al-naẓar* (rational demonstration). According to him, appealing to such a justification involves disregard of an important religious and historical fact. The Prophet ﷺ attested that the first generations of Muslims were the best batch of believers that had ever lived and will ever live. However, there is neither a report to the effect that he asked them to rationally prove their *īmān* to him, nor is there any evidence that anyone of the companions tried to provide such a proof.[18]

Contrary to the claim of many *mutakallimūn*, especially the Mu'tazilah, al-Ghazālī argued that *al-naẓar* (rational demonstration), based on the dialectical method of *kalām* instead of increasing *īmān*, just creates confusion and may even lead simple-minded believers to disbelief.[19] It is because of this possibility of creating confusion that earlier Muslims rejected *kalām*. Citing such a possibility of *kalām* leading to doctrinal confusion, al-Ghazālī agrees with Ibn Ḥanbal who cautioned that

---

quoted by Subhi, *Fī 'Ilm al-Kalām*, 1: 203-205.

[18] Al-Ghazālī, *al-Kashf wa 'l-Tabyīn fī Ghurūr al-Khalq Ajma'īn*, p. 169. The views stated here are not significantly different from those expressed by the traditionalist opponents of *kalām*. See for instance, al-Anṣārī al-Harawī, *Dhamm al-Kalām*, ed. Sarni: Daghīm (Beirut: Dar al-Fikr al-Lubnānī, 1994), and Jalāl al-Dīn al-Suyūṭī, *Ṣawn al-Manṭiq wa 'l-Kalām 'an Fannay al-Manṭiq wa 'l-Kalām*, ed. 'Ali Sāmī: al-Nashshār (Cairo: Maṭba'ah al-Sa'ādah, 1947).

[19] *Fayṣal*, McCarthy's translation, p. 168.

by using the dialectical method in refuting the opponents' claims, it is possible that the common believers may stop at your restatement of the opponents' arguments without proceeding to your refutation of those arguments. Alternatively, they may not understand the refutation. The result of all this is further doctrinal confusion and ultimate deviation.[20]

Al-Ghazālī pushes his point further by arguing that as far as the intensity of *īmān* is concerned, good believers among the common people may even be in a better position than many of the *mutakallimūn*.[21] The *īmān* of the *mutakallimūn* is very weak and is always subject to change. Moreover, they are not different from ordinary believers when it comes to *taqlīd* (following the opinions of others): In fact, the *taqlīd* of the *mutakallimūn* is even worse than that of the common people. This is because the *mutakallimūn* not only blindly follow the *madhab* (school), but they also accept without question other proofs (*adillah*) of scholars.[22] This explains why al-Ghazālī considered many of the *mutakallimūn* to be too rigid, inflexible and confused to lead people in matters of *'aqīdah*.[23]

With the above methodological issues in mind, al-Ghazālī observes that any science can be either praiseworthy (*maḥmud*) or blame-worthy (*madhmūm*). A science is considered blameworthy (*madhmūm*) if: (1) it harms the one who practices it or others, (2) it leads to harm most of the time, or (3) it is useless for one who studies it to go deeply into it (*al-khawḍ fīh*).[24] Among the examples of blameworthy sciences is 'the search for the secrets of divinity' which many philosophers and *mutakallimūn* are engaged

[20] *Munqidh*, McCarthy's translation, p. 82.

[21] *Iḥyā'*, 1:36; 1:94.

[22] Ibid., 1: 36; 1: 73. *Al-Iqtiṣād*, 107; *Fayṣal*, McCarthy's translation, 149.

[23] Ibid.

[24] *Iḥyā'*, 1: 30.

in.[25] This apparently implies that *kalām* is a blameworthy science. Al-Ghazālī laments that because of too much emphasis on dialectics and disputation, *kalām* had become an incurable sickness (*dā'un 'uḍāl*), which his reader is strongly advised to avoid.[26] Al-Ghazālī expresses regret over having spent too much time in dialectical *kalām*, although he does not seem to totally denounce it or even reject the works he had earlier written about on the subject.

In a related text, he discusses at length the views of earlier scholars such as al-Shāfi'ī, Mālik, Abu Ḥanīfah and Aḥmad Ibn Ḥanbal, about *kalām*. According to him, they all considered *kalām* an unlawful pursuit for Muslims.[27] Although he fundamentally agrees with those scholars, he maintains that dialectical *kalām* has to be considered like a harmful drug: It is useful only when it is needed. Otherwise, it can be catastrophic.[28] According to him, permission to deal with the dangerous drug of *kalām* is only given to two categories of people: **1.** one who is facing doubts and does not accept the evidence of revelation but insists on rational discourse, and **2.** one who is highly qualified in presenting rational proofs. *Kalām* is useful for this one so that he can administer the 'medicine to the sick'.[29]

All this seems as though al-Ghazālī was contradicting his conviction that *kalām* is useless and has never corrected any doctrinal deviation. If it is incapable of treating the disease, then why should he allow its use as medicine? To find a solution to this apparent contradiction, a holistic approach to al-Ghazālī's views

---

[25] Ibid.

[26] Ibid., I: 41.

[27] Ibid., 1: 94-96; See also *Fayṣal*, McCarthy's translation, 168.

[28] *Iḥyā'*, 1:97-100; Idem, *Iljām al-'Awām 'an 'ilm al-Kalām, In Majmū'āt Rasā'il al-Imām al-Ghazālī*, vol. 5. (Beirut: Dar al-Kutub al-'Ilmiyyah, 1994), 59. Henceforth cited as *Iljām*.

[29] Ibid., 83. *Fayṣal*, McCarthy's translation, 168.

regarding the nature and methods of *kalām* is necessary: In al-Ghazālī's view, dialectical *kalām* was incapable of removing any doubts (*shubhāt*).[30] However, if its methods are refined and rigorous proofs are employed, it can be useful in allaying the doubts of the doubters. In this case, however, it is only applicable to those who are suffering from such doubts and are capable of grasping the rigorous rational proofs. Moreover, it can only be used for that purpose by a competent *mutakallim* who has a strong faith and has mastered the religious sciences as well as the most powerful rational methods of argument. However, circumstances can allow the existence of only one or a few such capable *mutakallimūn* at a time. Ordinary Muslims (*al-'awām*), have to refrain from dialectical *kalām*, as it may lead them to confusion.

Thus, in addition to strengthening the methods of dialectical *kalām*, al-Ghazālī seriously narrowed down its area of application. He considered *kalām*, thus strengthened, the greatest and most general of all religious sciences on which all other religious sciences rely.[31] However, specialists of other religious sciences need not be masters of *kalām*.[32] Mastery of *kalām* is just a communal obligation (*farḍ kifāyah*), and if there is one good *mutakallim* to defend the religion and remove doubts, that is

---

[30] Apparently, al-Ghazālī considered himself one of the very few who are qualified to deal with *kalām*. This is made clear, for instance, in his *al-Risālah al-Wa'ẓiyyah*, in *Majmū'āt rasā'il al-imām al-Ghazālī*. vol. 3. (Beirut: Dar al-Kutub al-'Ilmiyyah, 1994), 40. Henceforth cited as *Wa'ẓiyyah*. See also Mustafa Abū Sway, Al- Ghazālīyy: *A Study in Islamic Epistemology*, (Kuala Lumpur: Dewan Bahasa dan Pustaka, 1996), pp. 110-118.

[31] Al-Ghazālī, *al-Mustaṣfā min 'ilmi 'l-'uṣūl*, 6. Henceforth cited as al-*Mustaṣfā*.

[32] Ibid., 7.

enough for the community.[33]

Although al-Ghazālī agrees that attaining knowledge of God's Essence, Attributes, Actions and Commands is a personal duty for every intelligent human being, he cautions that such knowledge should not be confused with *kalām*.[34] In the *Iḥyā'* he points out that the science of affirming Allah's unity (*al-tawhīd*) is one of the sciences which had been corrupted, mixed with other things and diverted from their original purpose. The true science of *tawhīd* involves knowledge, action and spiritual experience. It is directly based on the guidance of the Qur'an, *Sunnah* and the examples of the early Muslims and not on the dialectics of the *mutakallimūn*.[35] All this was apparently a result of al-Ghazālī's conversion to *taṣawwuf* which led to a change of emphasis in his thought.[36]

Although al-Ghazālī's discussion of the legitimacy of *kalām*, especially with respect to its dialectical method, involves many apparent inconsistencies, a general direction of his thought about this subject can still be identified. The general picture so far established is that the dialectical method used by the *mutakallimūn* is incapable of leading to *yaqīn* (certain

---

[33] *Iqtiṣād*, 11.

[34] Idem, *al-Risālatu al-Laduniyyah*, In *Majmū'āt Rasā'il al-imām al-Ghazālī*, vol. 3. (Beirut: Dar al-Kutub al-'Ilmiyyah, 1994), 58. Henceforth cited as *Laduniyyah*.

[35] Ibid. See also *Iḥyā'*, 1: 32-33. For a recent discussion of al-Ghazālī's criticism of dialectical *kalām*, see Josef Puig Montada, "lbn Rushd Versus al-Ghazālī: Reconsideration of a Polemic," *The Muslim World*, 82 (1992): pp. 115-118.

[36] Fazlur Rahman attributes the apparent inconsistencies in al-Ghazālī's evaluation of *kalām* to the possibility that his "mind was gripped by a certain mood at a given time, and also due to his prolific speed of writing, he sometimes expressed himself in an exaggerated manner about certain matters." See *Revival and Reform in Islam: A Study of Islamic Fundamentalism* (Oxford: One World, 2000), 119-120.

knowledge). It is therefore useless to use this method in confronting the ultra-rationalist skeptics and in guiding the simple-minded common believers. However, far from totally rejecting dialectical *kalām*, al-Ghazālī refined and strengthened its methodology[37] mainly by advocating the rigorous analytical method of demonstrative reasoning (*al-burhān*), which he considered to be based on the Qur'an. In addition, he advocated paying direct attention to the teachings of the Qur'an and the *Sunnah* as well as trying to attain divine intuition (*al-'Ilm al-laduniy*), by following the Sufi methods of *'ibādah* (worship) and *tazkiyat al-nafs* (self-purification).

Using *Manṭiq* (Logic) in *Kalām*

Al-Ghazālī has been rightly considered the first Muslim thinker to force-fully and systematically adopt and incorporate logical reasoning into *kalām*.[38] As part of his project of refuting the philosophers' arguments, al-Ghazālī studied and summarized Greek logic (*al-manṭiq*), which he presented, together with other parts of Greek philosophy, in his *Maqāṣid al-Falāsifah*. Apparently impressed by the strength of this tool, al-Ghazālī declared it neutral and independent of the philosophers' metaphysical views, which he found incompatible with the teachings of Islam. The philosophers' mistakes did not stem from the use of logic, but rather from following its dictates improperly, thereby causing them to commit serious errors. Al-Ghazālī subsequently wrote several works on logic including *Miḥakk al-Naẓar* and *Mi'yār al-'Ilm*. These were followed by *al-Qisṭās al-*

[37] For instance, he maintains that although his *Iqtiṣād* looks like the traditional *kalām* manuals, he had tried to improve its methods by using deeper probing and more rigorous arguments. See his *Kitāb al-Arba'īn fi 'Uṣūl al-Dīn*, 27. Henceforth cited as al- *Arba'īn*.

[38] See James Pavlin, *Sunni Kalam*, pp. 107-108.

Mustaqīm in which he attempted to vindicate logic as a truly Islamic method both in spirit and content. Having satisfied himself with such vindication, he went on to include it as a prolegomena to his work on the principles of Islamic jurisprudence.[39]

Al-Ghazālī argues that logic is available to and is used by all mankind. All human beings use the cognitive powers in their souls which depend on logic for their proper functioning.[40] It is logic which aids the systematic arrangement in the mind of the empirical and sensible principles. Nevertheless, many of us take it for granted and are even not conscious of it.[41] Al-Ghazālī points out, however, that although the methods of systematic reasoning are inherent in our souls, their proper application does not come naturally without learning. Therefore, in order to be able to think properly and to avoid all the pitfalls of poor reasoning, we have to learn logic,[42] which is, therefore, useful for distinguishing true from false evidence and arguments. It is also useful as an aid for formulating strong arguments. This being the case, logic is applicable to all the sciences, be they religious sciences or otherwise.

Convinced of the efficacy of logic and its potential as a tool for formulating as well as for evaluating arguments and considering the reluctance of traditional Muslim scholars to adopt it, al-Ghazālī saw an urgent need for justifying the incorporation of this method in Islamic studies. This was, first of all, done by distinguishing it from the metaphysical and physical theories of the philosophers which he rejected. Thus in his restatement and

---

[39] See *al-Mustaṣfā*, pp. 1-6.

[40] *Qisṭās*, McCarthy's translation, 314.1.

[41] Ibid.

[42] al-Ghazālī, *Mi'yār al-'Ilm fi'l-Manṭiq*, (Beirut: Dar al-Kutub al-'Ilmiyyah, 1990), 26. Henceforth cited as *Mi'yār*.

subsequent refutation of the philosophers' theories, he tried hard to distinguish their doctrines from their logical methods.[43] To this effect, he asserts that by itself, logic is a very useful tool. It is a neutral science which has nothing to do with religion by way of negation and affirmation.[44] It is just a method of analyzing proofs and conditions governing the premises of apodictic demonstrations. If we reject it, people, especially those intellectuals who are inclined to the rationalistic sciences, may have a low opinion of religion and it would be difficult to guide them to the truth.[45] Moreover, logic had already been used by earlier theologians and jurists, although they referred to it using different names. Therefore, using it in *kalām* was not an innovation in Islam.[46]

In his *Qisṭās*, al-Ghazālī claims that he deduced the balances (i.e. logic) by himself from the Qur'an, while at the same time acknowledging that he was preceded by the philosophers in formulating their principles.[47] By this he implies that his contribution to logic was to present it using Islamic terminology derived from the Qur'an, apparently with the intention of making it acceptable to Muslims, especially the rigid traditionalists.[48]

---

[43] See for example his *Maqāṣid al-Falāsifah*, ed. Sulaymān Dunyā. (Cairo: Dar al- Ma'ārif, 1961), 32. Henceforth cited as *Maqāṣid*. See also *Munqidh*, McCarthy's translation, p. 74.

[44] Ibid.

[45] Ibid., 75.

[46] For a detailed discussion of al-Ghazālī's arguments for justifying the application of logic in *kalām*, see M. Marmura, "Al-Ghazālī's Attitude to Secular Sciences and Logic," in *Essays on Islamic Philosophy and Science*, ed. George F. Hourani, (Albany, New York: SUNY Press, 1975), 103. Henceforth cited as "*Ghazali's Attitude*."

[47] *Qisṭās*, McCarthy's translation, pp. 291-305.

[48] Ibid., 306. Marmura argues, citing Ibn Taymiyyah's criticism, that al-Ghazālī's attempt to 'sanctify' logic did not impress many Islamic scholars. See his "*Ghazālī's Attitude*," pp. 102-103.

Interestingly, he points out that if we know that this science was formulated by the Greeks, that does not decrease its value, as it is possible that the philosophers themselves acquired it from divine revelation, their only contribution being the introduction of their own technical terminology.[49]

One may want to ask: What is the implication of all this for al-Ghazālī's views on the legitimacy of *kalām*? That al-Ghazālī's reservations against dialectical *kalām* were mostly because, for him, its arguments were weak and incapable of proving the tenets of Islam has already been explained. It is apparently because of this that he advocated the use of logic which he considered to be the best method by which all sorts of cognitions and arguments—including *kalām* arguments—can be judged. Moreover, referring to the Qur'an, he asserts that logic is the divinely ordained method of distinguishing truth from falsehood.[50] This makes it the ideal method of inquiry into *kalām* problems.

Following the classification of theology into **a.** what we can call 'positive theology', being a basic presentation of the tenets of Islam as revealed in Qur'an and the *Sunnah*, and **b.** *kalām* (speculative theology), al-Ghazālī explains that only men of insight and special intelligence should deal with *kalām*. This is the science concerned with adducing proofs for the tenets of Islam and refuting the contrary arguments of the contentious wranglers.[51] Such men of insight are masters of the techniques of logical reasoning. It is only by mastering logic that they can avoid the kind of mistakes committed by the early *mutakallimūn* who relied entirely on the methods of rhetoric and dialectics. As for the common believers, al-Ghazālī advises them to get guidance about the tenets of Islam from the sermons and exhortations based on

---

[49] *Qisṭās*, McCarthy's translation, p. 306.

[50] Ibid., p. 317.

[51] *Qisṭās*, McCarthy's translation, p. 318.

the Qur'an and *Sunnah*.[52] For the *mujādil* (the contentious wrangler), al-Ghazālī advises that he should be taught "the balances" which will help him recognize the truth wherever it is. Otherwise, he has to be handled by force.[53]

Moreover, the logical approach can help to resolve the disagreements among Muslims which arose basically as a result of the application of dialectical methods to theological questions. To the possible objection that even those who use logic did not reach agreement on all their subject matter, al-Ghazālī observes that disagreements can arise even when logic is used, but this is because of factors outside logic itself.

Disagreement can arise because of:

1. the inability of some to grasp completely the balance's conditions;
2. disregarding the balance and resorting to using simple innate bent and nature;
3. differences about the cognitions which serve as premises for the apodictic proofs; some being empirical, and others being based on impeccable transmission, etc.;
4. mixing up judgments of imagination with those of reason; and
5. mistaking sayings which are accepted and esteemed for analytical judgments.[54]

In other words, disagreements arise because of logical fallacies. This is why it is important for any intelligent person, in order to be qualified to engage in *kalām* discourse, to master the science of logic, so that he can differentiate true arguments from

[52] Ibid, p. 219.

[53] Ibid., p. 323.

[54] *Fayṣal*, McCarthy's translation, pp. 158-159.

false arguments. Faulty reasoning, based on false arguments, leads to unnecessary disagreements among believers but true reasoning has to be agreed upon by all reasonable and rational thinkers.

All this implies that for *kalām* to really serve its purpose, it should use logic as its method. Al-Ghazālī stresses this even in his *Iljām al-'Awām 'an 'Ilm al-Kalām*, which is apparently an anti-*kalām* tract. In the context of discussing the claim of the *mutakallimūn* that true *īmān* has to be based on *al-naẓar* (rational contemplation), he argues that what is necessary for all believers is to have an *īmān jāzim* (unwavering faith) in the religious doctrines. This is made up of six levels:

1. The first and highest level is that established on clear apodictic proofs based on the demonstrative syllogism (*al-burhān*). **2.** The second level is based on imagined dialectical proofs (*adillah wahmiyyah kalāmiyyah*), which are based on generally accepted arguments (*musallamāt*). These are accepted simply because they are widespread among great scholars. **3.** The third level is based on rhetorical arguments. **4.** The fourth level is based on words of highly regarded individuals. **5.** The fifth level is based on circumstantial evidence which does not lead to certainty. **6.** The sixth and lowest level is based on accepting statements simply because they are in line with one's natural disposition personality (*al-ṭab'*).[55] This is the weakest level of assent, as it is not based on any kind of indicative signs or proofs (*dalīl*).

Taking the above points into consideration, we can understand why al-Ghazālī highly esteemed logic, showed pride of his mastery of this science, and even kept pointing to his logical works whenever he discussed the methods of acquisition of knowledge. Similarly, we can understand why he had such a low regard for the *mutakallimūn*. In the *Munqidh*, he explained how

---

[55] *Iljām*, pp. 78-80.

application of logic to *kalām* problems led him to certain knowledge:

> I learned the balances from the Qur'an, then weighed with them all the cognitions about God and even the circumstances of the afterlife and the punishment of the iniquitous and the reward of the obedient ... And I found they all conformed to what is in the Qur'an and what is in the traditions. Thus I knew for sure that Muhammad ﷺ is veracious and that the Qur'an is authentic ... So my knowledge of the veracity of the prophet was necessary ...[56]

Such a profound degree of certitude is to be contrasted with the feeble *īmān* of the masses and the *mutakallimūn*, which is based on weak methods of inquiry. All this illustrates al-Ghazālī's strong conviction about the value and efficacy of logic as a tool in Islamic studies particularly in the science of *kalām*. It is apparently because of such a strong conviction that he vigorously defended logic against the objections of traditionalists. Because of this vigorous defense and eventual incorporation of logic into *kalām*, al-Ghazālī has been rightly considered the pioneer of a new approach to *kalām*, which was later referred to as the 'approach of the recent scholars' (*ṭar'īqat al-muḥdathīn*).[57]

However, this is only part of the story. In addition to his adoption of logic as a substitute for dialectical argumentation, al-Ghazālī elaborated a Sufi spiritual approach to Islamic theology. This is based, first and foremost, on a profound spiritual insight into the difficult theological texts of the Qur'an and *Ḥadīth*.

---

[56] *Qisṭās*, McCarthy's translation, pp. 316-317.

[57] See for instance, Ibn Khaldūn, *The Muqaddimah*, 3: 53.

A Spiritual Approach to Qur'an and *Sunnah*

That al-Ghazālī had serious doubts about the legitimacy and efficacy of dialectical *kalām* has already been discussed. As a matter of fact, the search for a valid method of enquiry in *kalām* related questions and the attempt to defend the legitimacy of *kalām* can be rightly considered among al-Ghazālī's lifelong preoccupations. Apparently, it is all a result of his awareness of the dangers posed to Islamic doctrines by the encroachment of alien philosophies as well as the widespread heretical tendencies among some Muslims. It was, therefore, necessary to strengthen *kalām* by employing in it a method that he considered capable of generating the apodictic proofs needed for defending Islamic doctrines and refuting contrary allegations of the detractors.

In this context, his classification of people into common people (*al-'awām*) and the specially gifted elite (*al-khawās*) makes perfect sense. Such a classification is discernible in the various stages of his career, albeit with slight differences in emphasis. At the beginning, the qualification for being included in this special group seems to have been mastery of logic.[58] To this he later added mastery of the way of the Sūfis, which is basically an experiential endeavor. That classification is very important for understanding his contribution to the evaluation of *kalām*. Apparently, all his anti-*kalām* arguments are made in the context of protecting the common people from *kalām's* negative effects.[59]

In one of his final works, he went close to totally rejecting

---

[58] Contrary to the possible contention that this shows how much al-Ghazālī was influenced by the logicians, I would argue that he was just being realistic. We have to judge peoples' suitability for a task on their capacity to handle that task. Since *kalām* involved proving doctrines and refuting the opponent's proofs, it was very important that a *mutakallim* masters the science which enables him to do that.

[59] See *Iljām*, p. 78.

kalām. Surprisingly, he systematically refuted most of the justifications advanced by the *mutakallimūn* in support of their science, even the ones he himself had subscribed to elsewhere. For instance, he argued that defending the legitimacy of *kalām* on the basis of the necessity to counter the rampant innovations and doctrinal attacks against Islam by the infidels, is not entirely satisfactory. Such doctrinal attacks are not new: even during the time of the companions of the Prophet and their followers, doctrinal attacks on Islam by the Jews, Christians and pagans were wide-spread. However, the *ṣaḥābah* and the *tābi'ūn* never tried to counter those attacks by rational speculation. All they did was to use the strong arguments of the Qur'an and the *Sunnah*.[60] Moreover, any attempt to correct the doctrine of a few people by opening up *kalām* discussion to the rank and file may end up leading more people into confusion. Therefore, the majority of believers have to be protected by strictly restricting their access to *kalām* disputation.[61]

Does this mean that common believers do not have to know religious doctrines? If by knowing here we mean knowledge of the doctrines and all their supporting rational proofs, the answer is yes. However, if we mean a general kind of knowledge of the doctrines without knowing the detailed rational derivations and proofs, certainly common believers cannot be prevented from knowing. This latter kind of knowledge is what the *mutakallimūn* referred to as *taqlīd* (imitation) which, in their view, is not real knowledge.

For al-Ghazālī, there is a clear distinction between *'Ilm al-Kalām*, from which the common believers have to be protected,

[60] Ibid., p. 60. This apparently contradicts *Iḥyā'*, 1: 22, where he justifies *kalām* on the basis of the rampant innovations and even goes to the extent of considering it a communal obligation (*farḍ kifāyah*).

[61] Ibid., p. 61.

and *'Ilm al-Tawhīd*, which is praiseworthy and accessible to all believers without any restriction.[62] This latter science involves a sincere unconditional assent to the contents of the Revelation. Thus there is no need for rationally proving any of the doctrines in question.[63] Although those who are capable of adducing rational proofs in support of their faith are regarded to be at a higher level, this is not the sole measure of salvation. In fact common believers who just follow the content of the Revelation are safer from confusion.[64]

In contrast to rationalistic dialectical *kalām*, which al-Ghazālī equated with "harmful medicine" which should only be resorted to when absolutely necessary, *'Ilm al-Tawhīd* which is based entirely, on Revelation is like water: it is useful both for the healthy and the sick.[65] This is why the first generation of Muslims who followed this latter approach were safe from doubts and doctrinal confusions which became common among later Muslims. All of al-Ghazālī's traditional as well as logical proofs in support of the approach of the pious ancestors (*al-salaf*) seem to imply that he was advocating some kind of traditionalist approach to *kalām*.[66] Nevertheless, his explanation of what he understood by the method of the *salaf* is clearly different from the Ḥanbalite approach, for instance, that propagated by Ibn Taymiyyah.

For al-Ghazālī, the approach of the *salaf* to the *mutashabihāt* (the apparently ambiguous Qur'an and *Ḥadīth* texts) involved seven steps:

1. *al-taqdīs* (sanctification): **2.** *al-taṣdīq* (assent to their truth);

---

[62] *Iḥyā'*, 1:39-39; al-*Risālatu 'l-Wa'ẓiyyah*, 39; *Iljām*, 82.

[63] al-*Risālatu 'l-Wa'ẓiyyah*, 39 39; *Iljām*, 82.

[64] Ibid.

[65] Ibid., 60.

[66] Ibid., 63-65. See also *Iḥyā'*, I; 31. By the salaf he refers to the *ṣaḥābah* and the *tābi'ūn*. See Iljām, 42.

3. *al-i'tirāf bi al-'ajz* (acknowledging incapacity to reach their real meaning); **4.** *al-sukūt* (keeping silent about the intended meaning); **5.** *al-kaff* (refraining from pointing out their meanings); **6.** *al-imsāk* (abstention from interpretation); and **7.** *al-taslīm li ahl al-ma'rifah* (leaving the task of interpretation to the people of knowledge).[67] That these steps are intended, for the common believers (*al-'awām*) is evident from his insistence that they should leave the detailed knowledge of doctrinal matters to the highly qualified masters. He attacks the Ḥanbalites for failing to properly observe the above steps which led them into anthropomorphism.

That *'Ilm al-tawhīd* has to be based on the Qur'an and the *Sunnah* is almost self-evident.[68] What may seem surprising, however, is al- Ghazālī's insistence that even the logico-dialectical *kalām*, where that is allowed, has to be based on the revelation. Even in such circumstances whereby the *mutakallim* is confronting an attack or is trying to help a doctrinally 'sick' person, the solution has to be sought from the compelling arguments of the Qur'an and the clear explanation of the *Sunnah*. As a matter of fact, all remedies for doubts and confusions are in the revelation, and the Prophets are "the physicians for treating all the maladies of the hearts."[69] The role of reason here is simply to understand the remedy prescribed by the revelation, rather than

---

[67] Ibid.

[68] In Islam, the source of all knowledge is believed to be God. This is even more evident with respect to knowledge of God Himself. In this respect, the primacy of revealed knowledge cannot be overemphasized. "Since it comes directly from God, it is unique in certitude and has a fundamentally beneficial nature" Wan Mohd. Nor Wan Daud, *The Concept of Knowledge in Islam*, (London: Mansell, 1994), 68. For a discussion about the importance of the Qur'an and *Sunnah* as sources of knowledge in Islam, see pages, 35-58.

[69] *Iḥyā'*, 1: 40; 99. *Munqidh*, McCarthy's translation, p. 102.

initiating the remedy by itself. Thus the Qur'an and *Sunnah* contain the basics of all the relevant arguments in support of Islamic doctrines. Any addition on that is simply a matter of detail, and, according to al-Ghazālī, for such detail to be really compelling, it has to be based on logic (the correct balance). On this basis, it is justified for the specially qualified few to interpret the Qur'an and *Sunnah* in order to derive the Islamic doctrines as well as the arguments in support of those doctrines.

It is clear from the aforegoing discussion that the meaning of many theological texts of the Qur'an and Ḥadīth is not always self-evident. To deal with the difficult texts of the revelation, theologians devised the technique of *ta'wīl* (allegorical interpretation of the Revelation), based mainly upon linguistic foundations. For al-Ghazālī, determining the meanings of the *mutashabihāt* involves logical and spiritual procedures, in addition to linguistic considerations.

In line with his general attitude towards *kalām*, al-Ghazālī follows his dual classification of believers in his approach to the question of allegorical interpretation of the *mutashabihāt*. With his advice to the common people regarding the best way of dealing with *kalām* questions in mind, he insisted that they should refrain from any allegorical interpretation of the revelation. Instead they should stick to the literal meaning and only refer to the explanation given by the Prophet and the pious ancestors (*al-salaf*). They have to avoid engaging in discussion and enquiry about the apparently ambiguous texts (*al-mutashabihāt*) of the Qur'an and the *Sunnah*.[70]

As for the men of speculation, whose traditional beliefs have been troubled, they are allowed to rationally investigate the meanings of any apparently ambiguous statement in the

---

[70] *Fayṣal*, McCarthy's translation, p. 158.

revelation, as long as there is a necessity for doing so, established upon apodictic proof.[71] Whenever there is an apparent conflict between reason and revelation, rational interpretation of the revelation is necessary. It is only when the conclusion of the revelation is categorical that it is not amenable to allegorical interpretation. In cases where the text of revelation is categorical (*naṣṣ*), revelation must be given preponderance over reason and a metaphorical interpretation cannot be justified merely on the basis of conflict with reason.[72] In such circumstances, additional evidence must be presented to justify the allegorical interpretation.

Against that, al-Ghazālī laid down guidelines by which a *mutakallim* can identify statements of the revelation which can be understood in their literal sense. This was by dividing existence into five hierarchical degrees. The first and the highest degree is that of essential existence (*al-wujūd al-dhātī*). It is the real existence that stands outside of sense and intellect. The second degree is that of sensible existence (*al-wujūd al-ḥissī*), which represents itself in the visual faculty of the eye, but does not exist outside the eye. The third degree is the imaginative existence (*al-wujūd al-khayālī*). This is the image of sensible objects in the mind when those objects are absent from sensation. The fourth degree is the mental existence (*al-wujūd al-'aqlī*). This occurs only when something has a soul (*ruḥ*), an objective reality (*ḥaqiqah*), and a meaning (*ma'nā*), but the intellect acquires only its meaning without its image being present in the imagination or the senses or externally at all. The fifth is analogical existence whereby the thing itself does not exist in its form, in the senses or in external reality, but what is seen or felt in any of these is something else

---

[71] Ibid.

[72] Ibid., See also *Iqtiṣād*, p. 212, *Mustaṣfā*, pp. 388-389; and *al-Qisṭās al-Mustaqīm* (Cairo, 1900), pp. 111-112.

which resembles it in one of its qualities or characteristics.[73]

The degrees of textual interpretation are parallel to the above degrees of existence. Therefore, if any text of the Qur'an or the *Sunnah* mentions existence which is real, that is essential existence, it should not be allegorically interpreted. This category includes the texts dealing with the basic principles of Islam. Any attempt to allegorically interpret them may lead to disbelief. Examples of those basic doctrines are the creation of the world in time (*ḥudūth al-'ālam*), corporeal resurrection and God's knowledge of the particulars. Texts dealing with those topics should not be allegorically interpreted because, the proof of the Qur'an and the *Sunnah* in support of making understood the assembly of bodies and the detailed connection of God Most High's knowledge with everything which happens to individuals are [facts] surpassing a limit which admits no interpretation.[74]

Obviously, al-Ghazālī's discussion here is aimed at justifying his action of accusing the philosophers of infidelity, precisely with respect to their views concerning the doctrines cited. If we should ask why interpretation of only those doctrines is proscribed and not other more basic doctrines of Islam such as the Essence of God, His attributes and His actions, al-Ghazālī would possibly refer us back to his degrees of existence. Moreover, since logical reasoning proves the absurdity of the ascription of anthropomorphic attributes to God, any text of the revelation wherein such ascriptions are made has to be allegorically interpreted.[75] This is clearly an attempt to discredit the *ta'wīl* done by the philosophers, while at the same time defending that done by the *mutakallimūn*. In line with his general approach to *kalām*,

---

[73] *Fayṣal*, McCarthy's translation, pp. 151-153.

[74] Ibid., 160.

[75] Ibid., pp. 150-155. See also Marmura, "Ghazālī's Attitude to Secular Sciences," p. 101.

al-Ghazālī cautions the *mutakallimūn* that although such allegorical interpretation is allowed when necessary, it should not be employed indiscriminately. He therefore laid down rules which have to be followed by anyone embarking on a rational interpretation of the Revelation. First and foremost, one should not attempt to interpret a text by reducing its meaning to a degree less than that of essential existence unless there is apodictic proof for the impossibility of that apparent essential meaning. This means that the meaning of any revealed text is presumed to be at the degree of essential existence unless it can be proved to be otherwise. Where the impossibility of the essential meaning is proved, interpretation must start from the highest degree of interpretation, that is sensible interpretation. It is only in the event of proving the impossibility of the essential interpretation that one should turn to the next degree and so on.[76]

In his epistle on *ta'wīl*, al-Ghazālī set down even more stringent rules for those who wished to do *ta'wīl*. Firstly, they should not try to interpret a text when the necessity of that interpretation has not been apodictically proven.[77] By this, he was apparently stating a prohibition of interpreting any text whose obvious meaning is at the level of essential existence. Secondly, they should never reject the apodictic proof of reason. Reason cannot deceive; for if it did, it would have possibly done so in affirming the veracity of the revelation. This means that if the apparent meaning of any text contradicts the dictates of reason, *ta'wīl* is necessary. Finally, where there are conflicting possibilities concerning the need for interpretation, they should not hasten to interpretation. This is because of the danger involved in trying to ascertain the intended meaning of divine speech based on

[76] Ibid., p. 157.

[77] *Qānūn al-Ta'wīl*, In *Majmū'āt Rasā'il al-Imām al-Ghazālī*, vol. 7, (Beirut: Dār al- Kutub al-'Ilmiyyah, 1994), p. 160. Henceforth cited as *Qānūn al-Ta'wīl.*

conjectures and guesswork.[78] He further cautions that:

> You can only know the intended [meaning] of the speaker where He states that intention. If He did not state it, how are you to know it? Unless you point out all the possibilities and falsify all except one which is then singled out by apodictic proof. However, there are several possibilities and several methods of expanding those possibilities. In such circumstances, suspending (*tawaqquf*) *ta'wīl* is the safest [option].[79]

Thus although al-Ghazālī considered the necessity of allegorically interpreting the revelation in order to derive the Islamic doctrines and arguments in defense of those doctrines, he did not consider it appropriate to do it indiscriminately. If allegorical interpretation is left to be used indiscriminately, the basis of *kalām* would no longer be Revelation, but human conjectures. Consequently, he classified people, with respect to their approach to the problem of *ta'wīl*, to five categories; the most successful being those who combined reason and Revelation. He observes, however, that combining the two is a very difficult, tricky and dangerous task.[80] In another place, he praised the group to which he belonged (Ash'arites and Sūfis), for taking the middle course and striking the optimum balance in their approach to the problem of *ta'wīl*. This is to be contrasted to the rigidity of the Ḥanbalites and the extreme conjectural interpretations of the Mu'tazilah and the *Falāsifah*.[81]

Al-Ghazālī introduces a spiritual approach to *ta'wīl* by asserting that on its own, reason can only identify texts of the revelation whose literal meaning cannot be taken; it cannot

---

[78] Ibid., p. 127.

[79] Ibid., p. 128.

[80] Ibid., 126.

[81] See *Iḥyā'*, 1: 104.

determine the intended meaning of any text. Although it is possible to point out the probable meaning of any given text by using linguistic means, the only means through which one can know the true meaning of a given text is spiritual. Al-Ghazālī explains that knowledge of the true meaning of the revelation is attainable only by those who have purified themselves, preparing their souls to receive the divine light which illuminates for them the essences of all things. This is what he calls *'Ilm al-mukāshafah* (the science of unveilment). He continues that,

> We therefore mean by the science of revelation [that science whereby] the cover is removed so that the truth regarding these things becomes as clear as if it were seen by the eye, leaving thereby no room for doubt ...[82]

This spiritual approach to understanding the meanings of the *mutashabihāt* represents al-Ghazālī's greatest contribution to Islamic theology. Through this method, he breathed new life into theological discourse and paved the way for the future development of a metaphysical tradition based on a direct intuition of existence. We shall now turn to his explanation of the experiential approach to theology.

Spiritual Unveiling (*Kashf*) and Direct Spiritual Tasting (*Dhawq*)

Considering that the purpose of theological discourse in Islam is not merely apologetic and defensive, but is, in the first place, for the believer to understand his position vis-a-vis his Creator as well as other beings, it becomes clear that such knowledge is not easily accessible by reason alone. Even when issues are clearly expressed in the Revelation, a true grasp of the underlying realities and their

[82] "Kitab al-'Ilm" in *Iḥyā'*, 1:18, Trans. Nabīh Amīn Faris, *The Book of Knowledge*, (Lahore: SH. Muhammad Ashraf, 1962. Repr. By SH. Shahzad Riaz, 1985), p. 47.

real significance is a divine gift. Disregard of this fact by many *mutakallimūn* and their almost entire reliance on rational discussions of theological questions had turned *kalām* into dry rational polemics. Thus al-Ghazālī's concern with this topic can be seen as an attempt to instill more life and dynamism into its methods and to reorient it to its original salvific goal.

One of the outcomes of al-Ghazālī's itinerary in search of sources of true and certain knowledge was the discovery or rediscovery that knowledge of the reality of things (*ḥaqā'iq al-ashyā'*) is within man's original nature (*al-fiṭrah*).[83] It is only because souls become corrupted as a result of their attachment to worldly beings that this original knowledge tends to be forgotten. Thus, seeking knowledge is an attempt to remove the effects of this corruption from the soul so that it can remember the truth and reality of things it once clearly grasped.[84] However, souls are different in their capacity to recover such knowledge: sick ones may take a life time without reaching them, whereas healthy souls may need only to exert minimal effort.

All this means that rather than being a purely rational endeavor, acquisition of knowledge is essentially a process of self-purification (*tazkiyat al-nafs*), in consequence of which uncovering of the truth and reality of things (*kashf*) may occur immediately, by the grace of God. For the purpose of the present study, we need not go into the depths of al-Ghazālī's mystical epistemology. It suffices to point out that his ultimate position about the question of the legitimacy and status of *kalām* was very much affected by his theory and practice of *'Ilm ladunnī*.[85] *Kalām*

---

[83] *Iḥyā'*, 1: 106.

[84] *Laduniyyah*, 73.

[85] *'Ilm Ladunni* is variously translated as "knowledge from on high" and "knowledge from the divine presence". It basically refers to the experience of spiritual unveilment whereby a person attains knowledge of the real

being a process of knowing the basic principles of religion and defending them against the contrary allegations of the enemies of Islam cannot be detached from the spiritual process of divine illumination. This partly explains why al-Ghazālī attacked some *mutakallimūn* who had turned *kalām* into an entirely rational discipline, even though they failed to reach the highest levels of rationality. In reality, truly legitimate *kalām* is not a matter of dry polemical or even logical discourse. On the contrary, it is an integral part of the spiritual process through which a believer seeks to be elevated to the highest degrees of *'ubūdiyyah* (servitude) to God, which is the *raison d 'etre* of human existence.

Basing himself on his personal experience in search of the truth, al-Ghazālī maintains that spiritual unveiling, resulting in the attainment of knowledge from the divine presence (*al-'ilm al-ladunnī*) is the most certain and most reliable source of knowledge. Such knowledge, according to al-Ghazālī, "is comparable to actual seeing and handling".[86] Thus, since it represents the highest degree of faith and knowledge, it should be the goal of all seekers after the truth. Since *kalām* is a science, by its very nature, concerned with uncovering the truths of divine doctrines in Islam, serious consideration has to be given in it to the experiential methods of attaining divine illumination.

Apparently challenging the rationalist approach of the *mutakallimūn*, al-Ghazālī maintained that with respect to divine matters, there are two kinds of knowledge; *'ilm al-mu'āmalah* (action-oriented knowledge) and *'ilm al-mukāshafah* (seeking the uncovering of divine truths). The former is concerned with details of the law (*Sharī'ah*) and spiritual practice. The latter is a result of

---

essences of things directly from God. See al-Ghazālī's *Al-Risālatu 'l-Laduniyyah*. Trans. Margaret Smith, *Journal of the Royal Asiatic Society*, 1938, 372.

[86] *Munqidh*, McCarthy's translation, p. 100.

the former whereby one attains direct knowledge about the Essence of God, His Attributes and His Actions and other celestial and terrestrial realities. The two have to go hand in hand.[87] Through this process, the believer attains an immediate knowledge of whatever was stated in the revelation about the truth and reality of divine Attributes, as well as the realities of all beings and events, in this world and in the hereafter.[88]

Without this holistic action and reflection, *kalām* loses its legitimacy and its status as a religious science. Hence,

> Any *mutakallim* who dedicates himself solely to disputation (*al-munaẓarah*) and polemics (*al-muāraḍah*), and does not travel on the path of the hereafter; or work upon taking care of his heart and its health, is basically not considered among the scholars of religion. This kind of *mutakallim* possesses nothing of the religion save the creed, which he shares with the common people, and which is simply no more than one of the external actions of the heart and tongue. Thus he tries to distinguish himself from the common people by [using] the techniques of dialectics and polemics. As for the [true] knowledge of God the almighty, and his Attributes and Actions, and whatever we have mentioned as part of *'ilm al-mukāshafah*, none of that is attainable through [ordinary] *'ilm al-kalām*. In fact *kalām* tends to be a veil and barrier preventing [one from reaching it].[89]

As for the exact nature of this illuminating knowledge, al-Ghazālī, apparently using Sufi terminology and explanation, maintains that it is a reflection of the knowledge in the mirrors of

---

[87] *Ghurūr al-Khalq*, p. 163.

[88] Ibid. See also *Laduniyyah*, p. 62; *Rauḍātu 'l-Ṭālibīn*, in *Majmū'āt Rasā'il al-Imām al- Ghazālī*, vol. 7, (Beirut: Dār al-Kutub al-'Ilmiyyah, 1994), p. 160. Henceforth cited as *Rauḍah*.

[89] *Iḥyā'*, 1: 23.

the preserved tablet (*al-lauḥ al-maḥfūẓ*) into the mirror of the heart. As a result of this reflection, the heart immediately grasps the content of the preserved tablet, thereby attaining knowledge of all the realities of beings.[90] This is the highest stage of knowledge attainable by human beings. It is only bestowed as a grace from God upon those who strive in purifying their souls and seeking God's pleasure by following His commands. It is not acquired through rational inquiry.[91]

The role of divine grace as the most reliable means of attaining certainty about the principles of religion cannot be overemphasized. In fact, asserts al-Ghazālī, the best kind of *īmān* (faith) is not that based on rational contemplation (i.e. that of the *mutakallimūn*), but the faith of ordinary men. Although their faith is based on imitation, it is accompanied by sincere worship and constant remembrance (*dhikr*) of Allah. Through worship (*'ibādah*) and remembrance of God (*dhikr*), the believer attains a direct knowledge of what he originally believed only by means of

---

[90] *Munqidh*, McCarthy's translation, pp. 62-66; 99; *Kimiyā' al-Sa'ādah*, in *Majmū'āt Rasā'il al-Imām al-Ghazālī*, vol. 7, (Beirut: Dar al-Kutub al-'Ilmiyyah, 1994), p. 160. Henceforth cited as *Kimiyā'*; See also *Laduniyyah*, pp. 69-71.

[91] *Laduniyyah*, pp. 69-71. See also *Mishkāt*, pp. 21-22; *Iḥyā'*, 1: 99 101, and *Munqidh*, McCarthy's translation, p. 94. See also *Iḥyā'*, 3: 119, where al-Ghazālī explains that the certitude derived from this kind of illuminative knowledge, when compared to the knowledge attained by the rational *kalām* methods, is like the knowledge attained about someone through the direct experience of being in his presence compared to one who only knows of that person's presence in another room by merely hearing his footsteps. Professor al-Attas has clearly explained that illuminative knowledge leads to the highest degree of certitude. Such knowledge leads to "truth of the highest degree of certainty (*ḥaqq al-yaqīn*), because it is gained by direct experience." *The Positive Aspects of Taṣawwuf*, (Kuala Lumpur: n.p., 1981), p. 9. See also Josep Puig Montada, *Ibn Rushd Versus Al-Ghazālī*, p. 118, and Subhi, *'Ilm al-Kalām*, 2: 197-198.

mere imitation (*taqlīd*).[92] Thus an ordinary believer, through sincerity and hard work, attains a level of gnosis (*ma'rifah*) that is not accessible to many *mutakallimūn*, in spite of their dialectical argumentation and logical proofs. From this we can infer that al-Ghazālī's negative remarks against the *mutakallimūn*, besides his opinion about the weakness of dialectical proofs, were also motivated by the fact that *kalām* had become worldly oriented. He held that many *mutakallimūn*, instead of seeking divine mercy and preparing for the hereafter, practiced their knowledge in pursuit of worldly fame.[93]

One may ask here whether al-Ghazālī by all this, wanted to totally replace *'ilm al-kalām* with this divinely inspired knowledge, which is more certain and reliable. In fact even his classification of people, at least in the later stages of his career, seems to depend on the degrees of spiritual elevation rather than intellectual development.[94] However, the fact that he restricts this kind of knowledge to the personal domain shows that it is not an alternative for, but complementary to *kalām*. Al-Ghazālī insists that divinely inspired knowledge is strictly personal. It is a secret that should not be divulged to anyone. In fact it should not even

---

[92] *Fayṣal*, McCarthy's translation, 169; *Kimiyā'*, p. 138. Although in his defense of logic al-Ghazālī seems to have elevated reason to a very high level, unlike the philosophers, he asserts that it is essentially a tool for receiving divine illumination. *Iḥyā'*, 1: 19 and 25. See also Massimo Companini, *Ghazzali*, p. 269.

[93] *Fayṣal*, McCarthy's translation, p.169.

[94] *Mishkāt*, pp. 3-4, *Iḥyā'* 1:20. Cf. *Iḥyā'*, 3: 115-119, where al-Ghazālī explains that acquiring knowledge of God takes place at three levels: following authority (*taqlīd*) for the common believers; looking for rational proofs (*istidlāl*) for the learned; and attaining direct illumination for the: gnostics (*'ārifūn*). This arrangement indicates that al-Ghazālī considered illuminative knowledge to be the highest of all in terms of certainty.

be written down in books.[95]

Considering the above comments, we can infer that for both the *mutakallimūn* and the common people, the most reliable means of attaining the highest degrees of certain knowledge is through the practice of spiritual self-discipline as taught by the Sūfis. By this, al-Ghazāli integrates theory and practice, and orients the entire intellectual endeavor of *kalām* towards the attainment of salvation in the hereafter.

In the light of the foregoing discussion. Professor Syed Muhammad Naquib al-Attas' evaluation of al-Ghazālī's contribution to the development of Islamic theology captures the gist of the seminal ideas of the great theologian. He writes that,

> Al-Ghazālī initiated a new movement in theology (*kalām*) by introducing the philosophical method as well as the metaphysics of the *ṣūfīs* as based on spiritual insight (*kashf*) and direct spiritual experience (*dhawq*) in the interpretation of Islamic theology in addition to reason, tradition, and consensus. The school of theology that developed out of this new movement of which Fakhr al-Din al-Rāzī (d.606) was another leader, became known as the 'later' school (*al-muta'akhkhirūn*) as distinguished from their earlier counterpart.[96]

---

[95] Ibid.

[96] Syed Muhammad Naquib al-Attas, *A Commentary on the Hujjat al-Siddiq of Nur al-Din al-Raniri*, (Kuala Lumpur: Ministry of Culture Malaysia, 1986), p. 212.

Biographies of Contributors

Prof. Dr. Muddathir 'Abd al-Raḥīm is Professor of Political Science and Chairman, Academic Board, African Research and Training Center, International University of Africa (IUA) in Khartoum, Sudan. In his rich academic and diplomatic career, he has held numerous posts and appointments: Distinguished Professor and Head, Human Rights Program, University Islam Malaysia, (UIM), Cyberjaya, Malaysia; Professor of Political Science and Islamic Studies and Distinguished Academic Fellow at the International Institute of Islamic Thought and Civilization (ISTAC), IIUM, Malaysia; Visiting Scholar, Northern Illinois University; Vice-Chancellor (Rector) Omdurman Islamic University, Sudan; and a Visiting Professor, School of Humanities, Temple University, among others. Prof. Muddathir was Sudan's Ambassador to Nordic Countries (Sweden, Norway, Denmark, and Finland), UNESCO Senior Expert, and a Member of the Sudanese Delegation to the U.N. General Assembly. He has authored and edited more than ten books and numerous scholarly articles, including *Human Rights in*

Islam (Preger, 2005) and *Imperialism and Nationalism in the Sudan—A Study in Constitutional and Political Development 1899-1956* (Oxford University Press, 1969). Prof. Muddathir is a Recipient of the Jordanian Royal Medal for Distinguished Contributions, "Wisam Al-Husayn li'l-'Atā'Al-Mutamayyiz," conferred by King Abdullah II, in Amman in 2013, and was honored as "Personality of the Year" in the Sudan in 2019 by the Ministry of Culture for his academic and cultural contributions, especially in connection with the promotion of Human Rights. Prof. Muddathir ʻAbd al-Raḥīm obtained his Ph.D. in Economics and Social Studies (Government) from the University of Manchester in 1964, a B.A. in Politics from Nottingham University in 1958, and another B.A. in Arabic, History, and Economics from the University of London in 1955.

Dr. Sabri Orman graduated from Istanbul University's Faculty of Economics, where he also received his Ph.D. He taught at Marmara University, worked as a research scholar at the London School of Economics and Political Sciences between 1989-1990, and became a professor in 1993. He was a professor of economics at the International Islamic University Malaysia (1992-1994) and the International Institute of Islamic Thought and Civilization (ISTAC) in Kuala Lumpur, 1995-1997 and 2002-2006. Dr. Orman authored or edited 12 books and wrote numerous scholarly articles. He served two terms as a Member of the Board of the Central Bank of the Republic of Turkey. Dr. Sabri Orman passed away in 2020 at the age of 72.

Dr. Cemil Akdogan obtained his Ph.D. in the history of science at the University of Wisconsin—Madison (USA) in 1978, with the dissertation on Optics in Albert the Great's De Sensu et sensato. He was a professor of the history of science at the

International Institute of Islamic Thought and Civilization (ISTAC) in Kuala Lumpur for almost a decade and a half, retiring in 2013. Dr. Akdogan wrote *Science in Islam & the West* (ISTAC, 2012), and published many articles in reputable international journals, mainly in the history of Islamic science.

Dr. Mustafa Mahmoud Abu-Sway is a Palestinian Islamic scholar and the first holder of the Integral Chair for the Study of al-Ghazali's work at al-Masjid al-Aqsa and al-Quds University in Jerusalem. Dr. Abu Sway received his education at Bethlehem University and Boston College. He taught at the International Islamic University Malaysia and was a visiting Fulbright scholar at Wilkes Honors College of Florida Atlantic University. He was a visiting professor of Islamic studies at Bard College in New York. A Senior Fellow of the Royal Aal al-Bayt Institute for Islamic Thought, Dr. Abu Sway was twice listed among the 500 Most Influential Muslims in the World. He is the author of several books on al-Ghazali, interfaith dialogue, and Islamic education, in both English and Arabic.

Dr. Mohd. Zaidi bin Ismail is currently the Deputy Director-General of the Institute of Islamic Understanding Malaysia (IKIM) and Editor-in-Chief of TAFHIM: IKIM Journal of Islam and the Contemporary World. He received his M.A. degree in Islamic Thought (Epistemology and Philosophy of Mind) in 1995 and a Ph.D. in the same field (Ontology) in 2006, both from the International Institute of Islamic Thought and Civilization (ISTAC) in Kuala Lumpur. He has authored and edited more than ten books, primarily in epistemology and philosophy of mind.

Dr. Asmaa' Mohd. Arshad has been a senior lecturer at the Academy of Contemporary Islamic Studies (ACIS), University of Technology Mara, Malaysia, since 2015. She began her career as a research fellow at the International Islamic Thought and Civilization (ISTAC) between 2001-2002, after graduating with her M.A. at the institute in 2000. Later, she became a lecturer at the International Islamic University Malaysia (IIUM) and pursued her Ph.D. at the University of Malaya, 2005-2010. Dr. Asmaa' had co-authored and edited several educational publications; besides co-organizing education lecture series for youth in Kuala Lumpur.

Dr. Ssekamanya Siraje Abdullah is an Associate Professor at the Kulliyah of Education, International Islamic University Malaysia (IIUM). After completing an M.A. in education at IIUM, he obtained his Ph.D. in Islamic Thought from the International Institute of Islamic Thought and Civilization (ISTAC) in Kuala Lumpur. Dr. Abdallah has published numerous book chapters and academic articles in education, Islamic thought, counseling, and higher education.

Index

A

a'yān mawjūdah, 41
Abbasid caliphate, 19
'Abd al-Amīr al-A'sam, 109, 123
Abd al-Dā'im al-Baqarī, 114, 115, 116
'Abd al-Raḥmān Sa'īd Dimashqiyyah, 109, 119
Abdul Qayyum, 6, 74
Abu al-Ḥusayn Ardashīr Ibn Manṣūr al-'Abbadī, 124
Abu al-Khaṭṭāb, 111
Abu Ḥanīfah, 203
Abu Ṭālib al-Makkī, 124
Abū Yazīd al-Bisṭāmī, 124
adab, 160, 163, 165, 167, 168, 169, 170, 172
  addabanā, 169
  ahl al-adab, 169
adāwat wa ālāt, 45
addabanī, 168
adillah, 136, 152, 153, 202, 211
af'āl, al-, 175
aḥkām, 17, 20, 29
Aḥmad Ibn Ḥanbal, 202, 203
  Ḥanbalite, 110, 111, 215, 216, 221
  Ḥanbalite school, 111
aḥwāl, 142, 153, 184
akhlāq, 168, 170, 171, 173, 174, 183, 185, 186, 191
akhlāq, al-, 168, 170, 171, 173, 174, 183, 185, 186, 191
ālāt, 52
al-awwaliyyāt, 141, 142, 145
Albert Einstein, 60
al-fiṭrah, 131, 164, 187, 193, 223
'Alī ibn Abī Ṭālib, 185, 193
Alnoor Dhanani, 75

Alp Arslān, 3
amīr, 48, 50
amwāl, 41, 52, 53
aqwāl, al-, 129, 175
ārā' maḥmūdah, 146
Aristotle, 67, 86, 167
  Aristotelian, 161, 167, 173
  Aristotelianism, 86, 87
Armstrong, David M., 96
Ash'arī, al-, 3, 64, 195, 196, 201, 221
Attas, Syed Muhammad Naquib al-, 59, 60, 68, 69, 70, 72, 73, 74, 80, 86, 87, 101, 103, 108, 128, 159, 160, 162, 164, 168, 170, 179, 181, 182, 186, 226, 228
a'yān, 52, 129
ayat, 70, 71

B

Bacon, Francis, 87
Baghdad, 3, 109, 110, 111, 113, 114, 115, 117, 119, 120, 121, 124, 125, 126
Barkyāruq, Sultan, 119, 123
Barzun, Jacques, 81, 101
baṭil, 128, 130, 190
  baṭil muṭlaqan, 128
bāṭin, 5, 166, 170
bay', 52, 56
Bergson, Henry, 69
Berkeleian, 101
bid'ah, 15
bilād, al-, 47
binā', 45
Boyle, Robert, 60, 62, 87, 92, 93, 94, 95, 96, 97, 98, 99, 105
Bryson, 163
burhān, 137, 141, 151, 192, 199, 206, 211
burhān, al-, 137, 141, 151, 192, 199, 206, 211
Burke, Edmund, 36
Buwayhid, 2, 3

C

caliphate, 2, 3, 4, 5, 12, 13, 17, 18, 19, 20, 21, 22, 23, 24, 25, 26, 27, 31, 113, 117, 120, 121
Carra de Vaux, 114, 115
Cartesians, 69, 82
Christian, 63, 136, 164, 197, 214
civil strife, 7, 9
Clatterbaugh, Kenneth, 96
Cook, Michael, 2
Copernican revolution, 102
Copleston, Frederick, 82

D

ḍa'īf, al-, 138
dalīl, 137, 211
Descartes, Rene, 59, 60, 61, 62, 63, 67, 69, 77, 78, 79, 80, 81, 82, 83, 87, 90, 91, 92, 95, 96, 99, 105, 107
Dewey, John, 101, 104
dhāt al-mu'taqad, 130
dhawq, 132, 222, 228

dhikr, 161, 226
dimāgh, al-, 179
dīn, 14, 23, 24, 26, 160, 168, 197
Drake, Stillman, 5, 88
dunyā, 11, 13, 14, 21, 31, 41, 42, 55
  al-bāṭinah, 42
  al-ẓāhirah, 43
  fi nafsihā, 41

E

ethic, 2, 35, 161, 162, 168, 184, 188, 191

F

Fakhr al-Din al-Rāzī, 228
fana' fī al-tawhīd, 134
farḍ kifāyah, 204, 214
Farid Jabre, 120, 121, 122, 123
Fārisī, al-, 117
Farrūkh, 114, 115, 118, 119
Fāṭimid, 120
Fazlur Rahman, 66, 69, 70, 71, 72, 73, 200, 205
Feyerabend, Paul, 107
Fichte, 101
filāḥah, 45
fiqh, 16, 18, 29, 49, 161
  uṣūl al-fiqh, 16
fiṭrah, 63, 131, 164, 187, 193, 223
fuqahā', 29

G

Galilei, Galileo, 9, 59, 60, 62, 87, 88, 89, 90, 91, 92, 95, 96, 99, 105
Geulincx, 82
ghaḍab, al-, 172, 184
ghaflah, 55
Gil'adi, 162

H

ḥadīth, 26, 117, 164, 168, 170, 212, 215, 217
ḥads, al-, 144, 156
ḥadsiyyāt, 144, 155
ḥadsiyyāt, al-, 144, 155
ḥāl, 39, 170, 184
ḥaq, al-, 128, 129, 188, 189, 190, 226
ḥaqīqah, 218
ḥaqq muṭlaqan, 128
ḥarām, 11, 15, 33
Ḥaramayn al-Juwaynī, al-, 3, 16, 22, 110, 199
Ḥārith al-Muḥāsibī, 124
Harūn al-Rashīd, 4
Ḥasan ibn al-Ṣabbāḥ, 4, 5
Ḥassān ibn Thābit, 180
ḥayawān, 41
Hayman, Arthur, 112, 113
Hegel, 101
hijrah, 169
ḥikmah, 161, 173, 175, 182, 185
ḥikmah, al-, 161, 173, 175, 182, 185
ḥiss, 137, 142
ḥiyākah, 45
Hobbes, Thomas, 2, 8, 18, 36

ḥudūth al-'ālam, 219
Hume, David, 59, 75, 83, 84, 85, 102, 107
ḥusn al-ẓann, 153
ḥuṣūl al-yaqīn, 142

I

i'tiqād, al-, 130, 135, 136
Ibn al-'Arabī, 110
Ibn al-Jawzī, 110
Ibn Kathīr, 125
Ibn Khaldūn, 2, 16, 115, 118, 161, 194, 195, 212
Ibn Taymiyyah, 2, 215
ijārah, 54
ijmā', 13
ijtihād, 5
ijtimā', 47, 49
ikhbār jamā'ah, 145
ikhtiyār, 164, 184
  ikhtiyār aḥwālihā, 184
ikrājuhū, 178
iktisāb, 54
ilhām, 139
Iljām, 129, 133, 134, 137, 140, 151, 152, 155, 203, 211, 213, 215
Ilm
  Ilm al-Tawhīd, 216
imāmate, 14
imān, 132, 151
īmān
  īmān jāzim, 211
Imre Lakatos, 107
imsāk, al-, 216
insān, 160, 168
iqtināṣ, 45
irādah, 140
iṣlāḥ, 36, 41, 44
Islamic
  atomism, 74
  history, 9
  order, 13, 14
  political institution, 2
  terminology, 36, 208
  theology, 63, 212, 222, 228
  tradition, 2, 7
istidlāl, 132, 137, 139, 227
istidlāl, al-, 132, 137, 139, 227
istikhrāj, 163
istiqrā', al-, 154
Itḥāf, 110, 172, 181, 184, 185
i'tidāl, 173, 174, 186
i'tidāl, al-, 173, 174, 186
i'tiqādāt, al-, 175
i'tirāf bi al-'ajz, al-, 216
i'tiyād, 165, 193
i'tiyād, al-, 165, 193
iṭṭirād al-'ādāt, 143

J

jadal, al-, 146
jadālī, al-, 141
jadaliyyan, 146
jalā', al-, 138
jihād, 15, 25, 26
jubāt, 50
Judaism, 63, 136, 164, 214

juhhāl, al-, 15
Junayd, al-, 124
jurisprudence, 2, 5, 16, 111, 207

K

kaff, al-, 216
kalām, 64, 74, 75, 107, 133, 196, 197, 199, 200, 201, 203, 204, 205, 206, 208, 209, 210, 211, 212, 213, 214, 215, 216, 217, 219, 221, 223, 224, 225, 226, 227, 228
  kamāl al-'aql, 186
  kamāl fiṭrī, 165
kāmil, 182
Kant, Immanuel, 59, 62, 67, 76, 80, 83, 84, 85, 88, 100, 101, 102, 103, 104, 105, 106, 107, 108
  Neo-Kantians, 107
  post-Kantian philosophy, 101
kashf, 132, 139, 200, 201, 222, 223, 228
kashf, al-, 132, 139, 223, 228
kathrah, al-, 24, 26, 37, 138
khafā', al-, 138
khalq, al-, 21, 166
kharāj, al-, 50
Kharijites, 7
khawās, al-, 213
khissat al-himmah, 55
khiṭābī, al-, 141
khiṭābiyan, 148
khuluq
  ḥusn al-khuluq, 167, 168, 171, 187
  sū' al-khuluq, 167
khuluq, al-, 163, 166, 167, 187
khuṭbah, 19
khuzzān, 50
kirā', 54
Kuhn, Thomas, 107

L

lā tajma'uhum rābiṭah, 50
lauḥ al-maḥfūẓ, al-, 226
law, 2, 9, 12, 14, 24, 31, 49, 84, 85, 143, 147, 224
lbn 'Aqil, 111
lbn Kathīr, 120
lbn Khallikān, 124
Locke, John, 61, 62, 87, 96, 97, 98, 99, 100, 104, 105, 106, 107

M

mā yuntafa' bih, 52
Macdonald, 119, 120, 122
madhab, 202
madhmūm, 202
madrasah, 3
maghrūrūn, 200
maḥmud, 202
maḥsūsāt, al-, 141, 142, 145, 155
Makkah, 113
Makkī, al-, 124
malik, 48, 50
Mālik, Imam, 203
ma'nā, 150, 218
manṭiq, al-, 129, 194, 201, 206,

207
Maqām, 184
maqāmāt, 184
maqbūlat, al-, 148, 149
ma'qūl, al-, 129
ma'rifah, 129, 136, 152, 160, 185, 227
ma'rifah ḥaqīqiyyah, 136
ma'rifah, al-, 129, 136, 152, 160, 185, 227
Marx, 2, 36
Marx, Karl, 2, 36
mashhūrāt, al-, 146, 148, 149, 197
maṣlaḥatan li 'l-'ibād, 55
masraḥiyyah fanniyyah, 115
Mawardī, al-, 2, 22
mawḍū', 168
mawjūd, al-, 130
mawjūdāt, al-, 44, 177
maẓnūnāt, al-, 148
McCarthy, R.J., 64, 114, 116, 121, 126, 129, 131, 189, 198
misāḥah, 49
Miskawayh, 162, 163, 164, 165, 167, 171, 172, 173, 174, 175, 176, 177, 179, 183, 184, 185, 186, 187, 193
mu'āmalah, 54, 224
muāraḍah, al-, 225
mu'āwadah, 53
mubṭil, 188
mufradah, 178
Muḥammad Ibn Malik Shāh, Sultan, 6
Muḥāsibī, al-, 124
mujaddid, 160
mujādil, 210
mujāhadah, 168, 171, 174, 184
mujāhadah, al-, 168, 171, 174, 184
mujarrabāt, al-, 143, 144, 145, 155
mujtahid, 17, 20
mukāshafah, al-, 132, 182, 222, 224, 225
mukhālaṭah, 193
mukhāṭabāt, al-, 148
mukhayyalāt, al-, 150
munāfiqūn, al-, 134
munaẓarah, al-, 225
muqallid, 154
muqarrabūn, al-, 132, 134, 138, 140
musallamāt, 146, 148, 211
musallamāt, al-, 146, 148, 211
mushāhadah, al-, 132
Mustaẓhir, Caliph al-, 6, 22, 24, 27, 121
muta'akhkhirūn, al-, 228
muta'allim, al-, 176, 178
mutakallim, 196, 204, 213, 216, 218, 225
mutakallimūn, 111, 134, 135, 196, 199, 200, 201, 202, 203, 204, 205, 209, 211, 212, 214, 219, 223, 224, 226, 228
mutakallimūn, al-, 134, 135, 196, 199, 200, 201, 202, 203, 204, 205, 209, 211, 212, 214, 219,

223, 224, 226, 228
mutaṣawwifah, 29
mutashabihāt, 150, 215, 217, 222
mutashabihāt, al-, 150, 215, 217, 222
mutawātirāt, al-, 141, 144
Mu'tazilah, 12, 200, 201, 221
Myers, Eugene A., 83

N

nafs, 70, 72, 73, 135, 138, 144, 166, 171, 172, 174, 176, 178, 179, 184
  ḥaml al-nafs, 171
  imtiḥāin al-nafs, 184
  nafs al-lawwama, al-, 70, 73
  nafs al-mutma'inna, al-, 70, 73
  tazkiyat al-nafs, 168, 206, 223
Najdite, 7
Nakamura, 114, 116, 122
Naquib al-Attas, Syed Muhammad, 59, 60, 68, 69, 70, 72, 73, 74, 80, 86, 87, 101, 103, 108, 128, 159, 160, 162, 164, 168, 170, 179, 181, 182, 186, 226, 228
naṣṣ, 218
naẓar, 5, 137, 200, 201, 211
naẓar, al-, 5, 137, 200, 201, 211
ni'mah, 32, 180
niẓām
  niẓām al-dīn, 13, 14
  niẓām al-islām, 13
Niẓām al-Mulk, 3, 4, 5, 6, 109, 110
niẓām al-tabī'ī, al-, 193
niẓāman li 'l-bilād, 55
Niẓāmiyyah, 3, 109, 110, 111, 113, 114, 120, 124
nubuwwah, 193
nuẓẓār, 135

P

philosophy, 2, 59, 60, 62, 63, 67, 72, 77, 79, 83, 96, 100, 101, 102, 103, 107, 117, 131, 206
Plato, 2, 67
Popper, Karl R., 102, 103, 107
Proctor, Robert N., 61, 86, 87
Prophet
  Adam, 178
  Companions, 23, 169
  Muḥammad, 11, 13, 15, 19, 23, 31, 160, 164, 168, 169, 170, 175, 192, 201, 214, 217
Pullman, Bernard, 74
Putnam, Hilary, 102, 107

Q

qāḍīs, 31, 32
qaḍiyyah 'āmmah, 143
qalb, 42, 138, 166, 179
qalb, al-, 42, 138, 166, 179
Qalqashandī, al-, 2
qillah, al-, 138
qiyās, 132, 143
  qiyās khafī, 143
  qiyāsan shi'riyyan, 150
qudrah, 173

Qur'an, 15, 17, 28, 68, 69, 70, 71, 72, 73, 152, 153, 166, 169, 174, 188, 190, 192, 194, 199, 205, 206, 208, 209, 212, 213, 214, 215, 216, 217, 219
Qurayshite, 20

R

Randall Jr., John Herman, 96, 97
Rava Lazarus-Yafeh, 161
ra'y, 5, 23
Renan, Ernest, 83
ri'āyah, 45
riyāḍah, 163, 164, 168, 170, 171, 172, 174, 175, 186, 187, 192
  riyaḍāt al-adab, 172
  riyaḍāt al-nafs, 184
  riyaḍāt al-ṭalab, 172
  riyāsah wa wilāyah, 48
riyāḍah, al-, 163, 164, 168, 171, 172, 174, 175, 186, 187, 192
Rorty, Richard, 107
rūḥ, 132, 166, 170, 179, 218
rūḥ, al-, 132, 166, 170, 179, 218

S

sa'ādah, al-, 187
Sa'ādī, 125
ṣabr, 184
ṣādiqatan, 141
Ṣaḥābah, 168, 169, 214, 215
sajiyyah, 164
salaf, al-, 215, 217
Schopenhauer, Arthur, 62, 105, 106, 107
Seljuk, 3, 4, 6, 9, 17, 25, 26, 31
Shāfi'ī, Imam, xii, 16, 110, 203
shahādah, al-, 130, 179
shahādāt, 146
shahwah, al-, 172, 184
shajā'ah, al-, 175
shajā'ah, 161, 173
shakk, 123, 135, 141
Shām, al-, 113
Shanker, Stuart G., 67, 83
Sharbāṣī, al-, 109, 111, 117
Sharī'ah, 2, 3, 12, 16, 17, 18, 21, 23, 26, 28, 31, 33, 111, 169, 175, 185, 224
  maqāṣid al-Sharī'ah, 13
Sharif, M.M., 69, 164
shaykh, 181
Shiblī, al-, 124
Shihab-ul-Islam, 74
Shī'ite, 2, 22, 23, 25
  Bābak of Adharbaijan, 4
  Bāṭinites, 4, 5, 6, 17, 22, 23, 24, 25, 26, 111, 120, 121, 122
  Ismā'ilites, 4
  Khurramādins of Isfahan, 5
  Qarāmiṭah (Carmathians), 4
  Sevener Shī'ites, 4
shubhah, 141, 200
shubhāt, 204
shūrā, 19
ṣiddīqūn, al-, 132, 134, 140
ṣinā'āt, 10, 49
siyāsah, al-, 9
Smith, A.D., 60

Smith, Margaret, 60, 66, 92, 114, 115, 135, 177, 224
Subkī, al-, 1, 109, 110, 117, 122
Sūfī, 29, 112, 120, 122, 124, 125, 138, 162, 179, 188, 190, 193, 206, 212, 213, 221, 225, 228
Sufism, 72, 172, 179
sukūt, al-, 216
Sultan, al-, 9, 17, 18, 19, 20, 21, 25, 26, 27, 30, 31, 32, 33, 34
Sunnah, 17, 28, 168, 169, 174, 188, 190, 192, 205, 206, 209, 213, 214, 216, 217, 219
Sunni
  Sunni caliphate, 22
  Sunni Muslims, 2, 3, 4, 5, 22, 174, 206
  Sunni *'ulamā'*, 5
surah, 70
Surah
  al-'Alaq, 160
  al-A'rāf, 178
  Al-Mu'minun, 70

T

ta'allum, 177, 178, 193
ta'ammul, 145
ṭab', al-, 145, 164, 167, 172, 211
Tabaqāt, 117
Tābi'ūn, 168, 169, 214, 215
Tabrīzī, al-, 125
tabula rasa, 87
tadarruj, al-, 172
tadhakkur, al-, 193
ta'dīb, 163, 165, 166, 167, 168, 170, 171, 179, 186, 192
tahdhīb, 163, 164, 165, 167, 168, 169, 171, 172, 173, 174, 175, 176, 177, 179, 182, 183, 184, 185, 187, 191, 192
  tahdhīb al-akhlāq, 168, 182, 183, 184, 187
taḥqiq, 154
tajribah, 137, 142
tajribiyyāt, al-, 141, 143
taklīf, 186, 193
ṭalab, 53, 178
ta'līm, 5, 163, 165, 176, 178, 186, 192
ta'līm, al-, 5, 163, 165, 176, 178, 186, 192
ta'līmāt, al-, 148
Ta'līmite-Bāṭinite, 131
Ta'līmiyyah, 5, 22
tamthīl, al-, 154
tamyīz, 176
taqdīs, al-, 215
taqlīd, 64, 131, 136, 139, 153, 154, 155, 202, 214, 227
taraddud, 54, 151
tarbiyah, 163, 168, 180, 181, 182, 183, 186, 192
taṣarruf al-'uqūl, 23
taṣawwuf, 109, 111, 116, 124, 196, 205
taṣdīq, al-, 128, 135, 136, 138, 151, 164, 193, 215
taslīm li ahl al-ma'rifah, al-, 216
tawaqquf, 221
tawātur, 137, 143, 145, 146, 148,

154, 155
tawātur, al-, 137, 143, 145, 146, 148, 154, 155
tawhīd, 59, 73, 74, 133, 134, 205
tawḥīd fī'lī, 134
ta'wīl, 217, 219, 220, 221
tazkiyah, 182, 183
theology, 1, 77, 131, 134, 195, 196, 197, 209, 222, 228
thiqah, 117
Tughrul-Beg, 3
Tutush, 119

U

Umar Farrūkh, 114, 115, 118, 119
ummah, 3, 16, 17, 20, 21, 23, 24, 26, 31, 34
umūr al-siyāsiyyah, al-, 50

V

Victor Sa'īd Bāsīl, 123

W

wahmiyyāt, al-, 150
wājibat al-qabūl, 141
walīs, 18, 27, 32
Walsh, James J., 112, 113
Watt, W. Montgomery, 5, 119, 120, 123, 188
wazīr, 3, 33
wilāyah, 32, 48
wujūd
wujūd al-'aqlī, al-, 218
wujūd al-dhātī, al-, 218
wujūd al-ḥissī, al-, 218
wujūd al-khayālī, al-, 218

Y

yaqīn, 111, 131, 135, 136, 137, 146, 205, 226
yaqīniyyatan, 141

Z

zāhid, 15
ẓāhir, 5, 148, 149, 166, 170
Zakariyya Bashir al-Imam, 115
ẓann, 135, 137, 150
ẓannun ghālibun, 148
Zoroastrian, 164
Zubaydī, al-, 110, 113
zuhhād, 55
ẓuhūr al-ḥaqq, 141
Zwemer, Samuel M., 114, 125